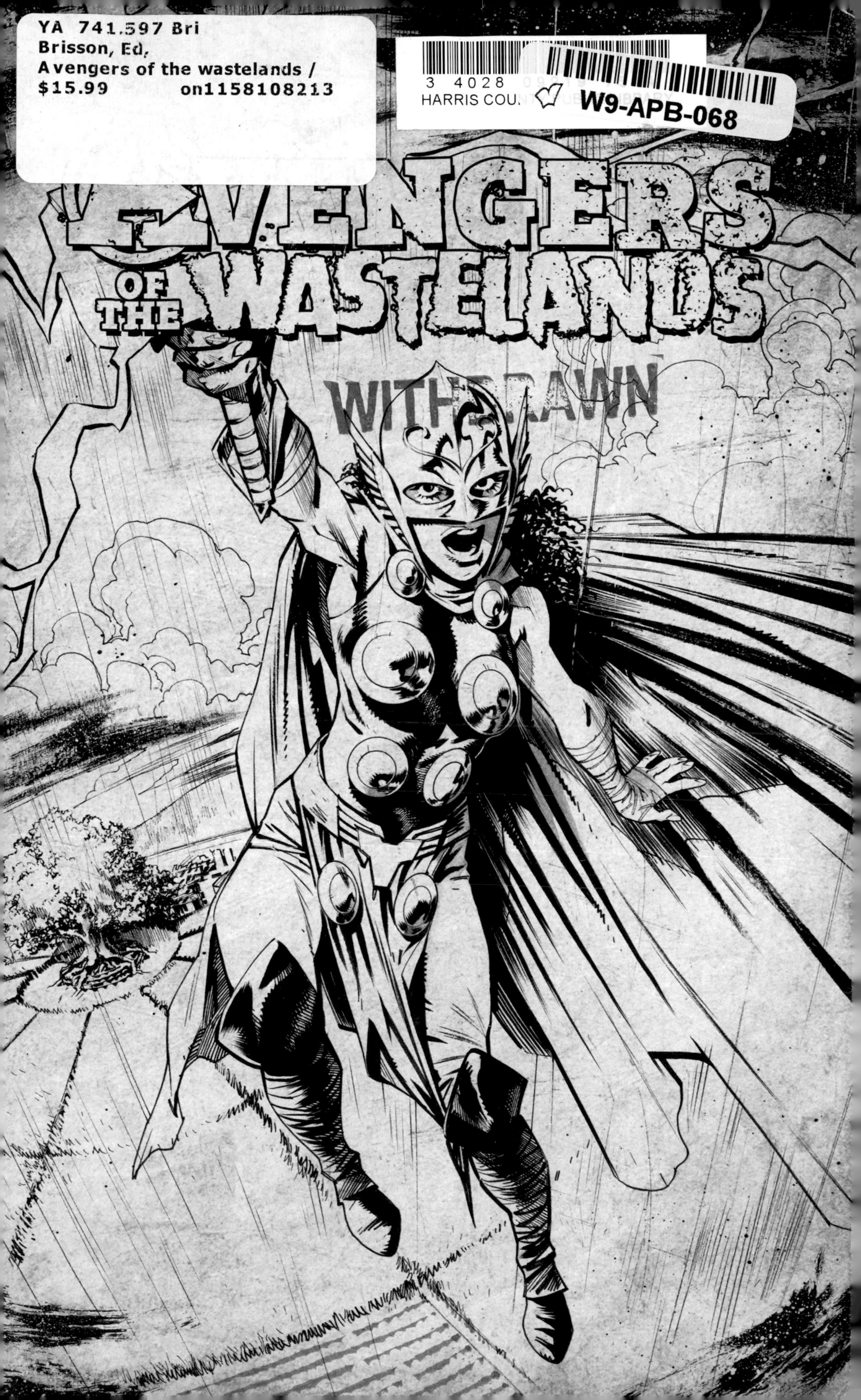
AVENGERS
OF THE WASTELANDS

JENNIFER GRÜNWALD.............................Collection Editor
MAIA LOY ....Assistant Managing Editor
LISA MONTALBANO ....Assistant Managing Editor
MARK D. BEAZLEY...........................Editor, Special Projects
JEFF YOUNGQUIST ....VP Production & Special Projects
JAY BOWEN with ANTHONY GAMBINO ....Book Designers
DAVID GABRIEL ....SVP Print, Sales & Marketing
C.B. CEBULSKI..Editor in Chief

AVENGERS OF THE WASTELANDS. Contains material originally published in magazine form as AVENGERS OF THE WASTELANDS (2020) #1-5. First printing 2020. ISBN 978-1-302-92004-3. Published by MARVEL WORLDWIDE, INC., a subsidiary of MARVEL ENTERTAINMENT, LLC. OFFICE OF PUBLICATION: 1290 Avenue of the Americas, New York, NY 10104. © 2020 MARVEL No similarity between any of the names, characters, persons, and/or institutions in this magazine with those of any living or dead person or institution is intended, and any such similarity which may exist is purely coincidental. **Printed in Canada.** KEVIN FEIGE, Chief Creative Officer; DAN BUCKLEY, President, Marvel Entertainment; JOHN NEE, Publisher; JOE QUESADA, EVP & Creative Director; TOM BREVOORT, SVP of Publishing; DAVID BOGART, Associate Publisher & SVP of Talent Affairs; Publishing & Partnership; DAVID GABRIEL, VP of Print & Digital Publishing; JEFF YOUNGQUIST, VP of Production & Special Projects; DAN CARR, Executive Director of Publishing Technology; ALEX MORALES, Director of Publishing Operations; DAN EDINGTON, Managing Editor; SUSAN CRESPI, Production Manager; STAN LEE, Chairman Emeritus. For information regarding advertising in Marvel Comics or on Marvel.com, please contact Vit DeBellis, Custom Solutions & Integrated Advertising Manager, at vdebellis@ marvel.com. For Marvel subscription inquiries, please call 888-511-5480. **Manufactured between 7/24/2020 and 8/25/2020 by SOLISCO PRINTERS, SCOTT, QC, CANADA.**

10 9 8 7 6 5 4 3 2 1

Decades ago, the world's super villains united and collectively wiped out nearly all super heroes. Dr. Doom now rules the wastelands that remain of the United States with an iron grip. But even in the bleakest of circumstances, heroes can arise and once more assemble...

AVENGERS *of the* WASTELANDS

ED BRISSON .... Writer
JONAS SCHARF .... Artist
NEERAJ MENON .... Colorist
VC's CORY PETIT .... Letterer
JUAN JOSÉ RYP & JESUS ABURTOV .... Cover Artists
JOE FRONTIRRE .... Logo Designer
MARTIN BIRO & SHANNON ANDREWS BALLESTEROS ....
.... Assistant Editors
MARK BASSO .... Editor

AVENGERS created by **STAN LEE & JACK KIRBY**

NOTE: The events of this story take place after
OLD MAN LOGAN, OLD MAN QUILL
& DEAD MAN LOGAN.

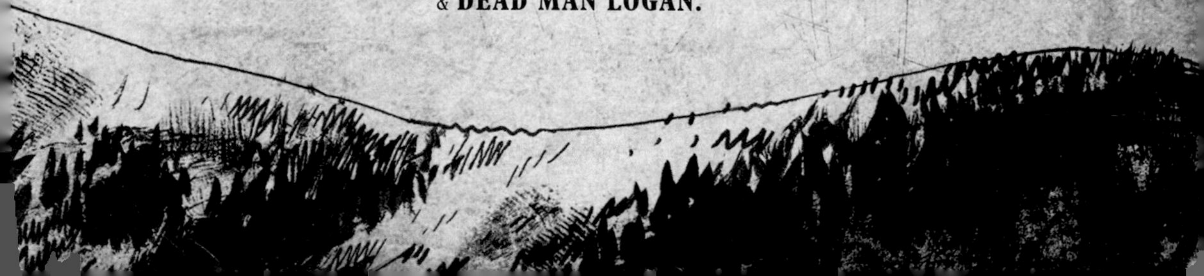

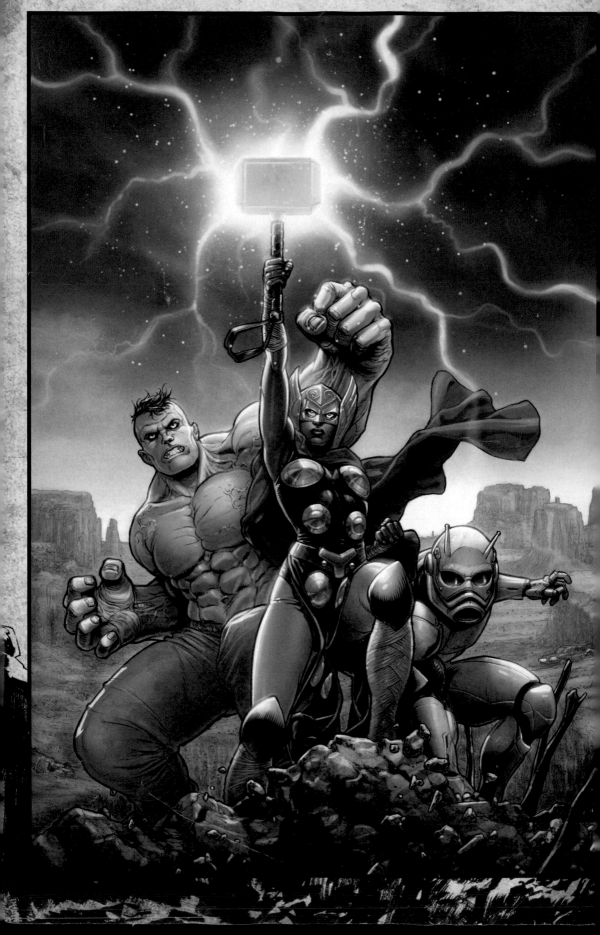

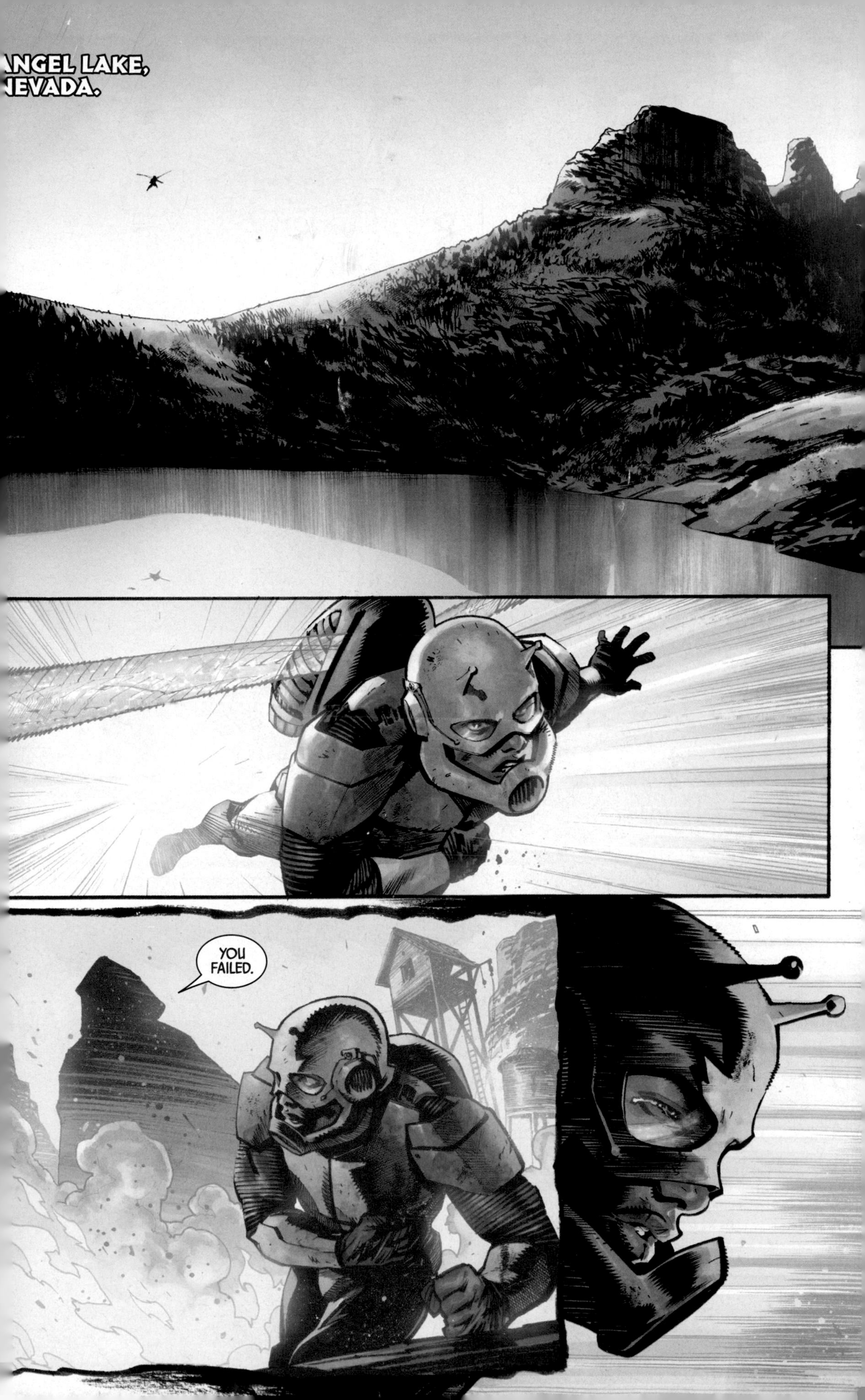

ANGEL LAKE,
NEVADA.
YOU FAILED.

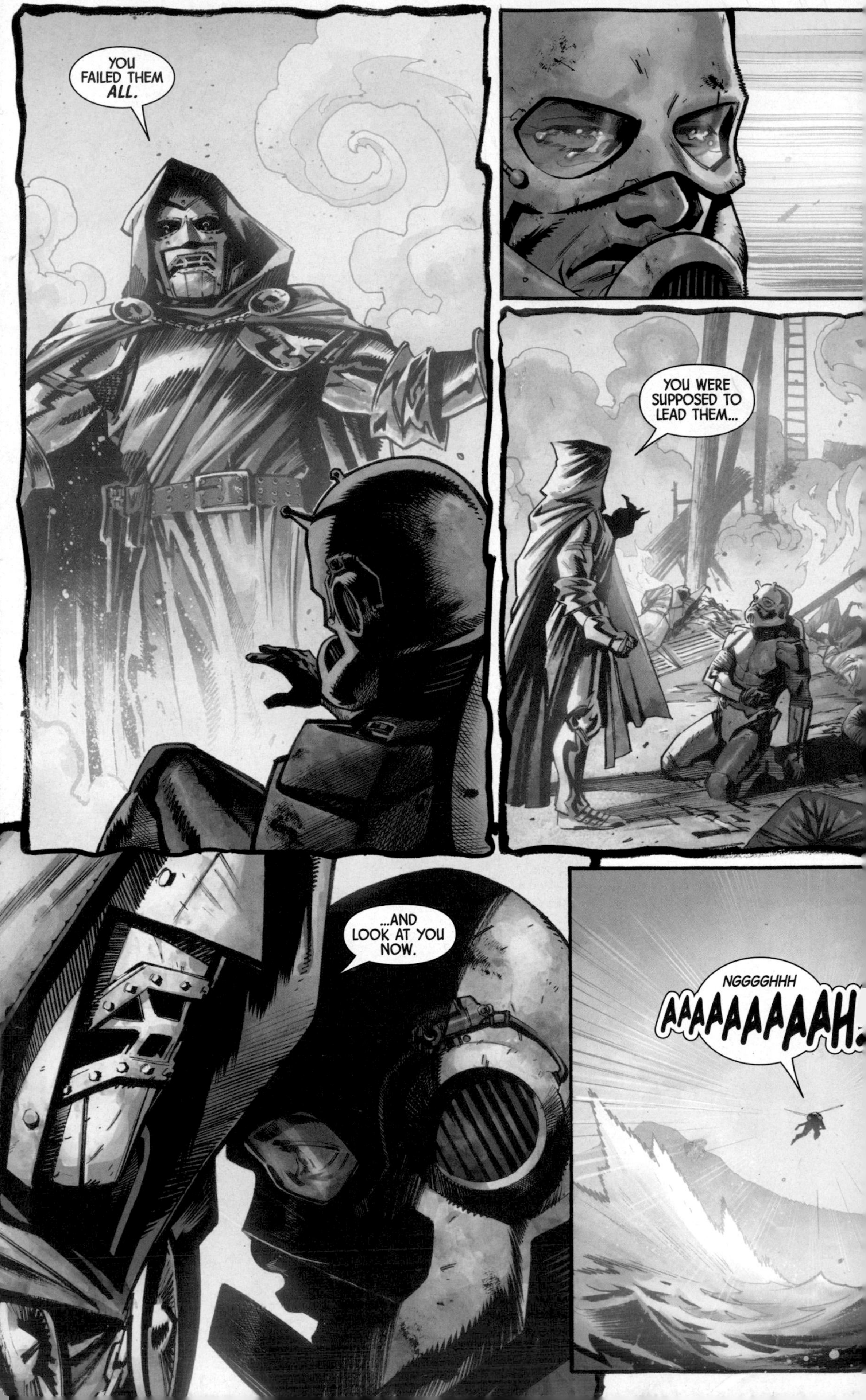
YOU FAILED THEM ALL.
YOU WERE SUPPOSED TO LEAD THEM...
...AND LOOK AT YOU NOW.
NGGGGHHH AAAAAAAAAH.

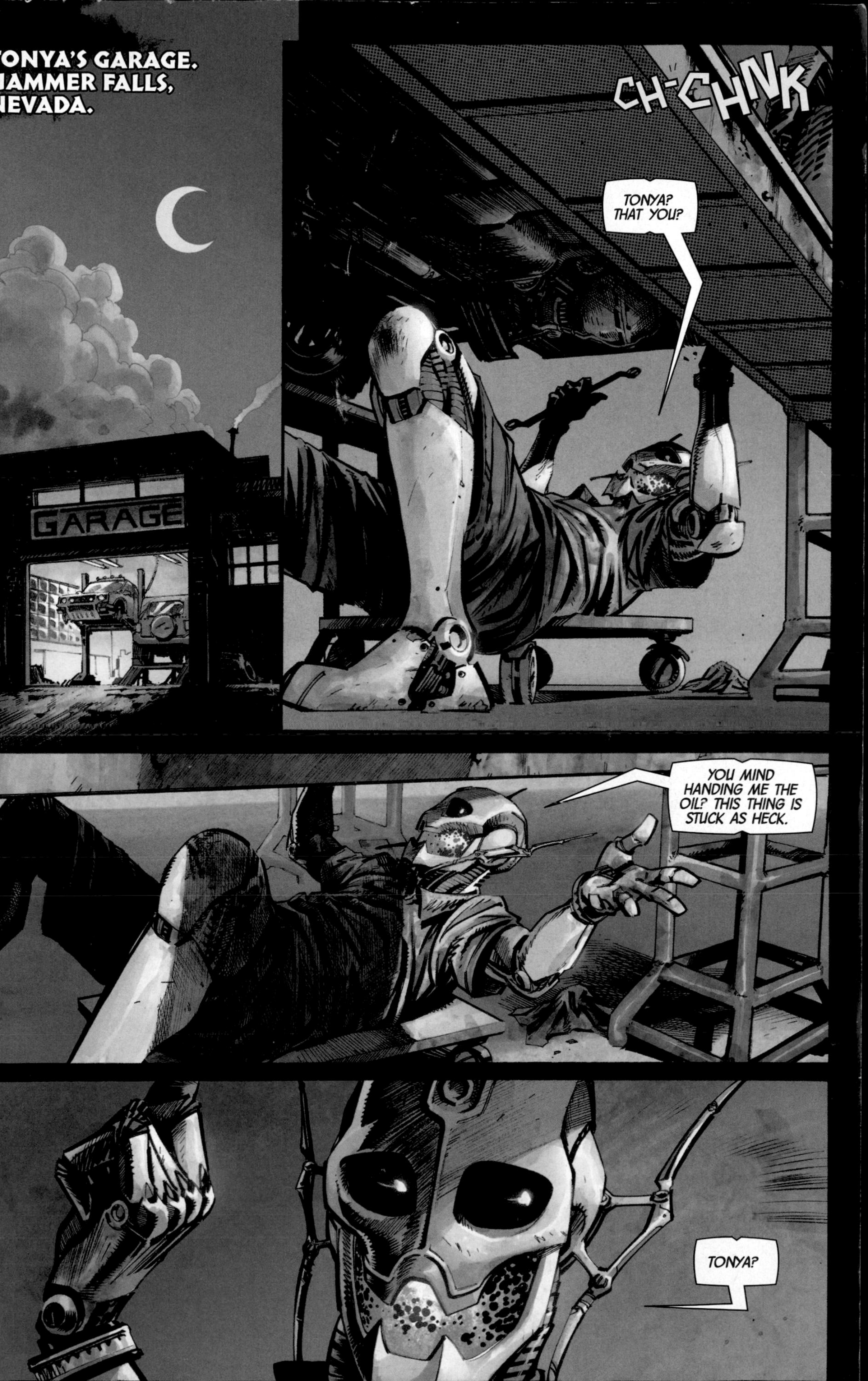
TONYA'S GARAGE. HAMMER FALLS, NEVADA.
GARAGE
CH-CHNK
TONYA? THAT YOU?
YOU MIND HANDING ME THE OIL? THIS THING IS STUCK AS HECK.
TONYA?

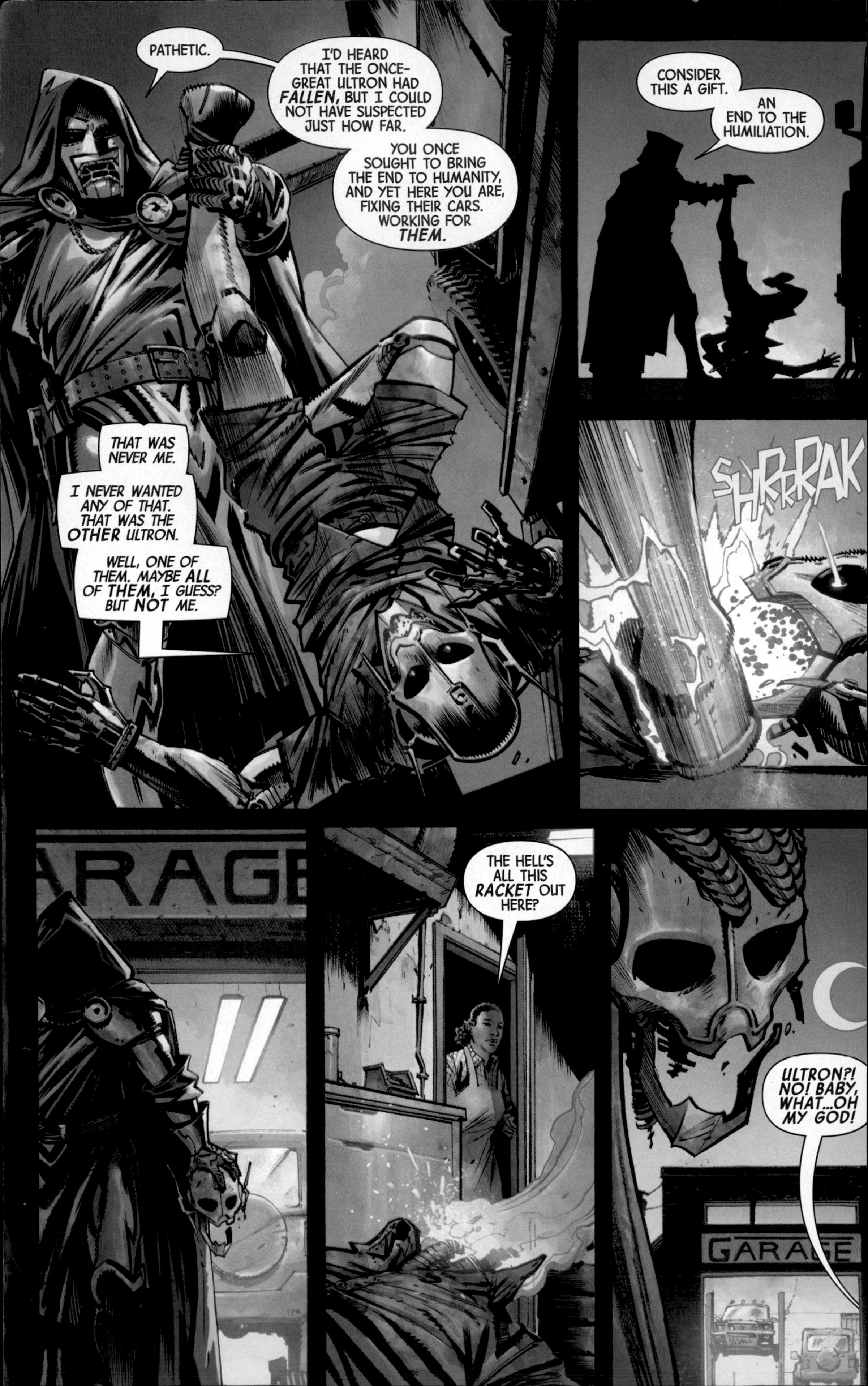
PATHETIC.
I'D HEARD THAT THE ONCE-GREAT ULTRON HAD FALLEN, BUT I COULD NOT HAVE SUSPECTED JUST HOW FAR.
YOU ONCE SOUGHT TO BRING THE END TO HUMANITY, AND YET HERE YOU ARE, FIXING THEIR CARS. WORKING FOR THEM.
THAT WAS NEVER ME.
I NEVER WANTED ANY OF THAT. THAT WAS THE OTHER ULTRON.
WELL, ONE OF THEM. MAYBE ALL OF THEM, I GUESS? BUT NOT ME.
CONSIDER THIS A GIFT.
AN END TO THE HUMILIATION.
SHRRRAK
GARAGE
THE HELL'S ALL THIS RACKET OUT HERE?
ULTRON?! NO! BABY, WHAT...OH MY GOD!
GARAGE

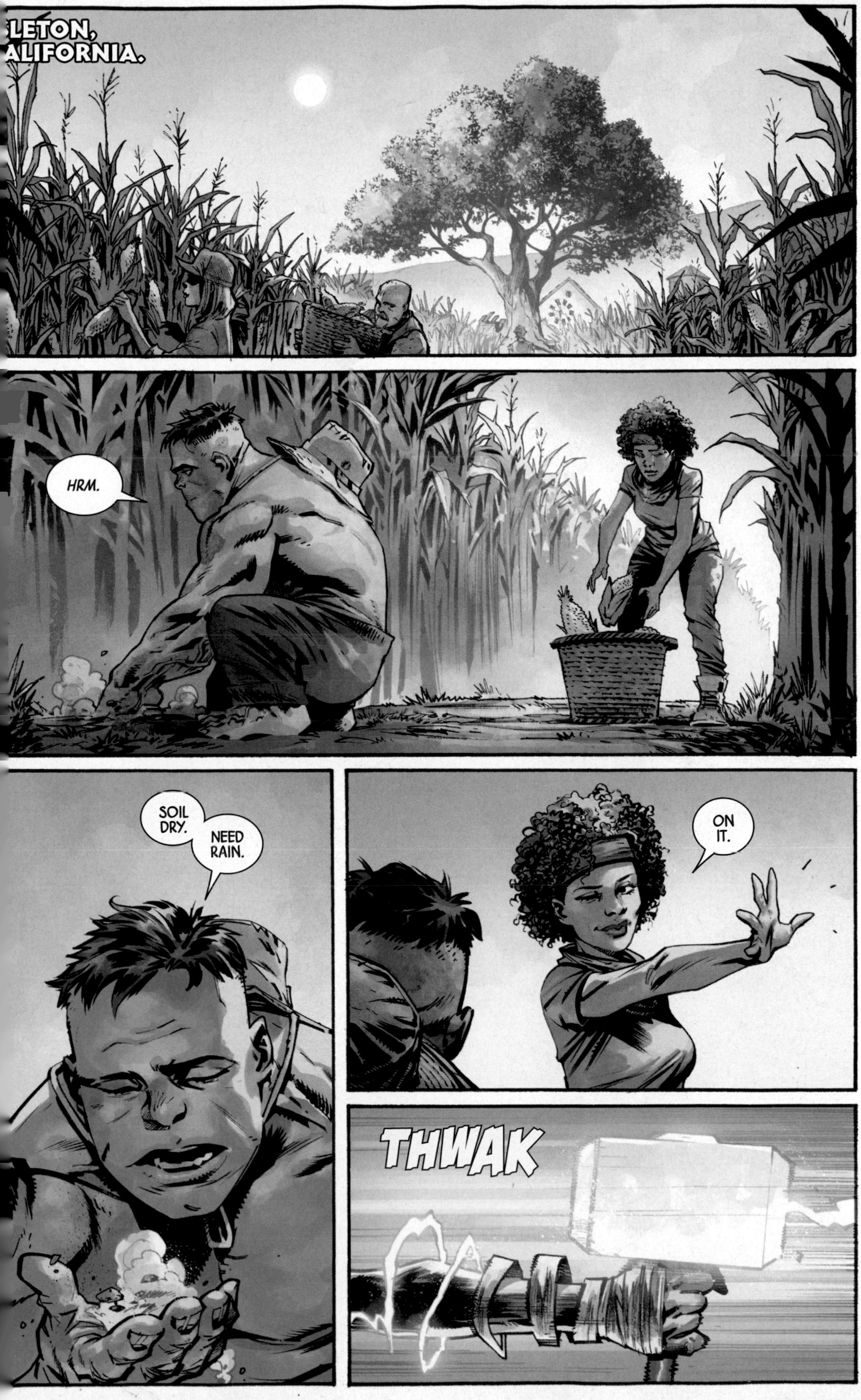
LETON,
ALIFORNIA.
HRM.
SOIL DRY.
NEED RAIN.
ON IT.
THWAK

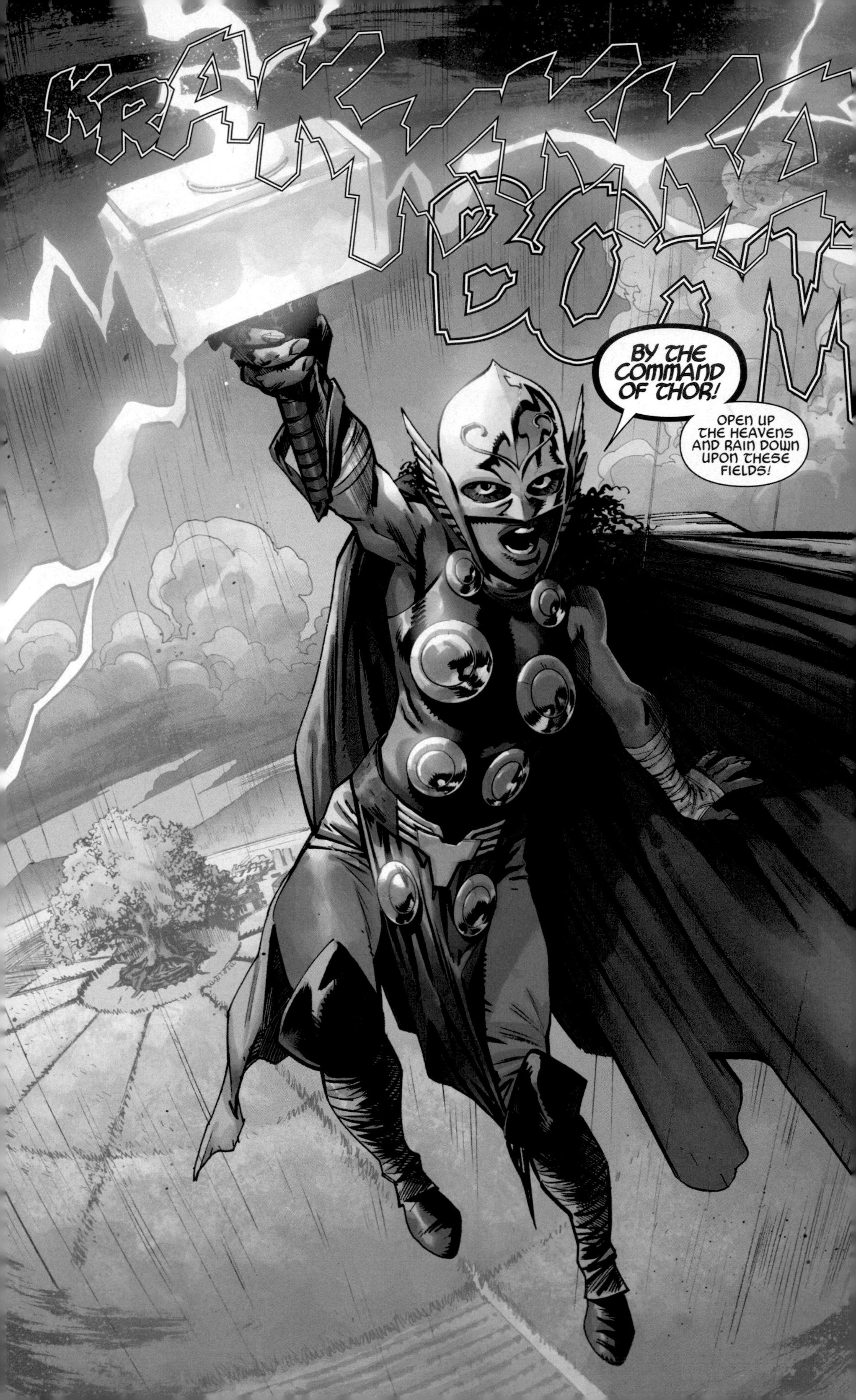
KRAKAWOOM
BOOM
BY THE COMMAND OF THOR!
OPEN UP THE HEAVENS AND RAIN DOWN UPON THESE FIELDS!

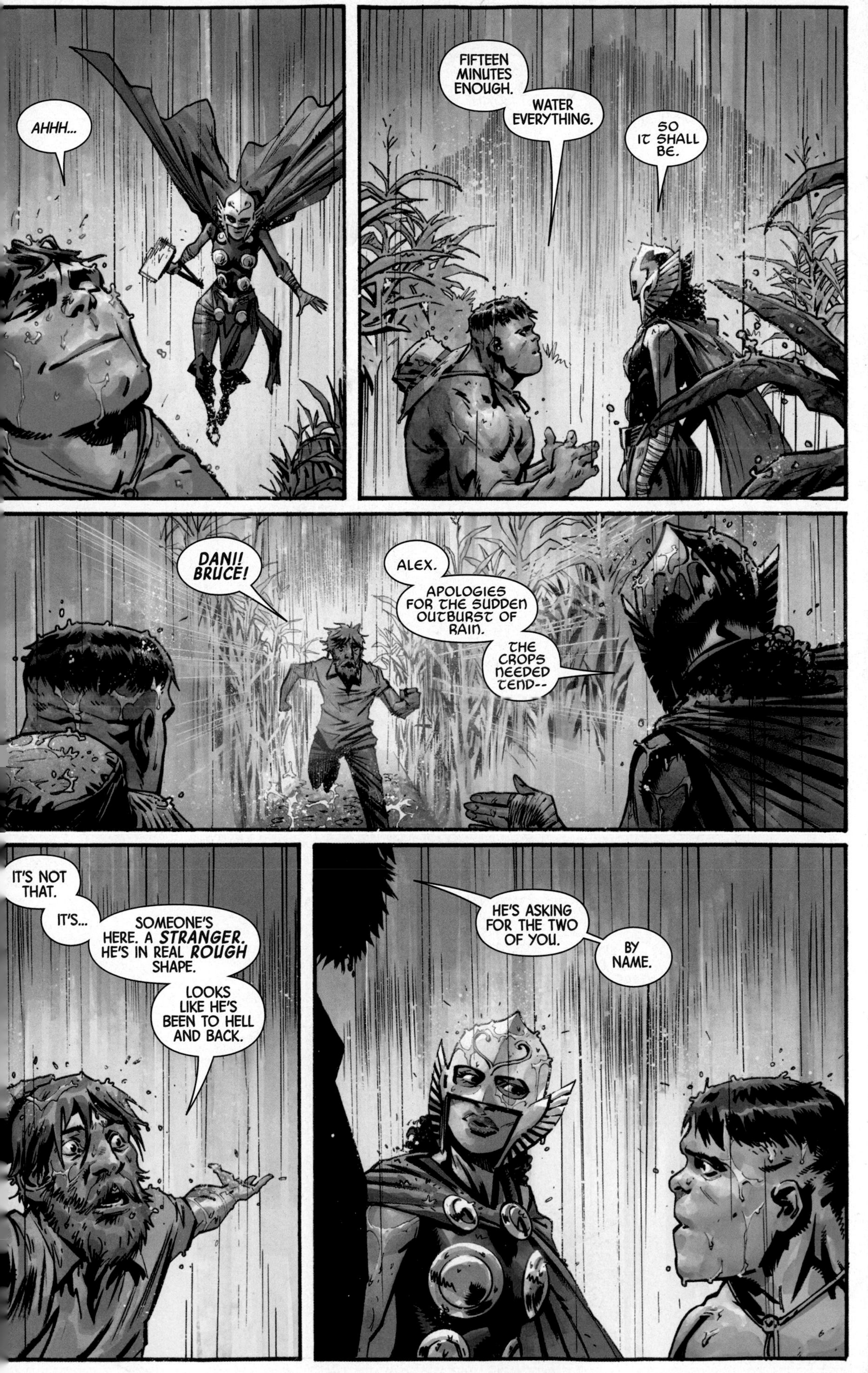
AHHH...
FIFTEEN MINUTES ENOUGH.
WATER EVERYTHING.
SO IT SHALL BE.
DANI! BRUCE!
ALEX.
APOLOGIES FOR THE SUDDEN OUTBURST OF RAIN.
THE CROPS NEEDED TEND--
IT'S NOT THAT.
IT'S...
SOMEONE'S HERE. A STRANGER. HE'S IN REAL ROUGH SHAPE.
LOOKS LIKE HE'S BEEN TO HELL AND BACK.
HE'S ASKING FOR THE TWO OF YOU.
BY NAME.

FINALLY.

I'VE BEEN TRYING TO GET HIM TO REST, BUT HE WON'T SIT STILL UNTIL HE TALKS TO YOU.

WHO?

WOULDN'T GIVE ME HIS NAME, JUST SAID YOU KNOW HIM.

DANI... IT'S BEEN A WHILE.

DWIGHT?

OH MY GOD. I THOUGHT...WHEN FORGE'S COMPOUND BLEW UP*...I THOUGHT EVERYONE WAS...

NOT EVERYONE.

*AS SEEN IN DEAD MAN LOGAN #10!

ME AND A COUPLE DOZEN OTHERS--WE SURVIVED.

SPENT THE LAST TWO YEARS REBUILDING AND THEN...

AND THEN...

DO YOU MIND IF WE HAVE THE ROOM FOR A MINUTE?

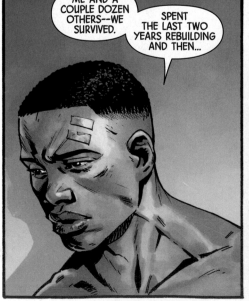

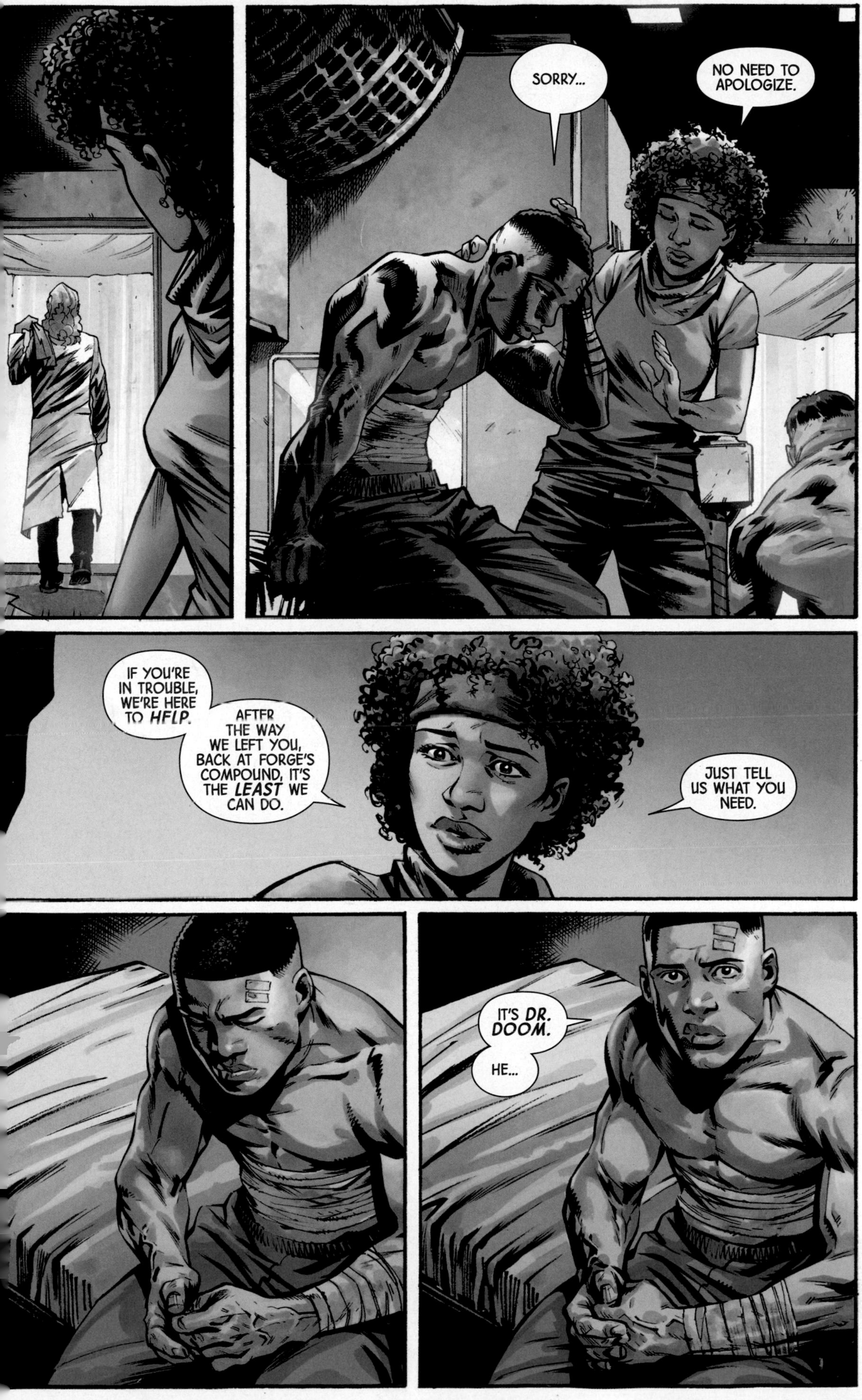
SORRY...
NO NEED TO APOLOGIZE.
IF YOU'RE IN TROUBLE, WE'RE HERE TO HELP.
AFTER THE WAY WE LEFT YOU, BACK AT FORGE'S COMPOUND, IT'S THE LEAST WE CAN DO.
JUST TELL US WHAT YOU NEED.
IT'S DR. DOOM.
HE...

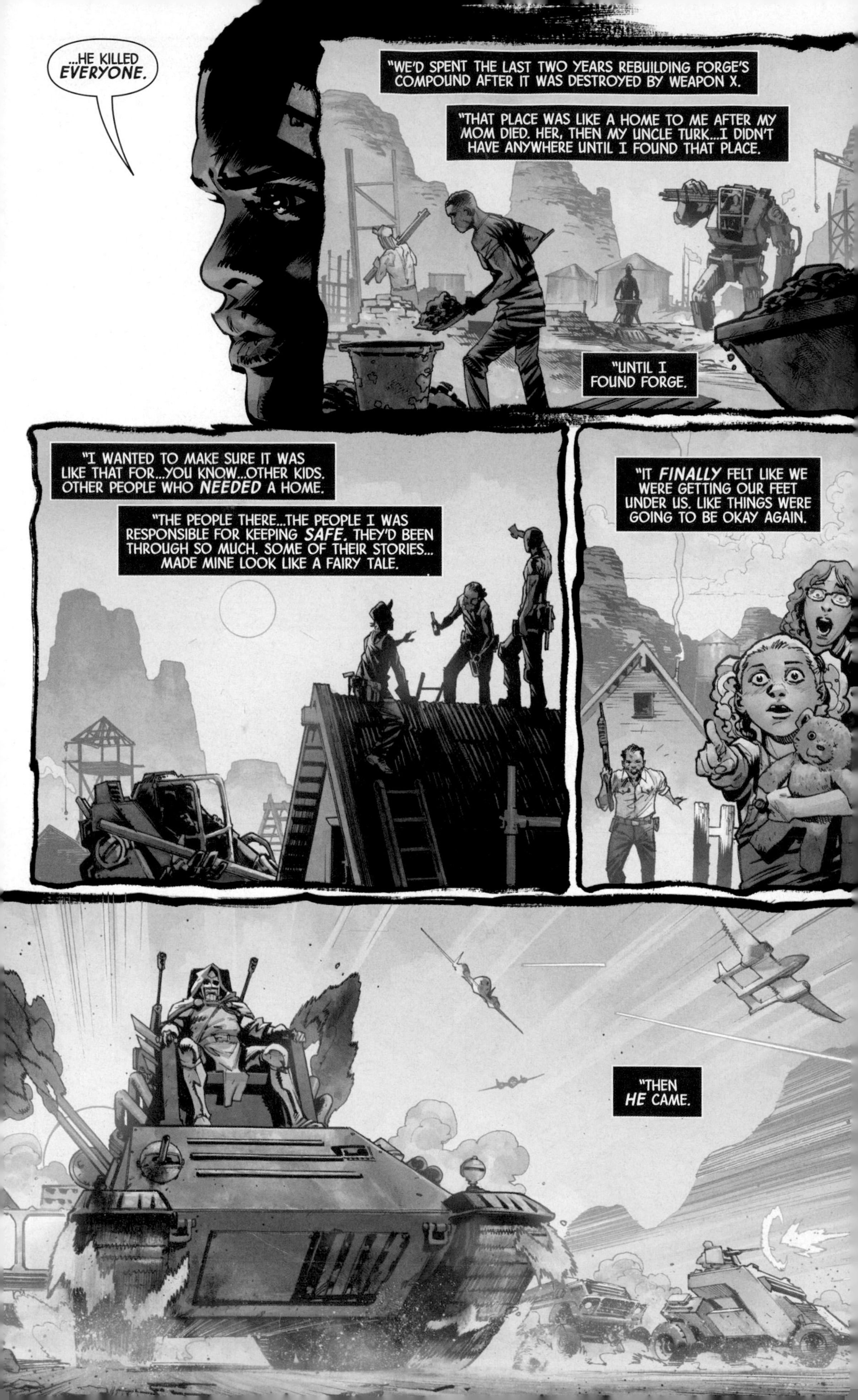
...HE KILLED EVERYONE.
"WE'D SPENT THE LAST TWO YEARS REBUILDING FORGE'S COMPOUND AFTER IT WAS DESTROYED BY WEAPON X.
"THAT PLACE WAS LIKE A HOME TO ME AFTER MY MOM DIED. HER, THEN MY UNCLE TURK...I DIDN'T HAVE ANYWHERE UNTIL I FOUND THAT PLACE.
"UNTIL I FOUND FORGE.
"I WANTED TO MAKE SURE IT WAS LIKE THAT FOR...YOU KNOW...OTHER KIDS. OTHER PEOPLE WHO NEEDED A HOME.
"THE PEOPLE THERE...THE PEOPLE I WAS RESPONSIBLE FOR KEEPING SAFE. THEY'D BEEN THROUGH SO MUCH. SOME OF THEIR STORIES... MADE MINE LOOK LIKE A FAIRY TALE.
"IT FINALLY FELT LIKE WE WERE GETTING OUR FEET UNDER US. LIKE THINGS WERE GOING TO BE OKAY AGAIN.
"THEN HE CAME.

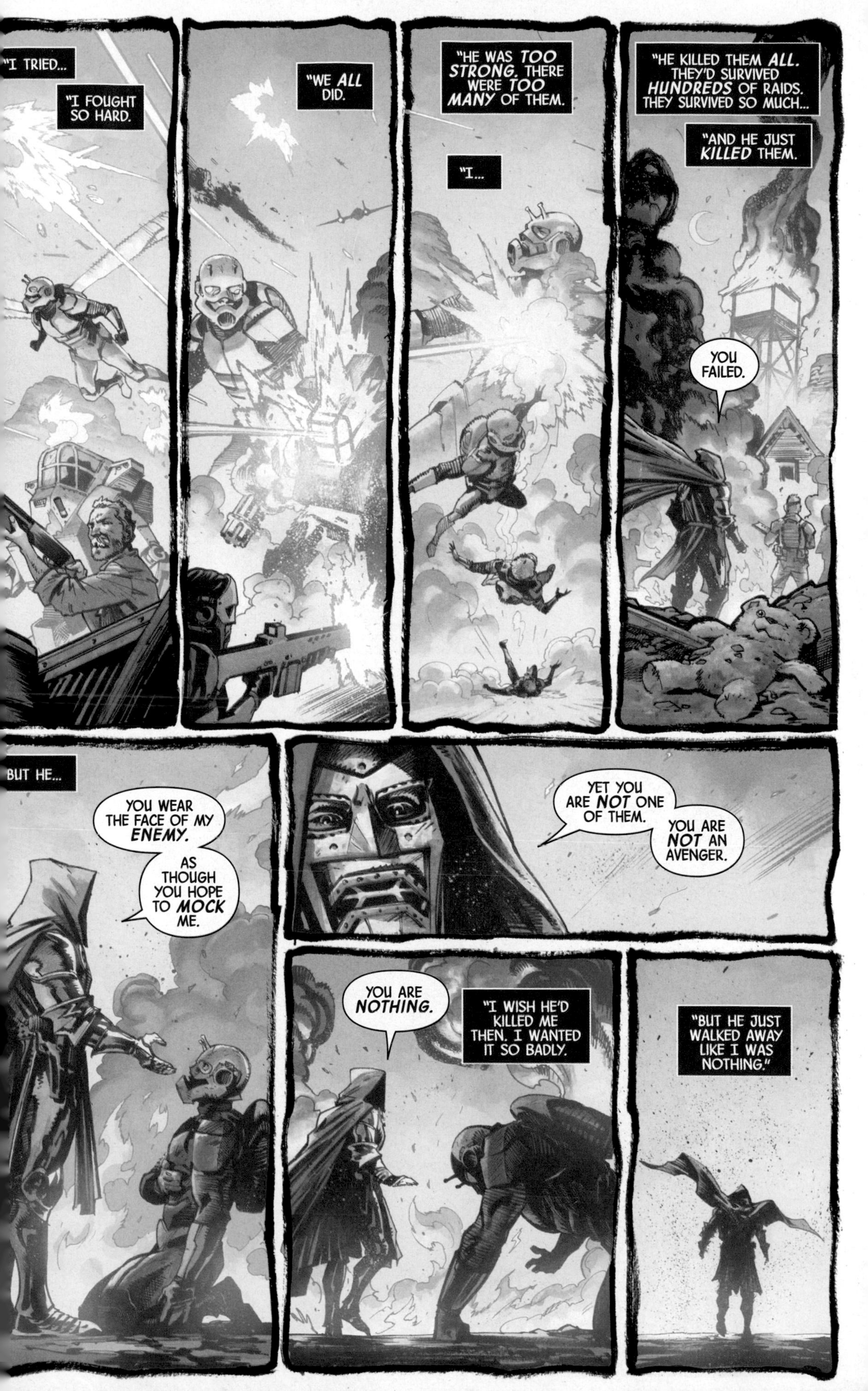
"I TRIED...
"I FOUGHT SO HARD.
"WE ALL DID.
"HE WAS TOO STRONG. THERE WERE TOO MANY OF THEM.
"I...
"HE KILLED THEM ALL. THEY'D SURVIVED HUNDREDS OF RAIDS. THEY SURVIVED SO MUCH...
"AND HE JUST KILLED THEM.
YOU FAILED.
BUT HE...
YOU WEAR THE FACE OF MY ENEMY.
AS THOUGH YOU HOPE TO MOCK ME.
YET YOU ARE NOT ONE OF THEM.
YOU ARE NOT AN AVENGER.
YOU ARE NOTHING.
"I WISH HE'D KILLED ME THEN. I WANTED IT SO BADLY.
"BUT HE JUST WALKED AWAY LIKE I WAS NOTHING."

OH MY GOD.

I'VE BEEN FIDDLING WITH THIS ANT-MAN ARMOR EVER SINCE FINDING THAT HELMET AS A KID.

THOUGHT MAYBE...MAYBE I COULD BE LIKE THE MAN WHO ORIGINALLY MADE IT.

THOUGHT MAYBE I COULD BE A *HERO*. THAT I COULD SAVE PEOPLE.

BUT WHEN IT MATTERED MOST?

I COULDN'T SAVE THEM.

LOOK...WE'VE GOT ENOUGH FOOD, RESOURCES, HOUSING... *WHATEVER* YOU NEED.

YOU CAN STAY HERE *AS LONG* AS YOU WANT. WE COULD USE SOMEONE LIKE YOU.

I KNOW IT'S NOT GOING TO CHANGE WH HAPPENED BUT--

I'M *NOT* STAYING.

I DIDN'T COME HERE TO *ESCAPE.*

I CAME HERE BECAUSE...

...BECAUSE I'M GOING TO *KILL* DOOM.

AND I *NEED* YOUR HELP.

I... UH...

DWIGHT, WE'VE BUILT SOMETHING HERE.

A *SAFE* PLACE, WITH MORE THAN ENOUGH FOOD TO FEED EVERYONE.

FOR THE DESTRUCTION THEY BROUGHT TO THIS PART OF THE COUNTRY. HE WANTED TO SHOW THAT HE WASN'T LIKE THEM. THAT THE BANNER REIGN OF TERROR WAS TRULY OVER.

THIS WHOLE WORLD HAS BEEN TWISTED AND SNARLED, CAUGHT UP IN ONE LONG WAR. DECADES OF BASHING IN EACH OTHERS' HEADS AND *NOTHING* HAS GOTTEN BETTER.

IT HAS TO STOP AT SOME POINT. WE'RE TRYING TO BUILD SOMETHING NEW, WITHOUT *VIOLENCE*. WITHOUT *BLOODSHED*.

YEAH?

DIDN'T *LOGAN* TRY THAT, TOO?

HOW'D *THAT* WORK OUT FOR HIM?

HELL, *I* TRIED IT AND IT DIDN'T WORK. THAT'S *NOT* THE WORLD WE LIVE IN. BURYING YOUR HEAD IN THE SAND ISN'T GOING TO CHANGE THAT.

DWIGHT--

DOOM KILLED THEM, DANI!

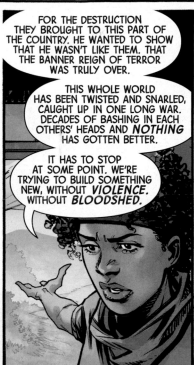

WE BUILT THIS PLACE BECAUSE BRUCE WANTED TO MAKE AMENDS FOR THE THINGS THAT HIS FATHER AND HIS FAMILY DID.

AND KILLING HIM *WON'T* BRING THEM BACK.

NOT JUST THEM! THIS IS HAPPENING *EVERYWHERE*. DOOM HAS KILLED SO MANY.

COMING HERE, I FOUND HOLDOUT AFTER HOLDOUT.

GUTTED. DESTROYED.

SO MANY BODIES THAT I LOST COUNT.

TOO LOUD. TOO LOUD! DON'T SHOUT!

BRUCE, IT'S ALL RIGHT. WE'RE JUST TALKING. THAT'S ALL.

NO SHOUTING.

I... DWIGHT... LOOK. WE'LL HELP YOU, BUT...

WE NEED TO TALK ABOUT IT. OKAY? YOU JUST GOT HERE AND IT'S A LOT TO TAKE IN.

WE NEED TO--

DANI! BRUCE!

WE'VE GOT A *PROBLEM*.

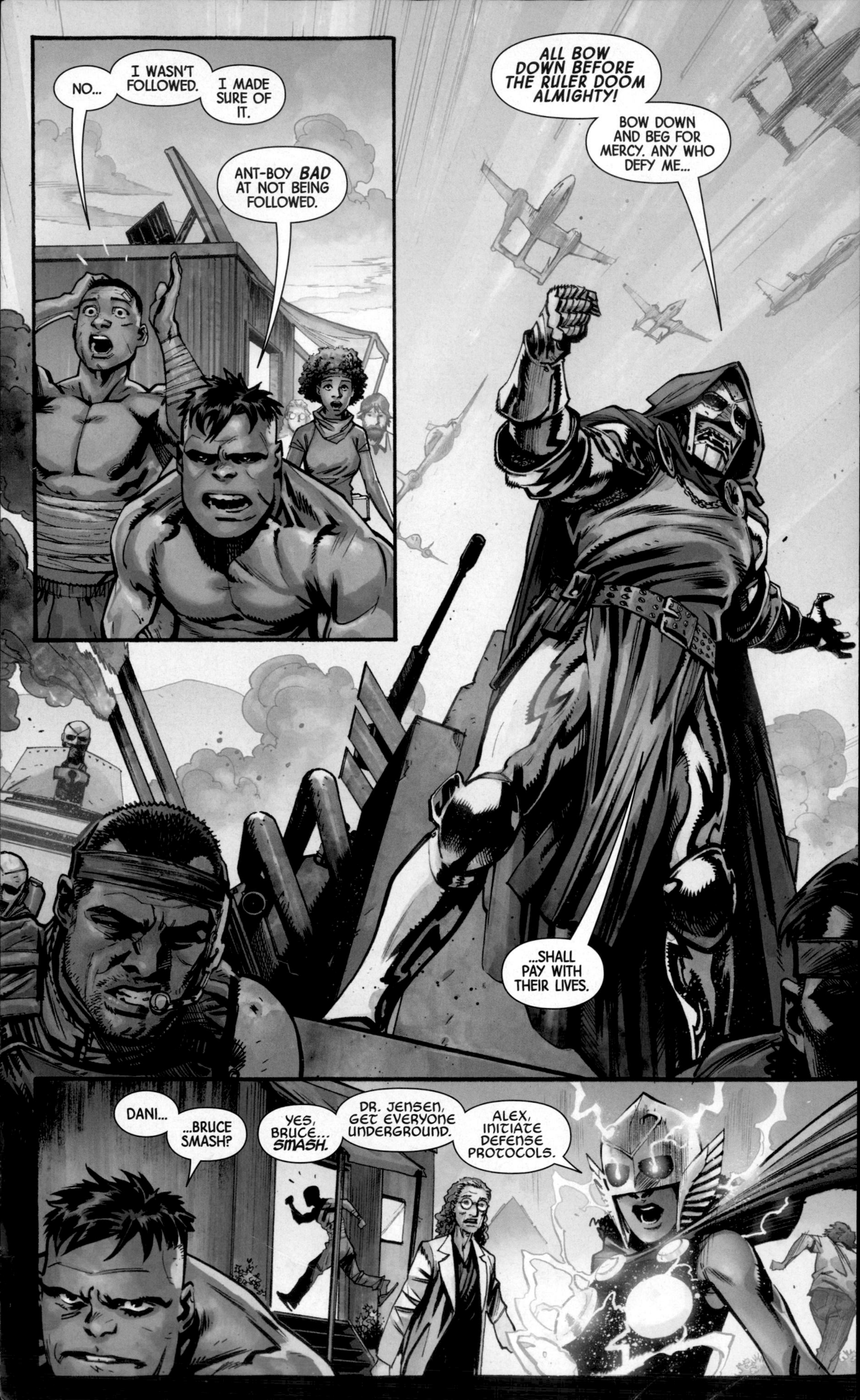
NO...
I WASN'T FOLLOWED.
I MADE SURE OF IT.
ANT-BOY *BAD* AT NOT BEING FOLLOWED.
ALL BOW DOWN BEFORE THE RULER DOOM ALMIGHTY!
BOW DOWN AND BEG FOR MERCY. ANY WHO DEFY ME...
...SHALL PAY WITH THEIR LIVES.
DANI...
...BRUCE SMASH?
YES, BRUCE... *SMASH.*
DR. JENSEN, GET EVERYONE UNDERGROUND.
ALEX, INITIATE DEFENSE PROTOCOLS.

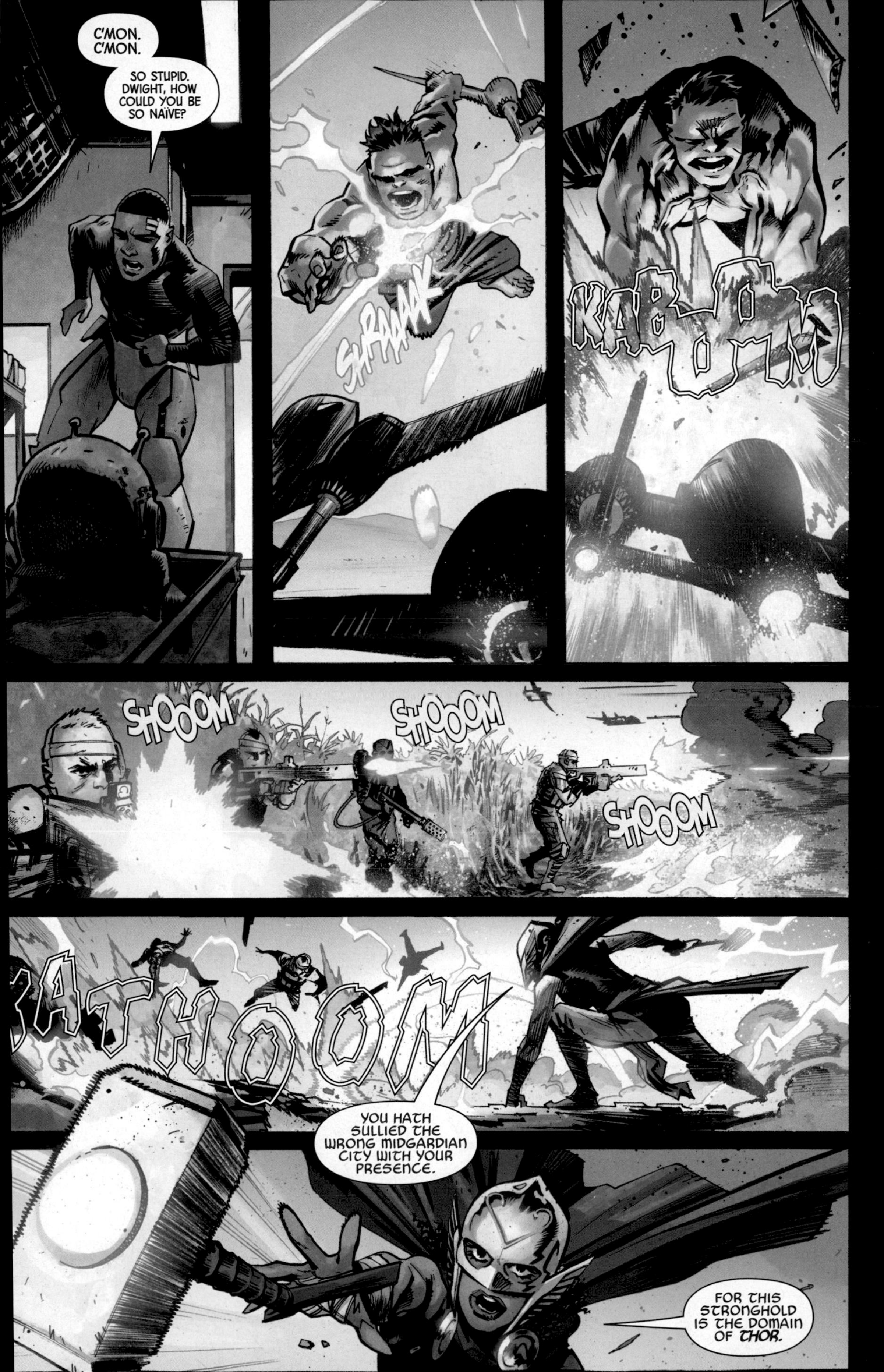
C'MON. C'MON.
SO STUPID. DWIGHT, HOW COULD YOU BE SO NAÏVE?
SHRAAAK
KABOOM
SHOOOM
SHOOOM
SHOOOM
ATHOOOM
YOU HATH SULLIED THE WRONG MIDGARDIAN CITY WITH YOUR PRESENCE.
FOR THIS STRONGHOLD IS THE DOMAIN OF *THOR.*

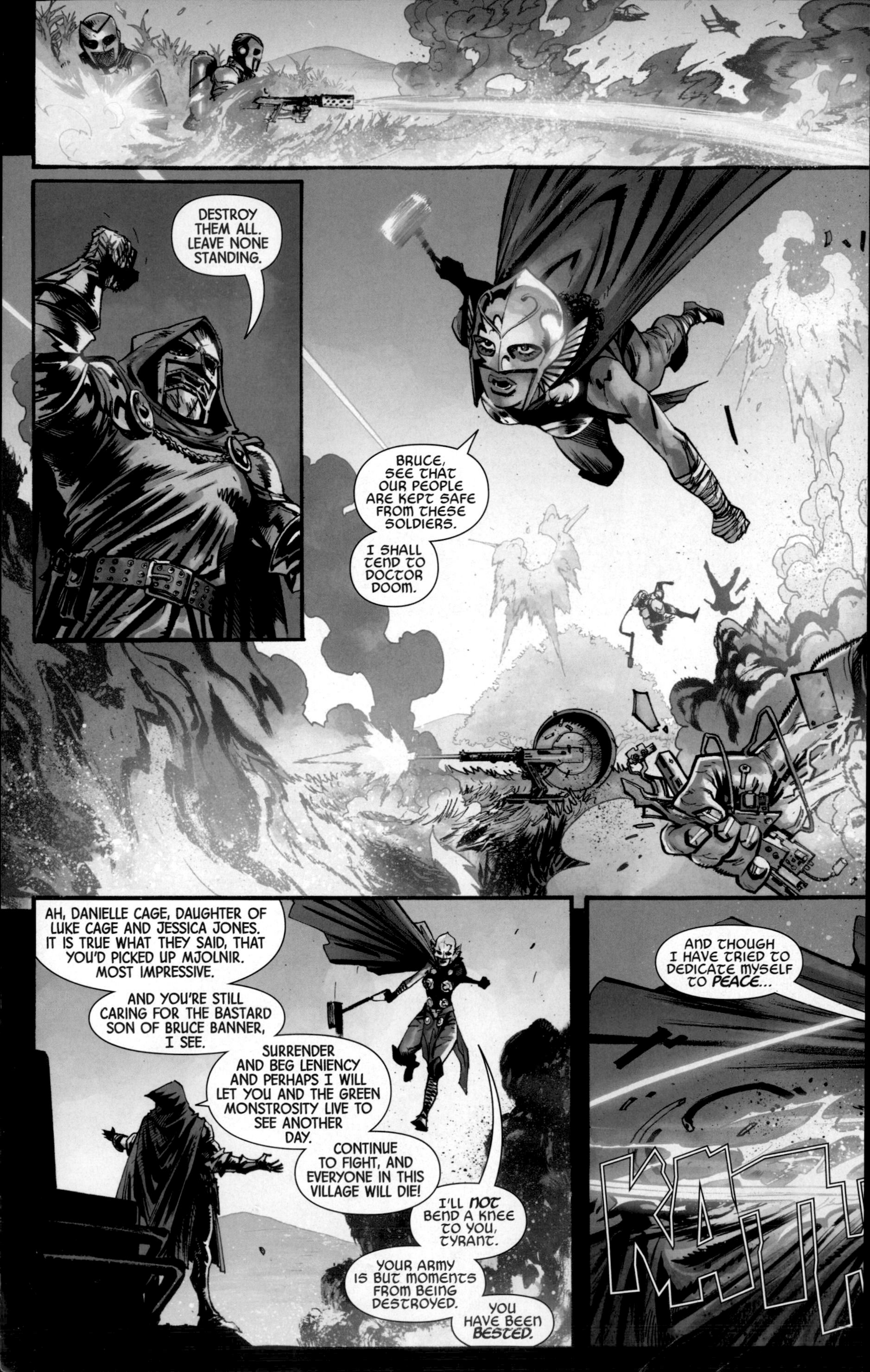
DESTROY THEM ALL. LEAVE NONE STANDING.
BRUCE, SEE THAT OUR PEOPLE ARE KEPT SAFE FROM THESE SOLDIERS.
I SHALL TEND TO DOCTOR DOOM.
AH, DANIELLE CAGE, DAUGHTER OF LUKE CAGE AND JESSICA JONES. IT IS TRUE WHAT THEY SAID, THAT YOU'D PICKED UP MJOLNIR. MOST IMPRESSIVE.
AND YOU'RE STILL CARING FOR THE BASTARD SON OF BRUCE BANNER, I SEE.
SURRENDER AND BEG LENIENCY AND PERHAPS I WILL LET YOU AND THE GREEN MONSTROSITY LIVE TO SEE ANOTHER DAY.
CONTINUE TO FIGHT, AND EVERYONE IN THIS VILLAGE WILL DIE!
I'LL NOT BEND A KNEE TO YOU, TYRANT.
YOUR ARMY IS BUT MOMENTS FROM BEING DESTROYED.
YOU HAVE BEEN BESTED.
AND THOUGH I HAVE TRIED TO DEDICATE MYSELF TO PEACE...

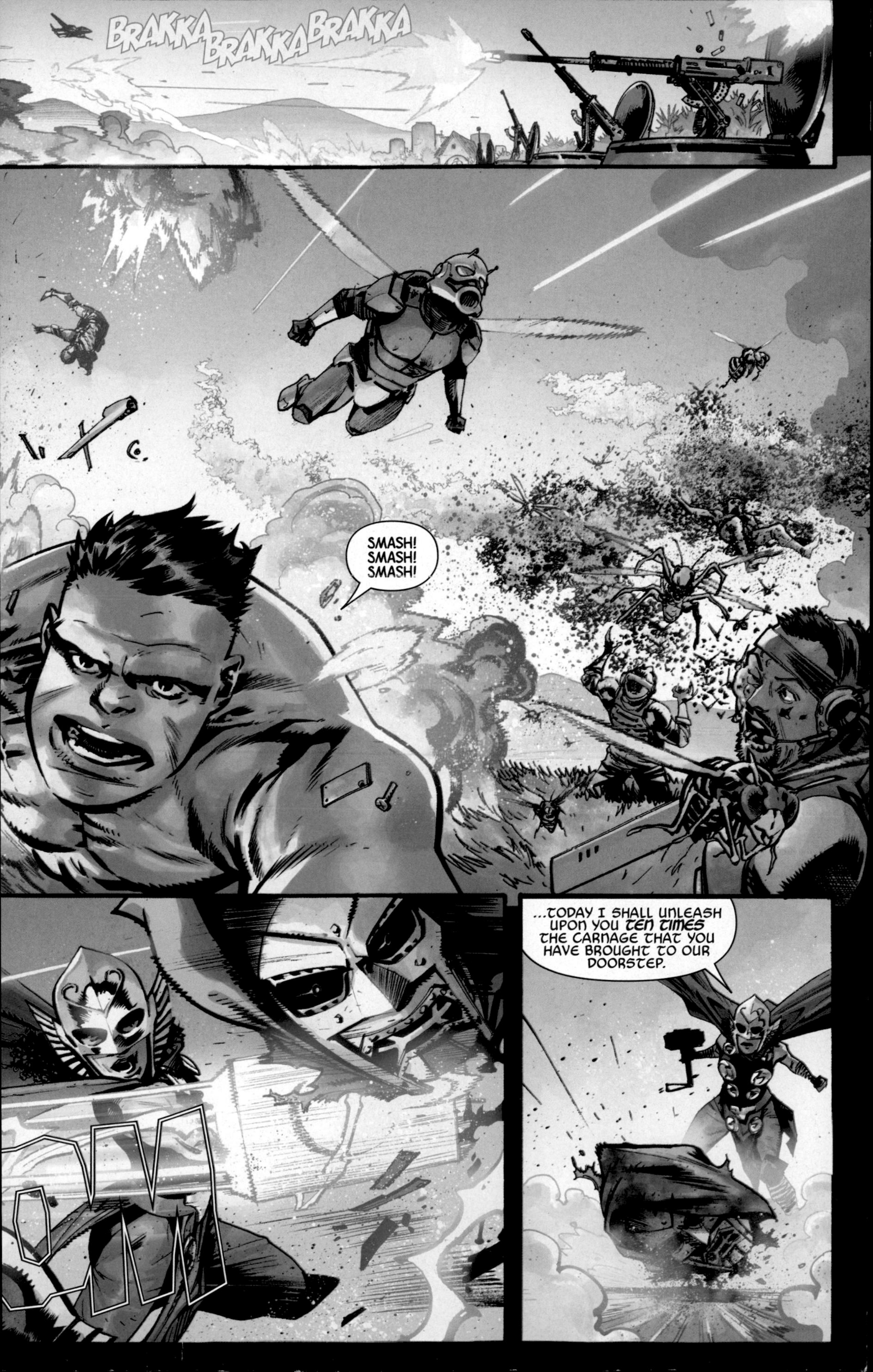
BRAKKA BRAKKA BRAKKA
SMASH! SMASH! SMASH!
...TODAY I SHALL UNLEASH UPON YOU *TEN TIMES* THE CARNAGE THAT YOU HAVE BROUGHT TO OUR DOORSTEP.

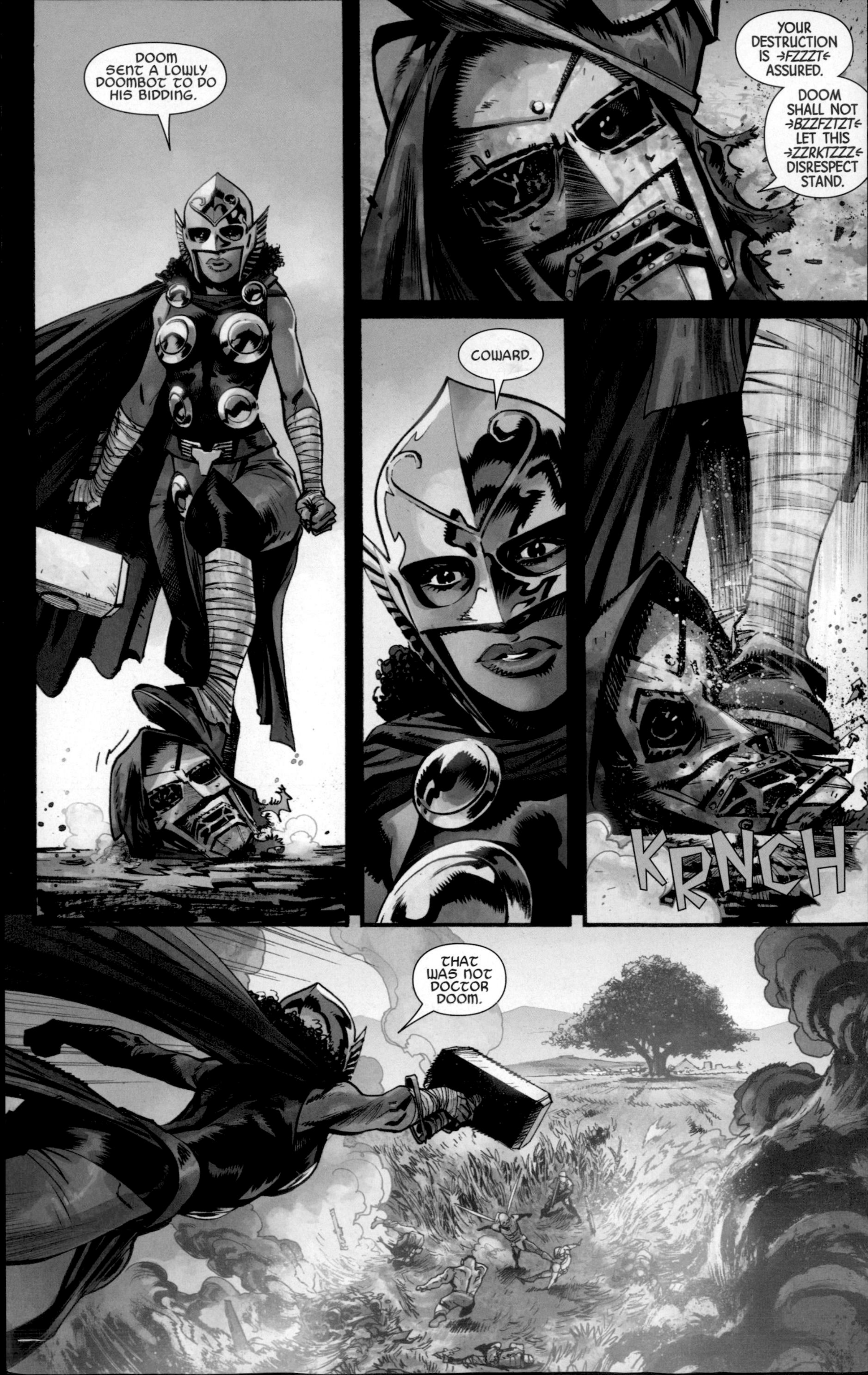
DOOM SENT A LOWLY DOOMBOT TO DO HIS BIDDING.
YOUR DESTRUCTION IS →FZZZT← ASSURED.
DOOM SHALL NOT →BZZFZTZT← LET THIS →ZZRKTZZZ← DISRESPECT STAND.
COWARD.
KRNCH
THAT WAS NOT DOCTOR DOOM.

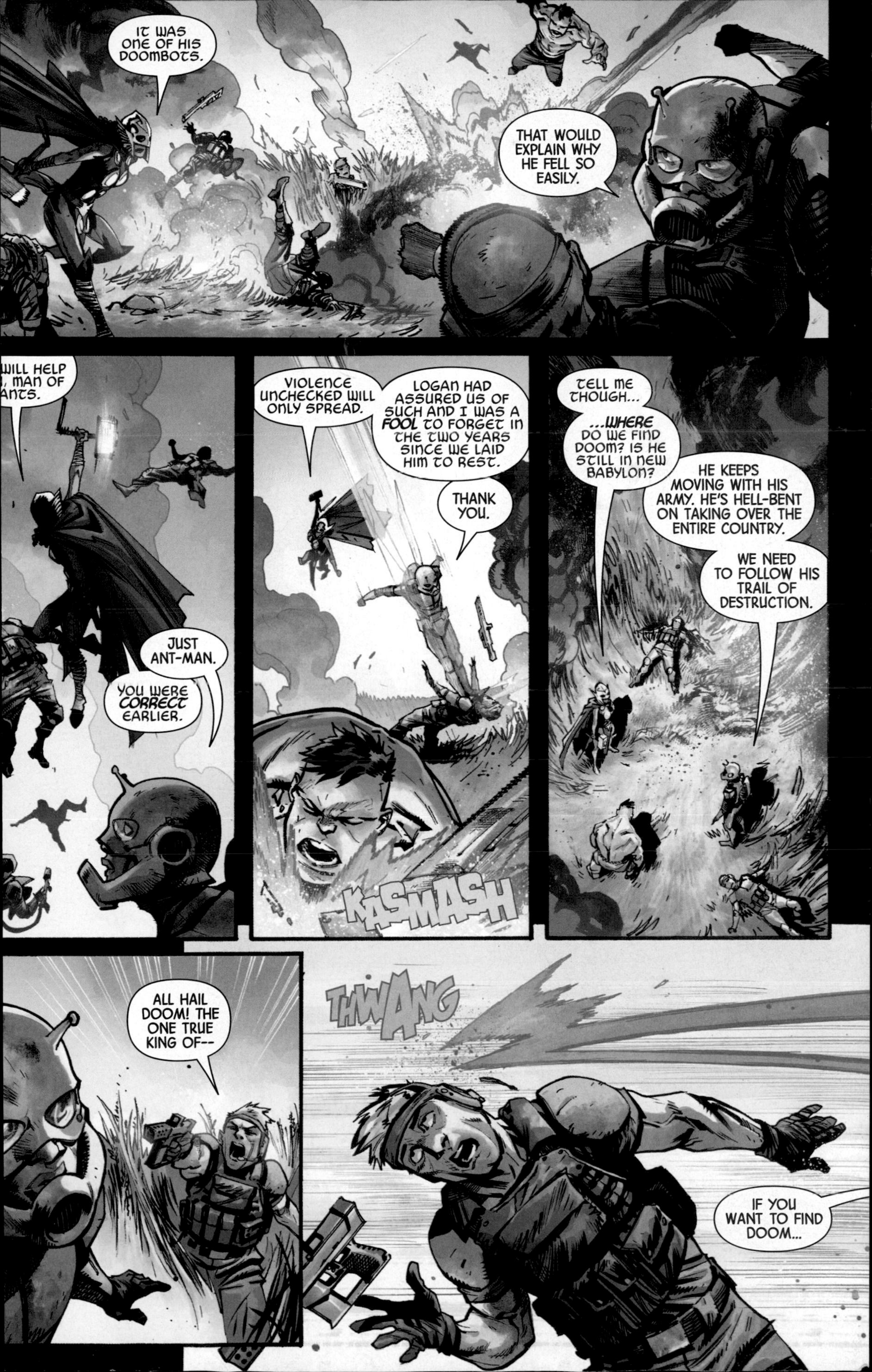
IT WAS ONE OF HIS DOOMBOTS.
THAT WOULD EXPLAIN WHY HE FELL SO EASILY.
WILL HELP , MAN OF ANTS.
JUST ANT-MAN.
YOU WERE CORRECT EARLIER.
VIOLENCE UNCHECKED WILL ONLY SPREAD.
LOGAN HAD ASSURED US OF SUCH AND I WAS A FOOL TO FORGET IN THE TWO YEARS SINCE WE LAID HIM TO REST.
THANK YOU.
KASMASH
TELL ME THOUGH...
...WHERE DO WE FIND DOOM? IS HE STILL IN NEW BABYLON?
HE KEEPS MOVING WITH HIS ARMY. HE'S HELL-BENT ON TAKING OVER THE ENTIRE COUNTRY.
WE NEED TO FOLLOW HIS TRAIL OF DESTRUCTION.
ALL HAIL DOOM! THE ONE TRUE KING OF--
THWANG
IF YOU WANT TO FIND DOOM...

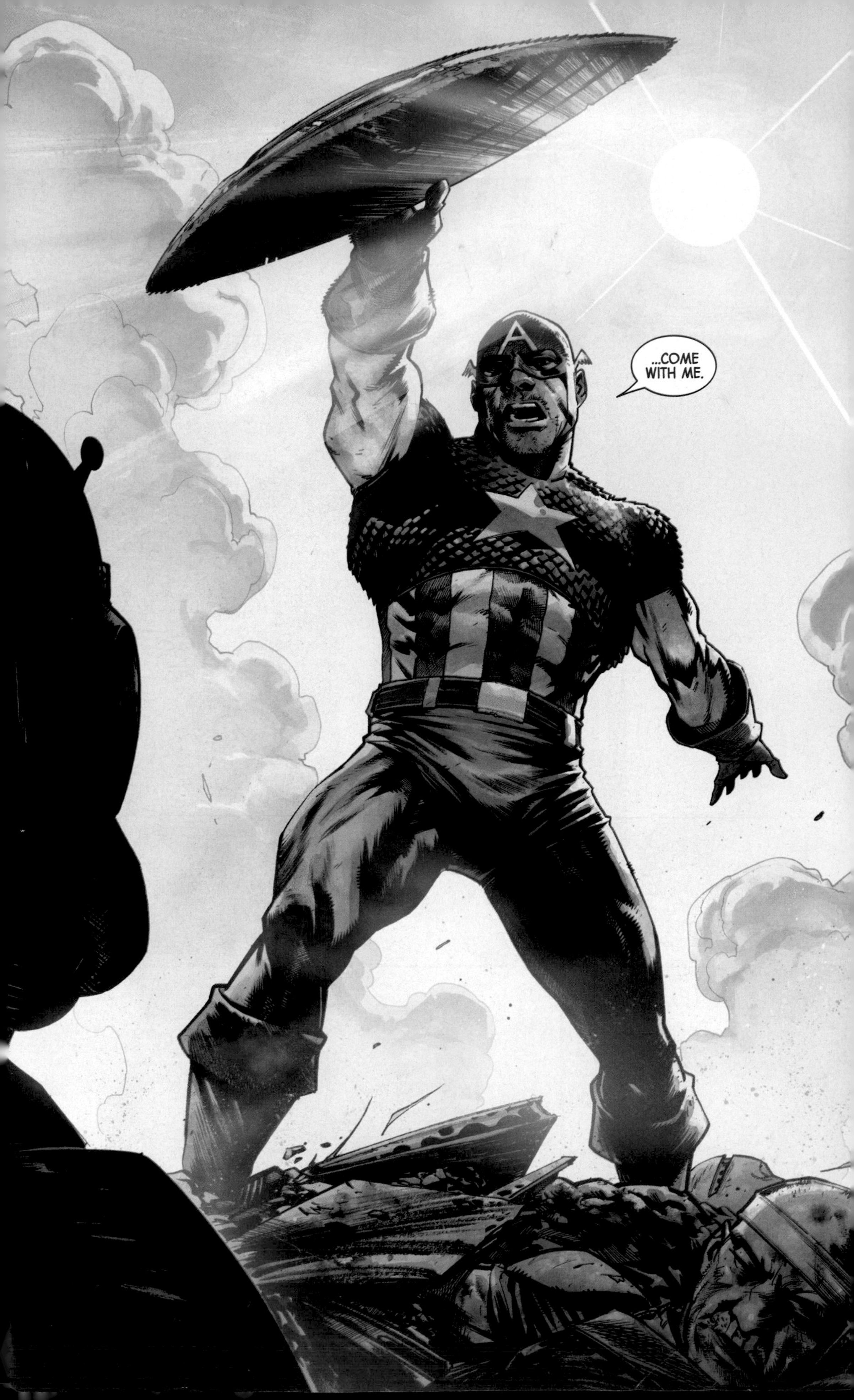
...COME WITH ME.

2.

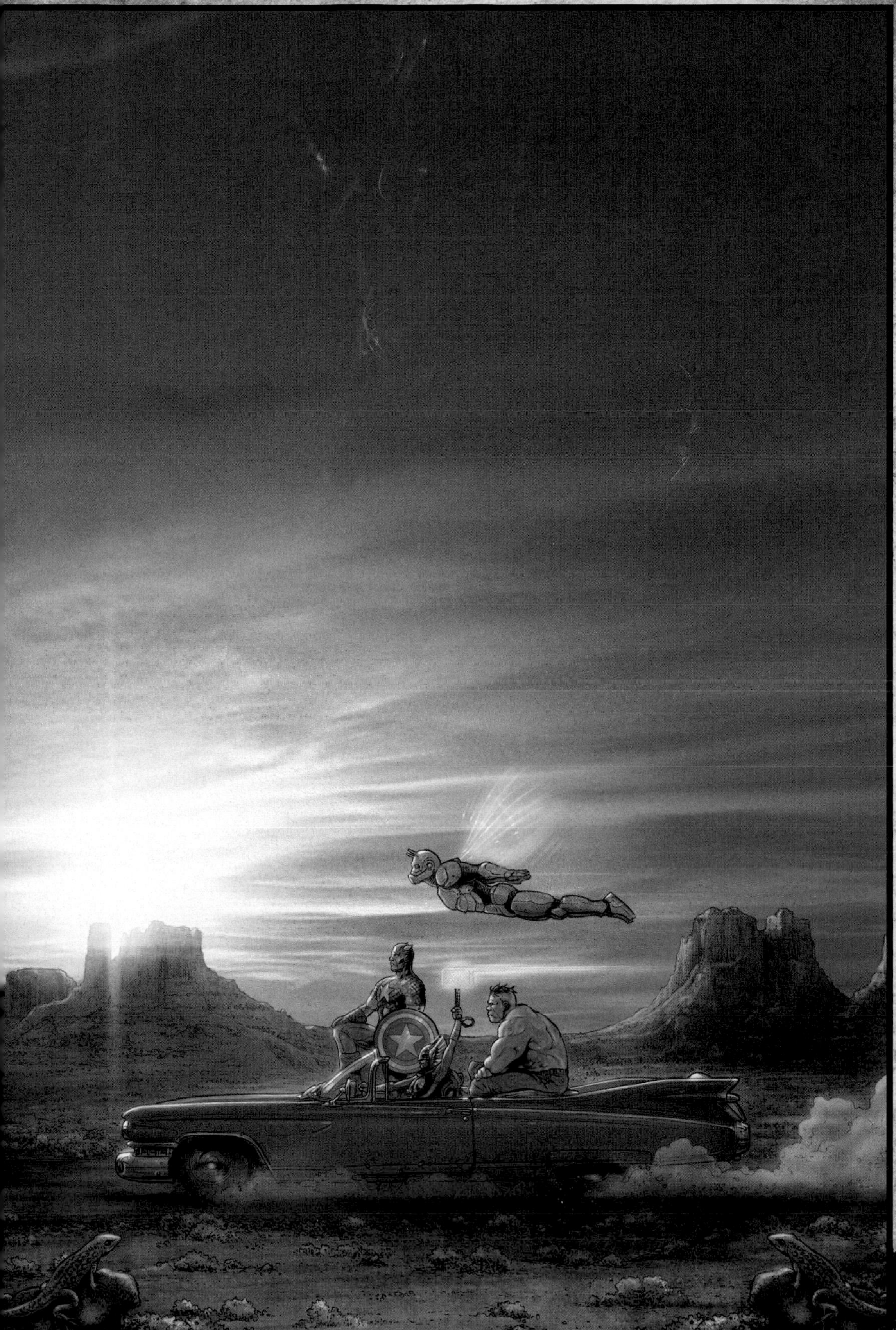

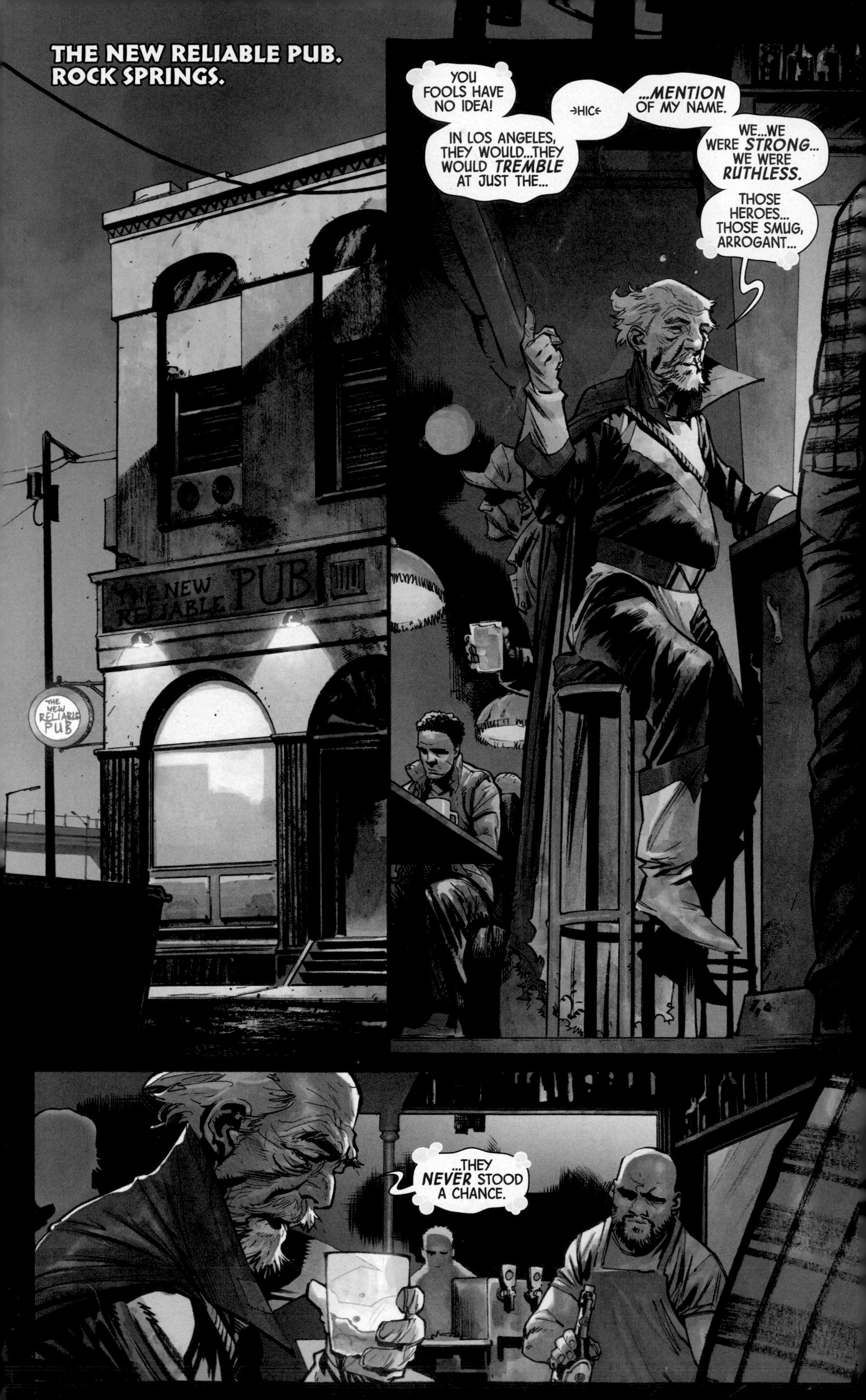
THE NEW RELIABLE PUB. ROCK SPRINGS.
THE NEW RELIABLE PUB
THE NEW RELIABLE PUB
YOU FOOLS HAVE NO IDEA!
IN LOS ANGELES, THEY WOULD...THEY WOULD TREMBLE AT JUST THE...
HIC
...MENTION OF MY NAME.
WE...WE WERE STRONG... WE WERE RUTHLESS.
THOSE HEROES... THOSE SMUG, ARROGANT...
...THEY NEVER STOOD A CHANCE.

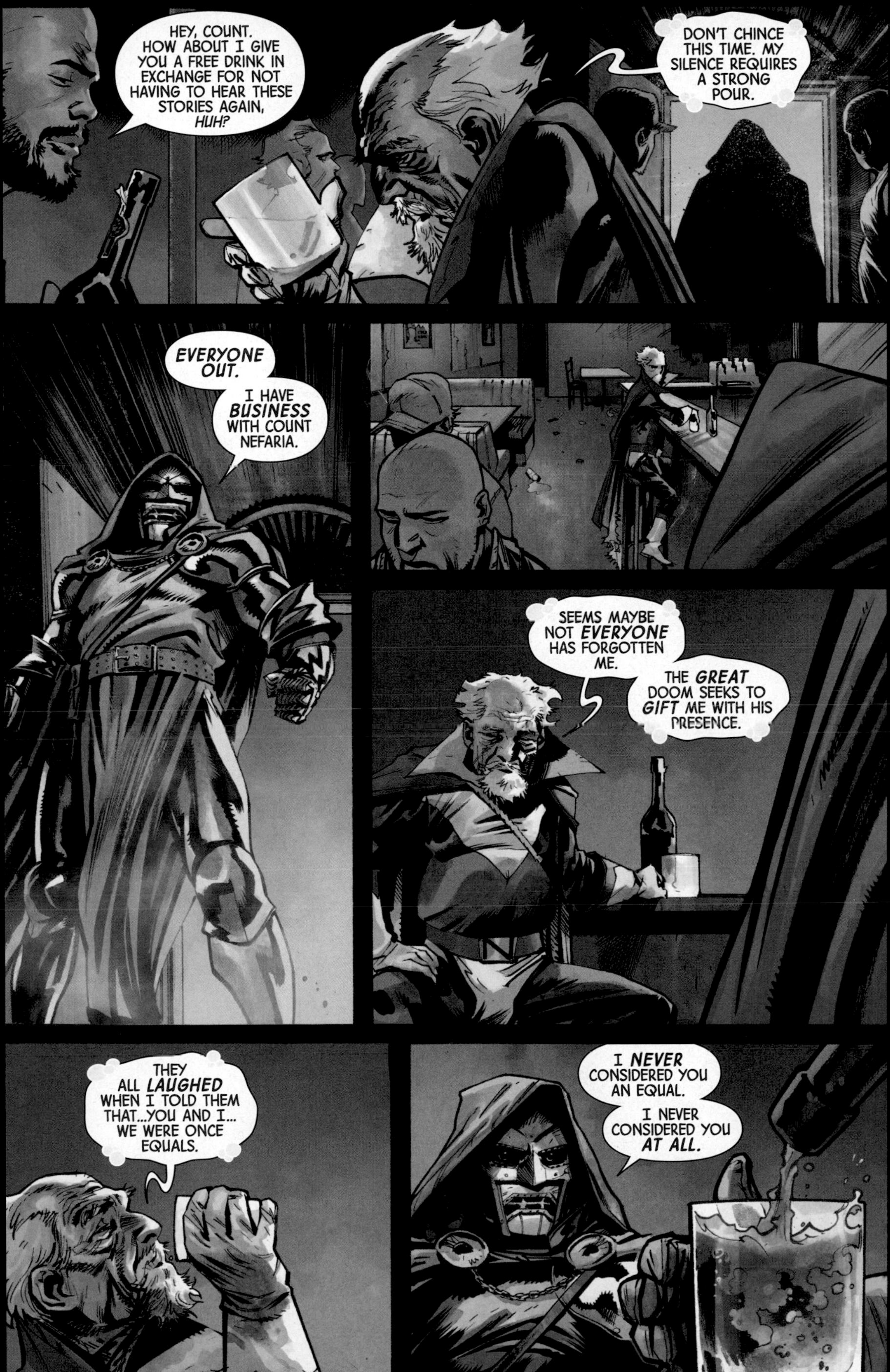
HEY, COUNT. HOW ABOUT I GIVE YOU A FREE DRINK IN EXCHANGE FOR NOT HAVING TO HEAR THESE STORIES AGAIN, HUH?
DON'T CHINCE THIS TIME. MY SILENCE REQUIRES A STRONG POUR.
EVERYONE OUT.
I HAVE BUSINESS WITH COUNT NEFARIA.
SEEMS MAYBE NOT EVERYONE HAS FORGOTTEN ME.
THE GREAT DOOM SEEKS TO GIFT ME WITH HIS PRESENCE.
THEY ALL LAUGHED WHEN I TOLD THEM THAT...YOU AND I... WE WERE ONCE EQUALS.
I NEVER CONSIDERED YOU AN EQUAL.
I NEVER CONSIDERED YOU AT ALL.

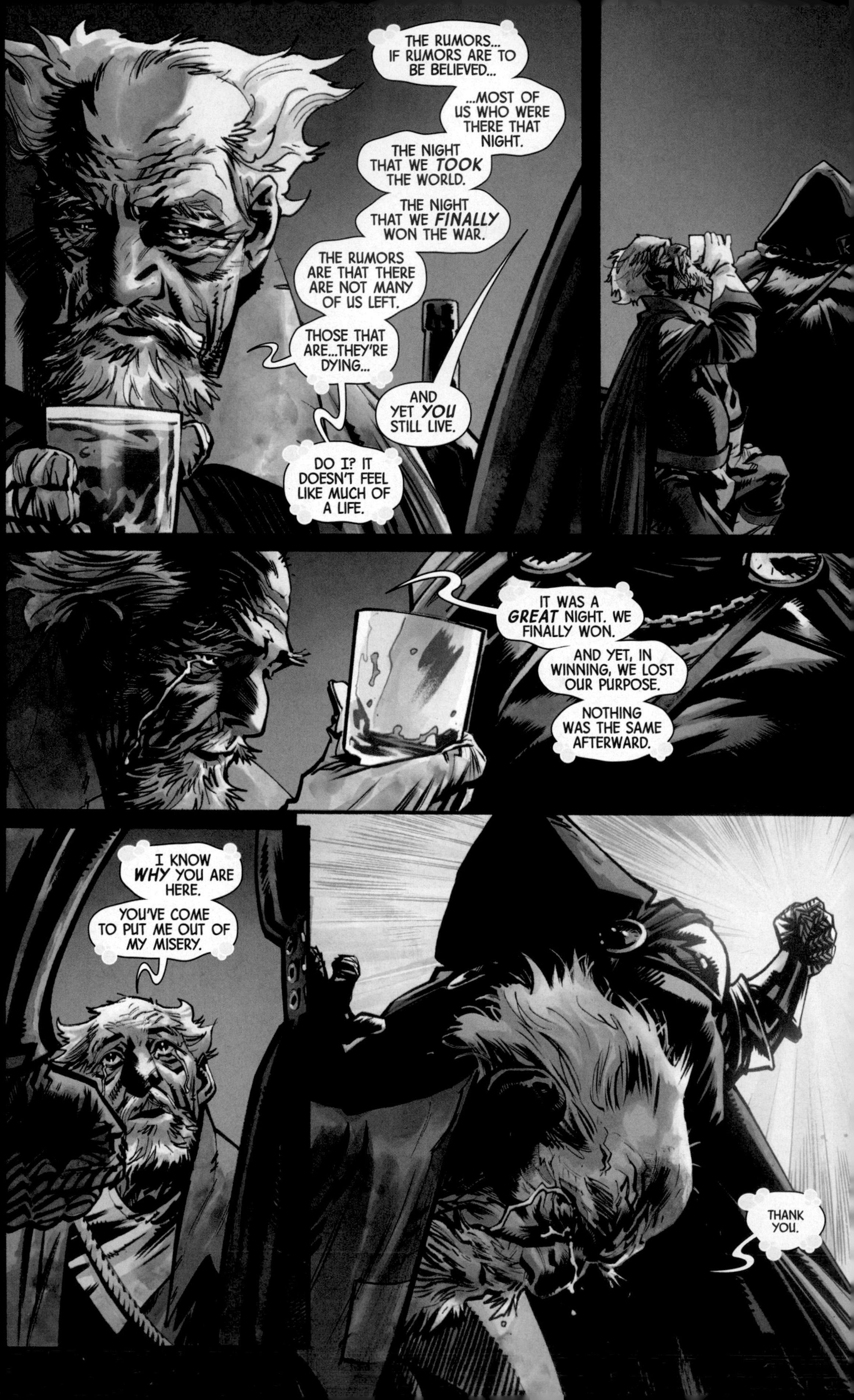
THE RUMORS... IF RUMORS ARE TO BE BELIEVED...
...MOST OF US WHO WERE THERE THAT NIGHT.
THE NIGHT THAT WE TOOK THE WORLD.
THE NIGHT THAT WE FINALLY WON THE WAR.
THE RUMORS ARE THAT THERE ARE NOT MANY OF US LEFT.
THOSE THAT ARE...THEY'RE DYING...
AND YET YOU STILL LIVE.
DO I? IT DOESN'T FEEL LIKE MUCH OF A LIFE.
IT WAS A GREAT NIGHT. WE FINALLY WON.
AND YET, IN WINNING, WE LOST OUR PURPOSE.
NOTHING WAS THE SAME AFTERWARD.
I KNOW WHY YOU ARE HERE.
YOU'VE COME TO PUT ME OUT OF MY MISERY.
THANK YOU.

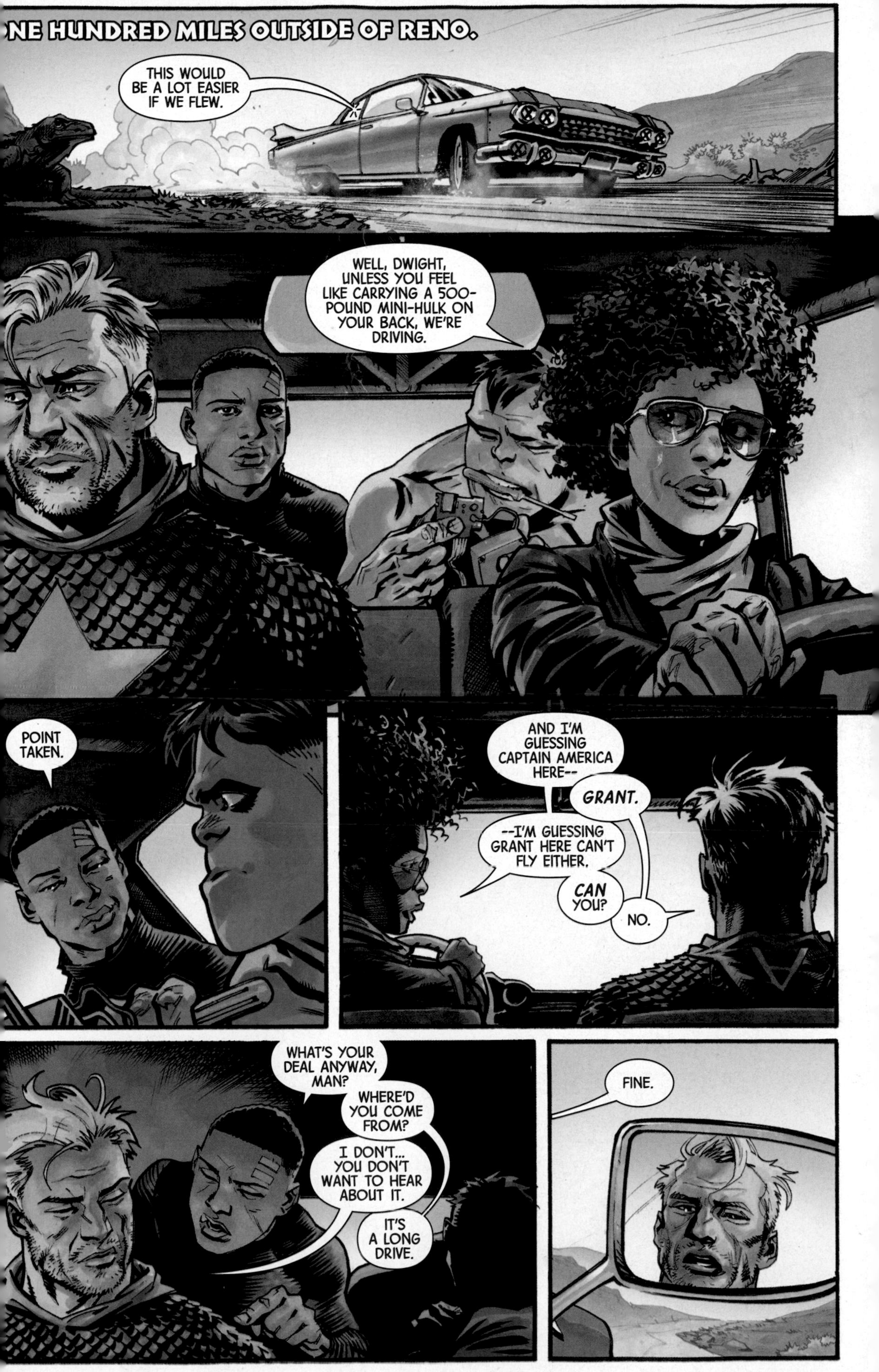
NE HUNDRED MILES OUTSIDE OF RENO.
THIS WOULD BE A LOT EASIER IF WE FLEW.
WELL, DWIGHT, UNLESS YOU FEEL LIKE CARRYING A 500-POUND MINI-HULK ON YOUR BACK, WE'RE DRIVING.
POINT TAKEN.
AND I'M GUESSING CAPTAIN AMERICA HERE--
GRANT.
--I'M GUESSING GRANT HERE CAN'T FLY EITHER.
CAN YOU?
NO.
WHAT'S YOUR DEAL ANYWAY, MAN?
WHERE'D YOU COME FROM?
I DON'T... YOU DON'T WANT TO HEAR ABOUT IT.
IT'S A LONG DRIVE.
FINE.

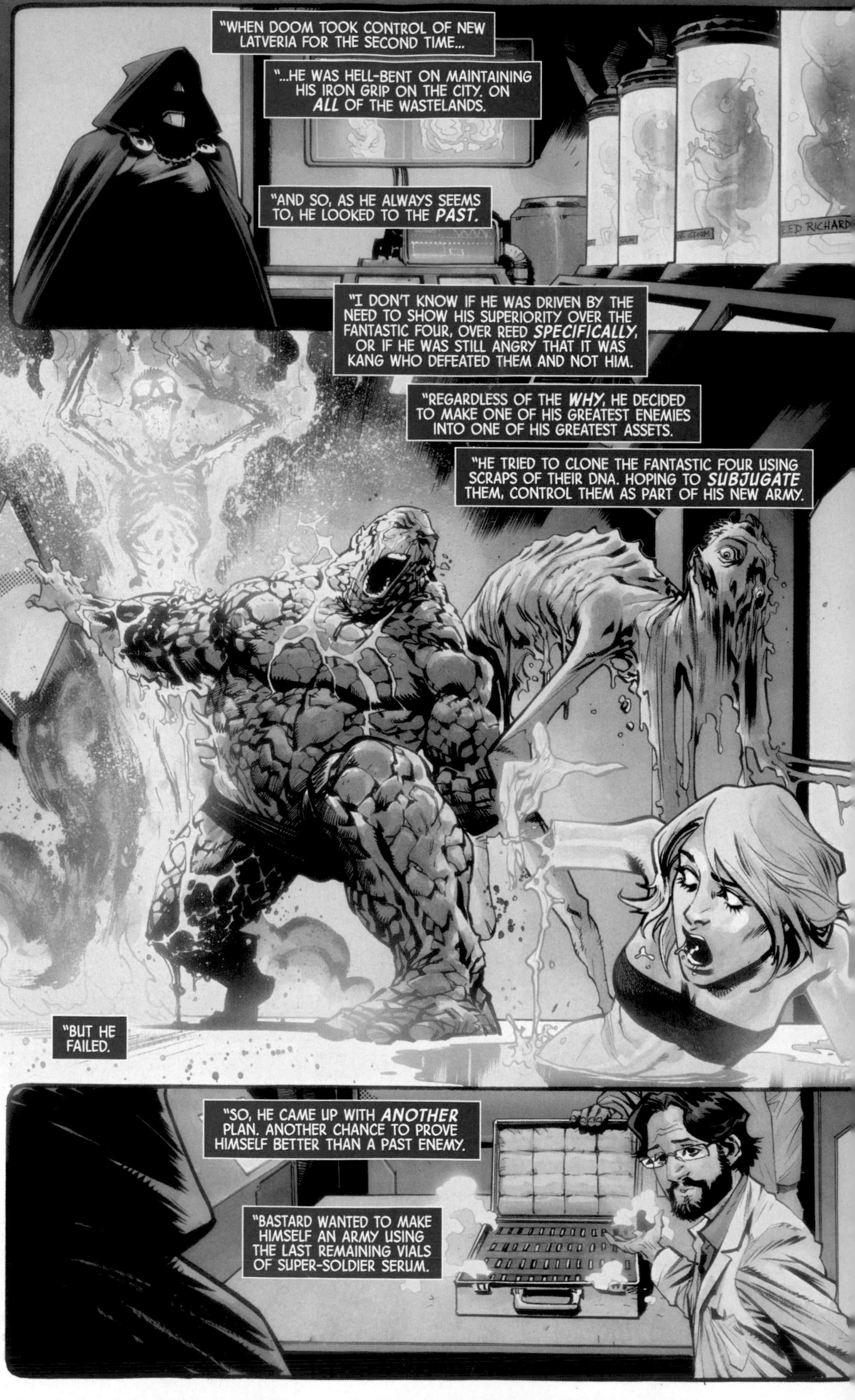
"WHEN DOOM TOOK CONTROL OF NEW LATVERIA FOR THE SECOND TIME...
"...HE WAS HELL-BENT ON MAINTAINING HIS IRON GRIP ON THE CITY. ON *ALL* OF THE WASTELANDS.
"AND SO, AS HE ALWAYS SEEMS TO, HE LOOKED TO THE *PAST*.
"I DON'T KNOW IF HE WAS DRIVEN BY THE NEED TO SHOW HIS SUPERIORITY OVER THE FANTASTIC FOUR, OVER REED *SPECIFICALLY*, OR IF HE WAS STILL ANGRY THAT IT WAS KANG WHO DEFEATED THEM AND NOT HIM.
"REGARDLESS OF THE *WHY*, HE DECIDED TO MAKE ONE OF HIS GREATEST ENEMIES INTO ONE OF HIS GREATEST ASSETS.
"HE TRIED TO CLONE THE FANTASTIC FOUR USING SCRAPS OF THEIR DNA. HOPING TO *SUBJUGATE* THEM, CONTROL THEM AS PART OF HIS NEW ARMY.
"BUT HE FAILED.
"SO, HE CAME UP WITH *ANOTHER* PLAN. ANOTHER CHANCE TO PROVE HIMSELF BETTER THAN A PAST ENEMY.
"BASTARD WANTED TO MAKE HIMSELF AN ARMY USING THE LAST REMAINING VIALS OF SUPER-SOLDIER SERUM.

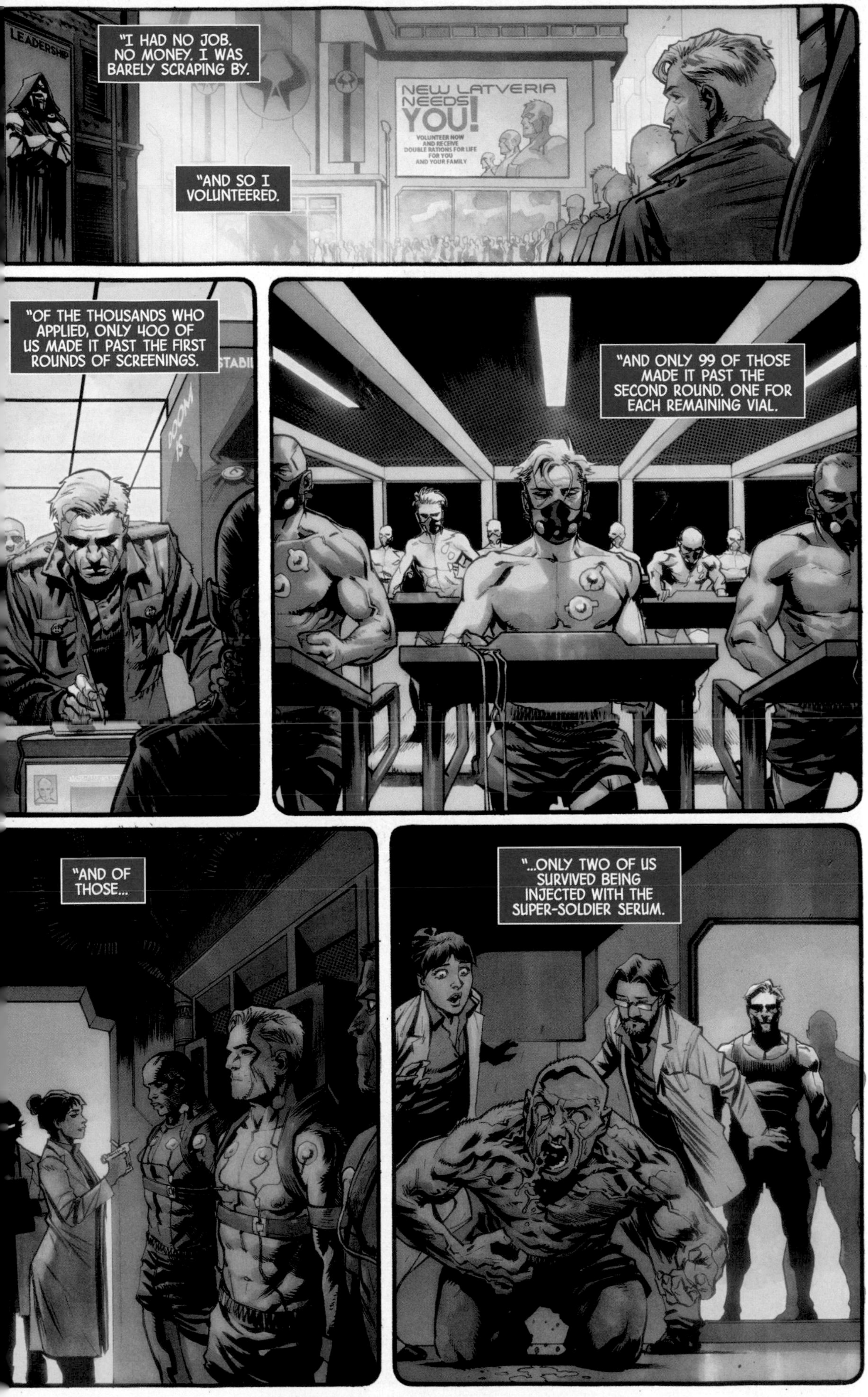

"I HAD NO JOB. NO MONEY. I WAS BARELY SCRAPING BY.
LEADERSHIP
NEW LATVERIA NEEDS YOU!
VOLUNTEER NOW AND RECEIVE DOUBLE RATIONS FOR LIFE FOR YOU AND YOUR FAMILY
"AND SO I VOLUNTEERED.
"OF THE THOUSANDS WHO APPLIED, ONLY 400 OF US MADE IT PAST THE FIRST ROUNDS OF SCREENINGS.
DOOM IS
"AND ONLY 99 OF THOSE MADE IT PAST THE SECOND ROUND. ONE FOR EACH REMAINING VIAL.
"AND OF THOSE...
"...ONLY TWO OF US SURVIVED BEING INJECTED WITH THE SUPER-SOLDIER SERUM.

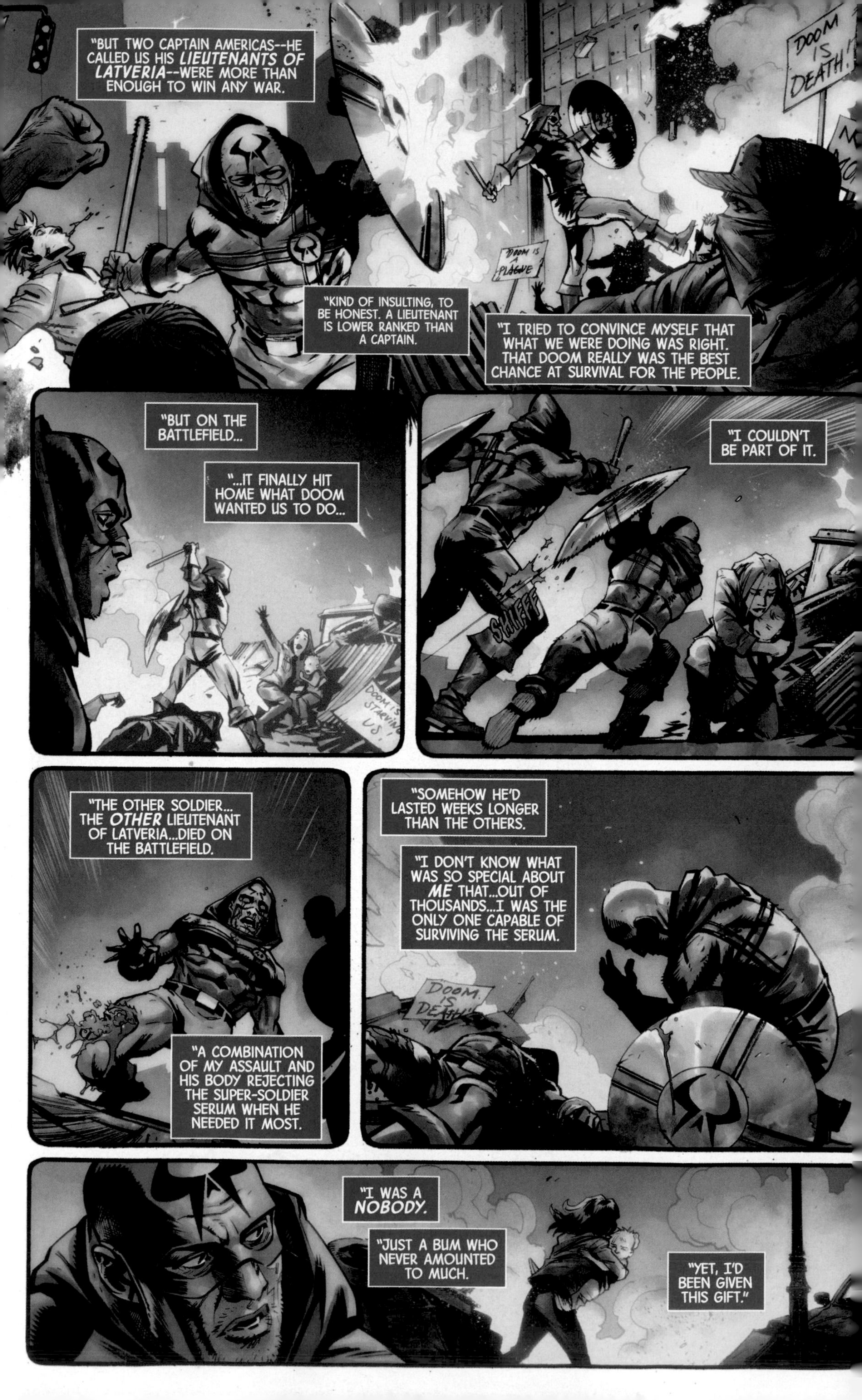
"BUT TWO CAPTAIN AMERICAS--HE CALLED US HIS *LIEUTENANTS OF LATVERIA*--WERE MORE THAN ENOUGH TO WIN ANY WAR.
DOOM IS DEATH!
DOOM IS A PLAGUE
"KIND OF INSULTING, TO BE HONEST. A LIEUTENANT IS LOWER RANKED THAN A CAPTAIN.
"I TRIED TO CONVINCE MYSELF THAT WHAT WE WERE DOING WAS RIGHT. THAT DOOM REALLY WAS THE BEST CHANCE AT SURVIVAL FOR THE PEOPLE.
"BUT ON THE BATTLEFIELD...
"...IT FINALLY HIT HOME WHAT DOOM WANTED US TO DO...
DOOM IS STARVING US.
"I COULDN'T BE PART OF IT.
SHHFFF
"THE OTHER SOLDIER... THE *OTHER* LIEUTENANT OF LATVERIA...DIED ON THE BATTLEFIELD.
"A COMBINATION OF MY ASSAULT AND HIS BODY REJECTING THE SUPER-SOLDIER SERUM WHEN HE NEEDED IT MOST.
"SOMEHOW HE'D LASTED WEEKS LONGER THAN THE OTHERS.
"I DON'T KNOW WHAT WAS SO SPECIAL ABOUT *ME* THAT...OUT OF THOUSANDS...I WAS THE ONLY ONE CAPABLE OF SURVIVING THE SERUM.
"I WAS A ***NOBODY.***
"JUST A BUM WHO NEVER AMOUNTED TO MUCH.
"YET, I'D BEEN GIVEN THIS GIFT."

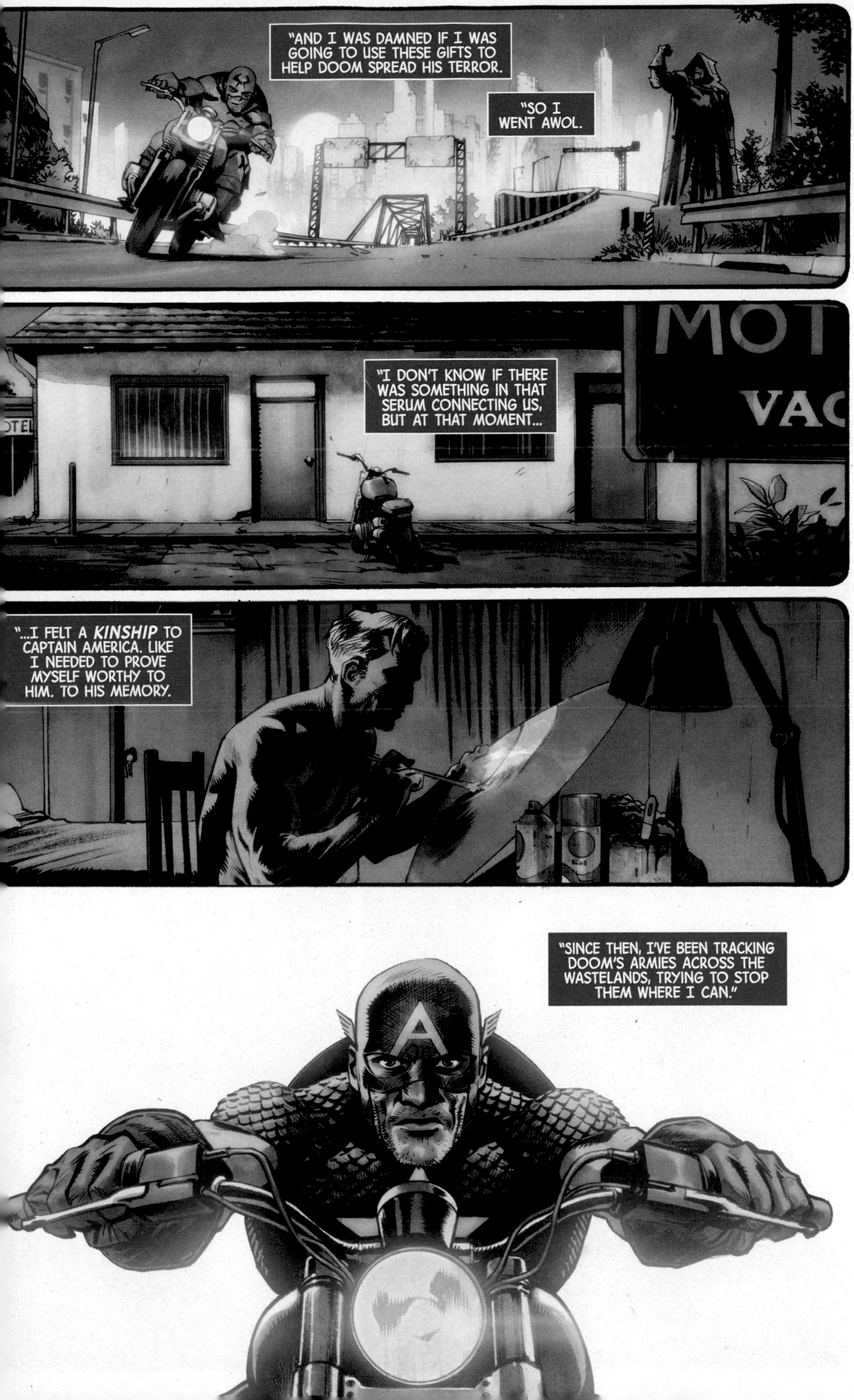

"AND I WAS DAMNED IF I WAS GOING TO USE THESE GIFTS TO HELP DOOM SPREAD HIS TERROR.
"SO I WENT AWOL.
MOT
VAC
OTEL
"I DON'T KNOW IF THERE WAS SOMETHING IN THAT SERUM CONNECTING US, BUT AT THAT MOMENT...
"...I FELT A *KINSHIP* TO CAPTAIN AMERICA. LIKE I NEEDED TO PROVE MYSELF WORTHY TO HIM. TO HIS MEMORY.
"SINCE THEN, I'VE BEEN TRACKING DOOM'S ARMIES ACROSS THE WASTELANDS, TRYING TO STOP THEM WHERE I CAN."

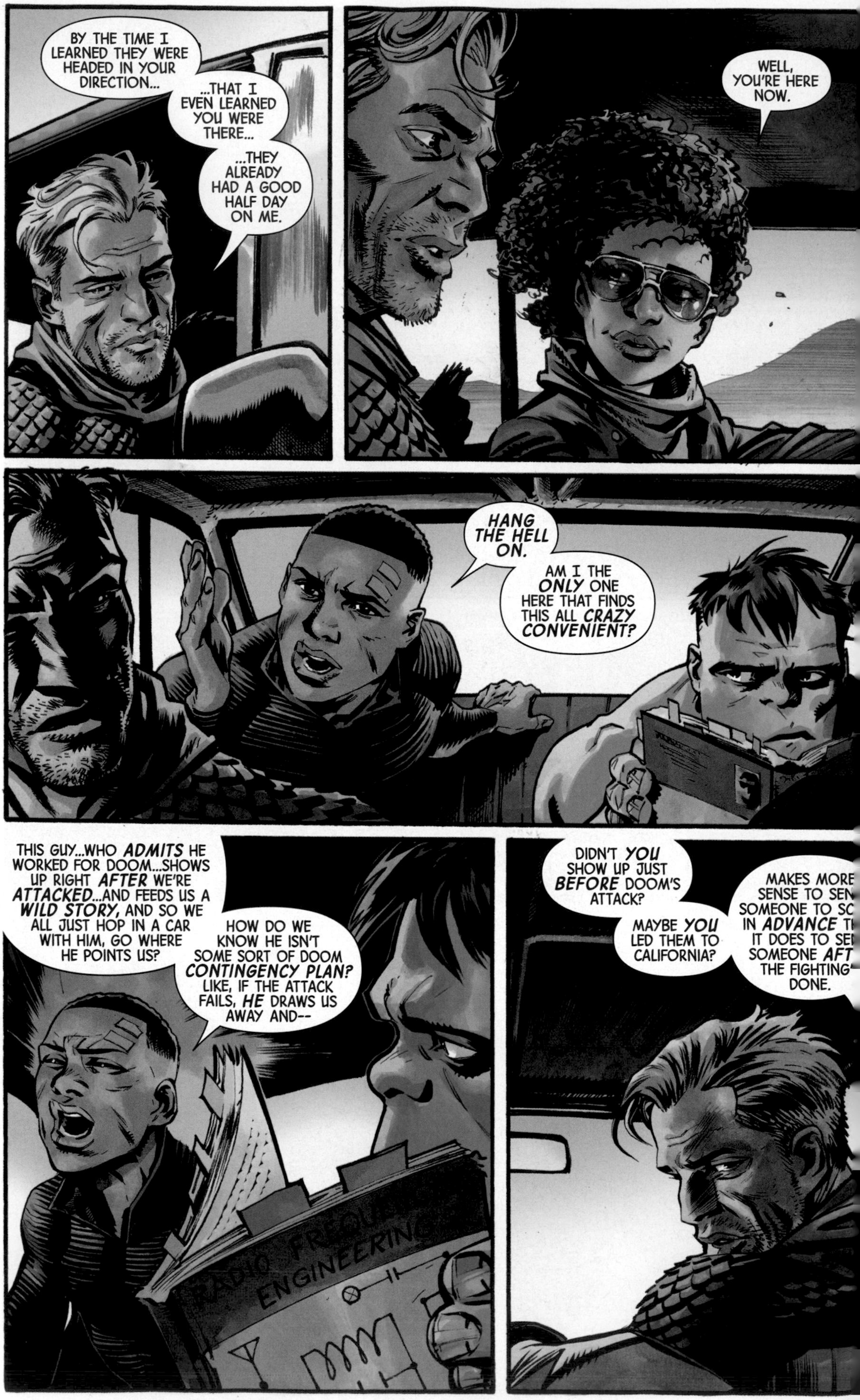
BY THE TIME I LEARNED THEY WERE HEADED IN YOUR DIRECTION...
...THAT I EVEN LEARNED YOU WERE THERE...
...THEY ALREADY HAD A GOOD HALF DAY ON ME.
WELL, YOU'RE HERE NOW.
HANG THE HELL ON.
AM I THE ONLY ONE HERE THAT FINDS THIS ALL CRAZY CONVENIENT?
THIS GUY...WHO ADMITS HE WORKED FOR DOOM...SHOWS UP RIGHT AFTER WE'RE ATTACKED...AND FEEDS US A WILD STORY, AND SO WE ALL JUST HOP IN A CAR WITH HIM, GO WHERE HE POINTS US?
HOW DO WE KNOW HE ISN'T SOME SORT OF DOOM CONTINGENCY PLAN? LIKE, IF THE ATTACK FAILS, HE DRAWS US AWAY AND--
RADIO FREQU
ENGINEERING
DIDN'T YOU SHOW UP JUST BEFORE DOOM'S ATTACK?
MAYBE YOU LED THEM TO CALIFORNIA?
MAKES MORE SENSE TO SEN SOMEONE TO SC IN ADVANCE T IT DOES TO SE SOMEONE AFT THE FIGHTING DONE.

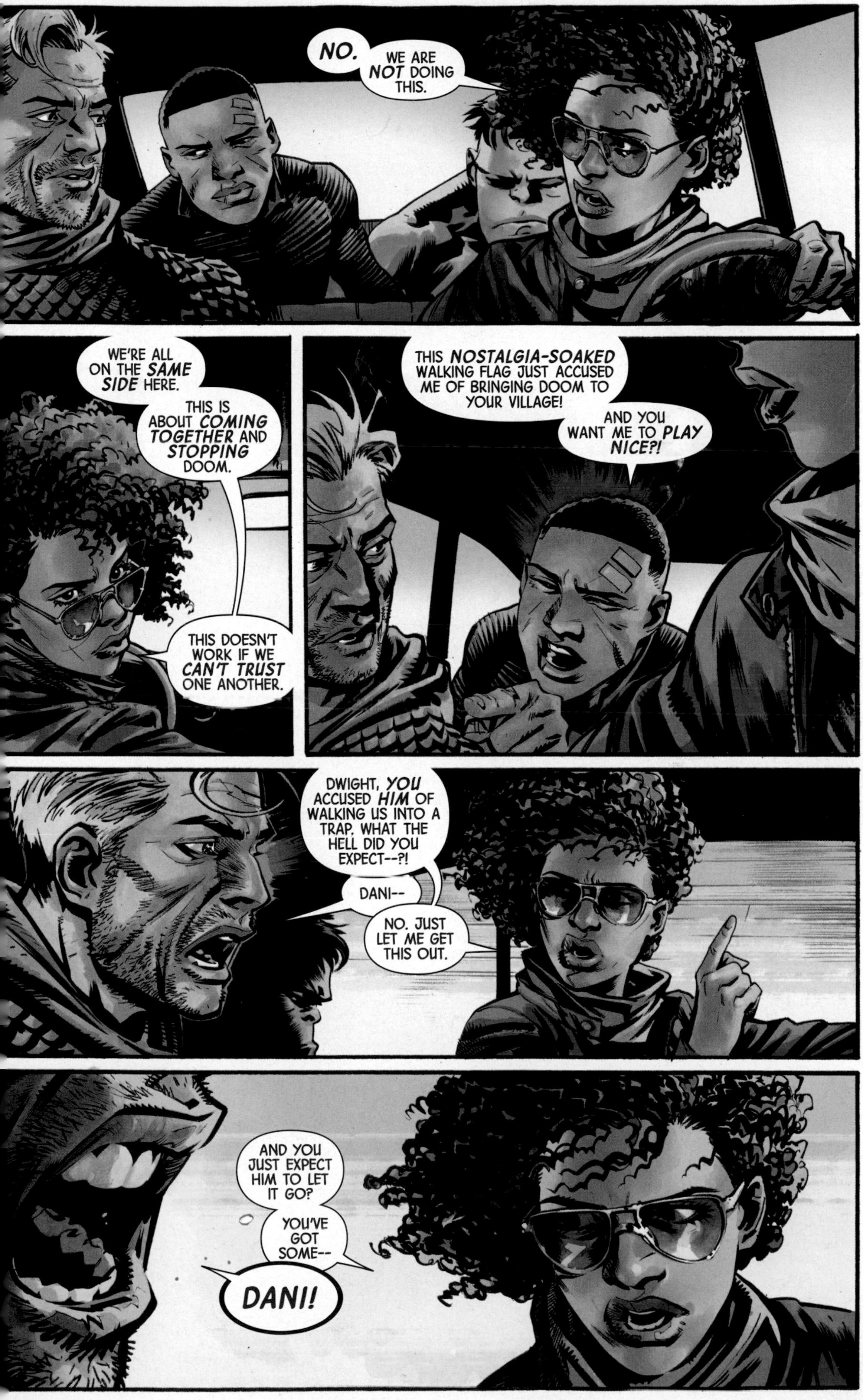
NO.
WE ARE NOT DOING THIS.
WE'RE ALL ON THE SAME SIDE HERE.
THIS IS ABOUT COMING TOGETHER AND STOPPING DOOM.
THIS DOESN'T WORK IF WE CAN'T TRUST ONE ANOTHER.
THIS NOSTALGIA-SOAKED WALKING FLAG JUST ACCUSED ME OF BRINGING DOOM TO YOUR VILLAGE!
AND YOU WANT ME TO PLAY NICE?!
DWIGHT, YOU ACCUSED HIM OF WALKING US INTO A TRAP. WHAT THE HELL DID YOU EXPECT--?!
DANI--
NO. JUST LET ME GET THIS OUT.
AND YOU JUST EXPECT HIM TO LET IT GO?
YOU'VE GOT SOME--
DANI!

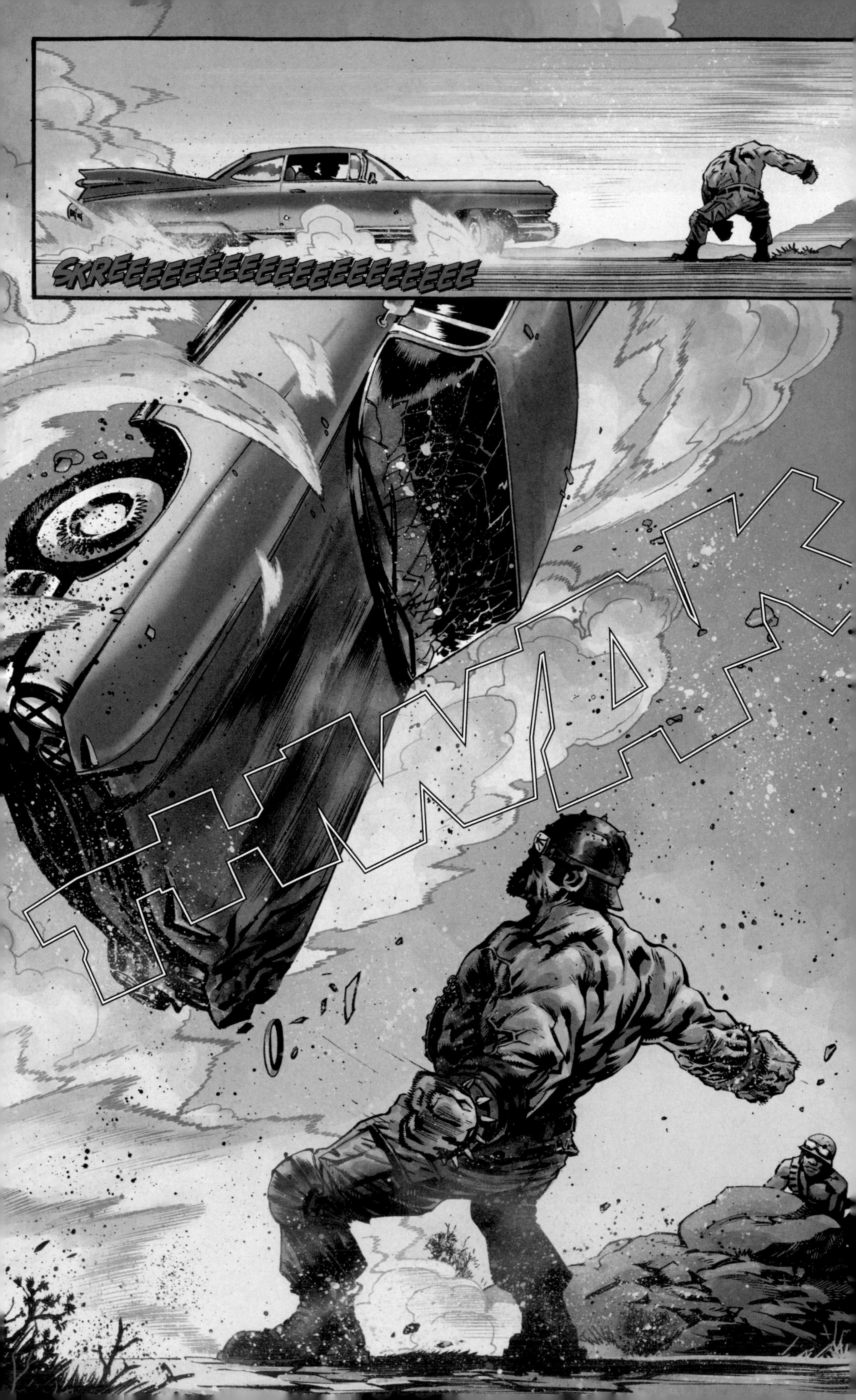
SKREEEEEEEEEEEEEEEEEEEE
THWAK

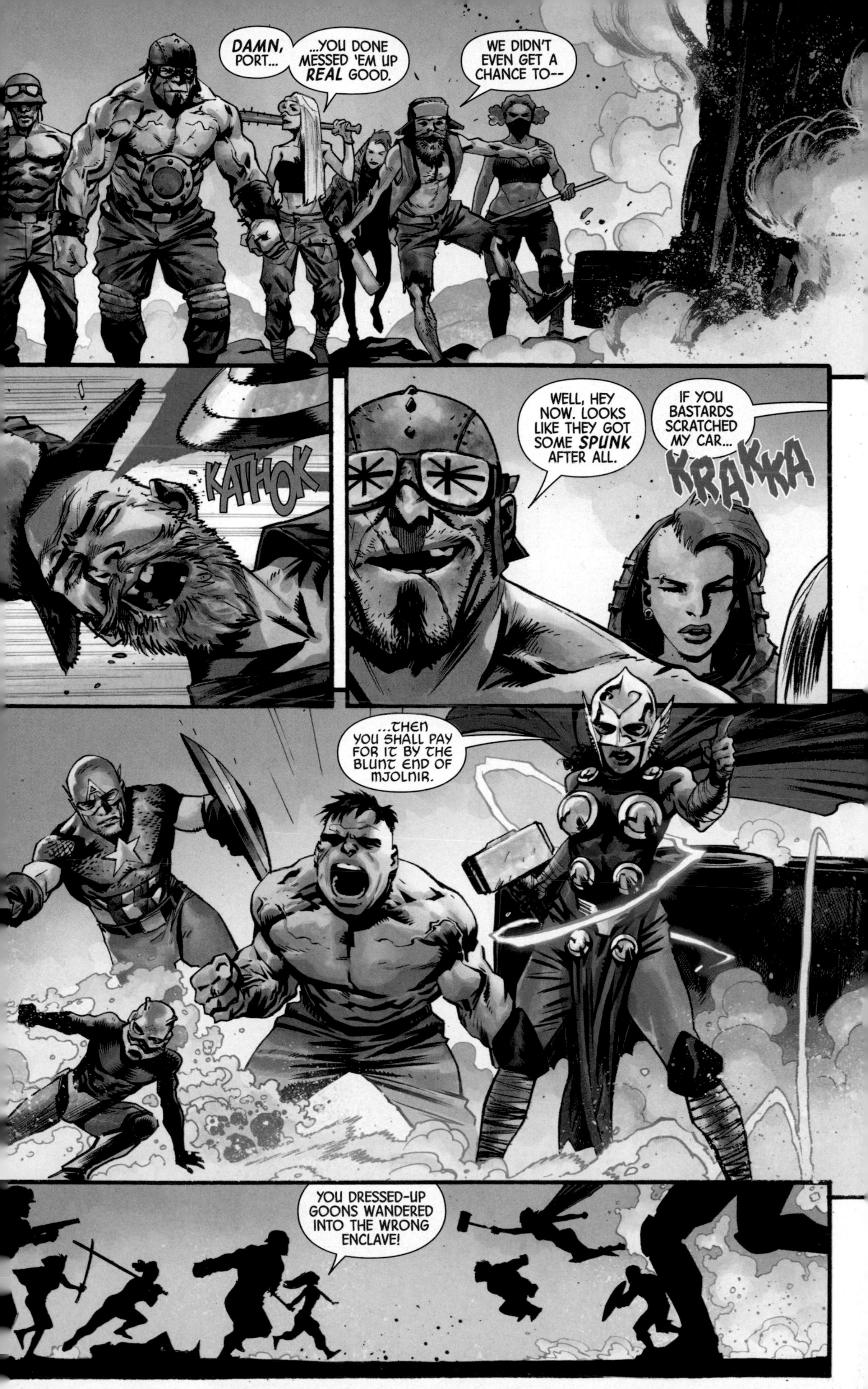

DAMN, PORT...
...YOU DONE MESSED 'EM UP REAL GOOD.
WE DIDN'T EVEN GET A CHANCE TO--
KATHOK
WELL, HEY NOW. LOOKS LIKE THEY GOT SOME SPUNK AFTER ALL.
IF YOU BASTARDS SCRATCHED MY CAR...
KRAKKA
...THEN YOU SHALL PAY FOR IT BY THE BLUNT END OF MJOLNIR.
YOU DRESSED-UP GOONS WANDERED INTO THE WRONG ENCLAVE!

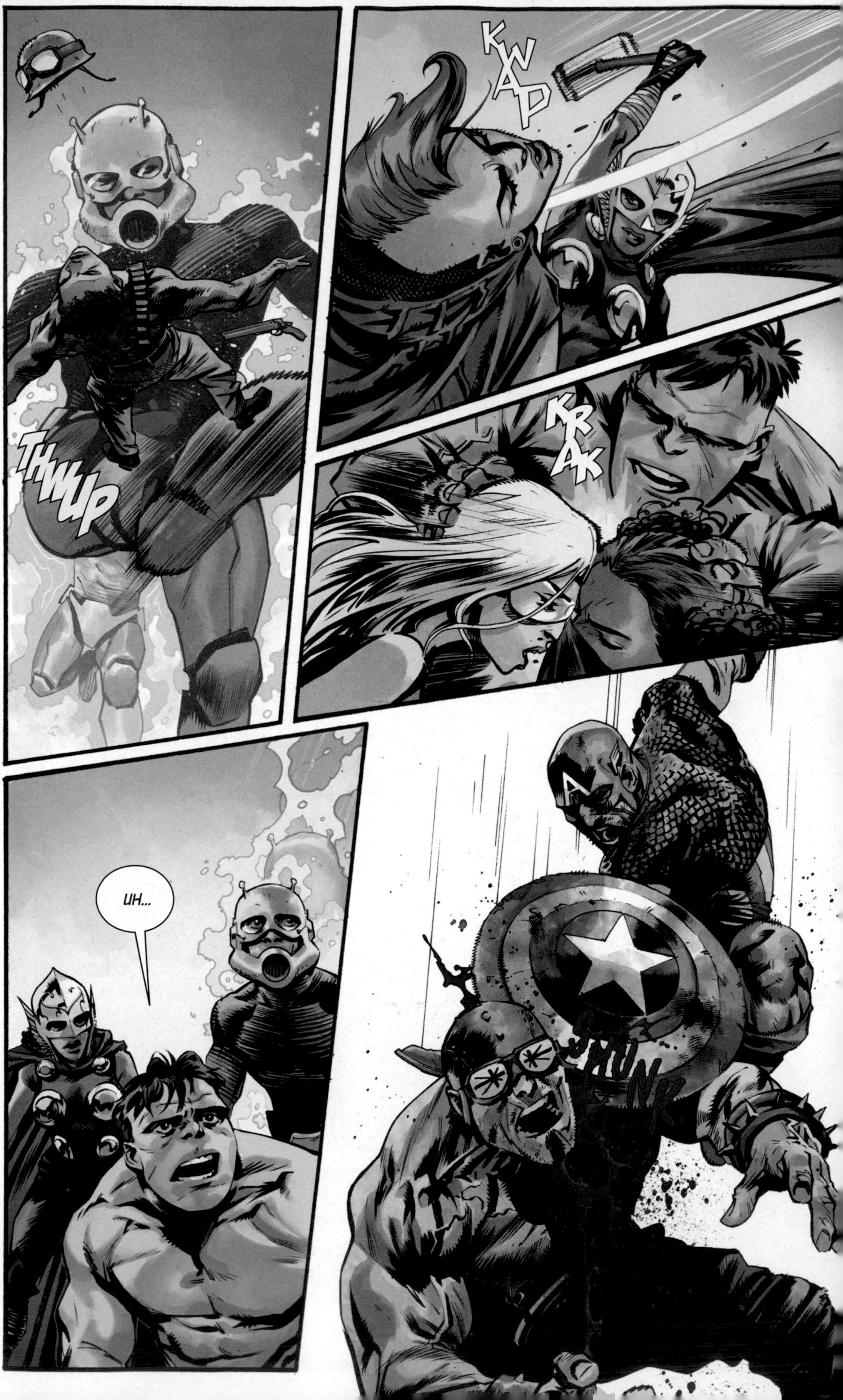

THWUP
KWAP
KRAK
UH...
SHUNK

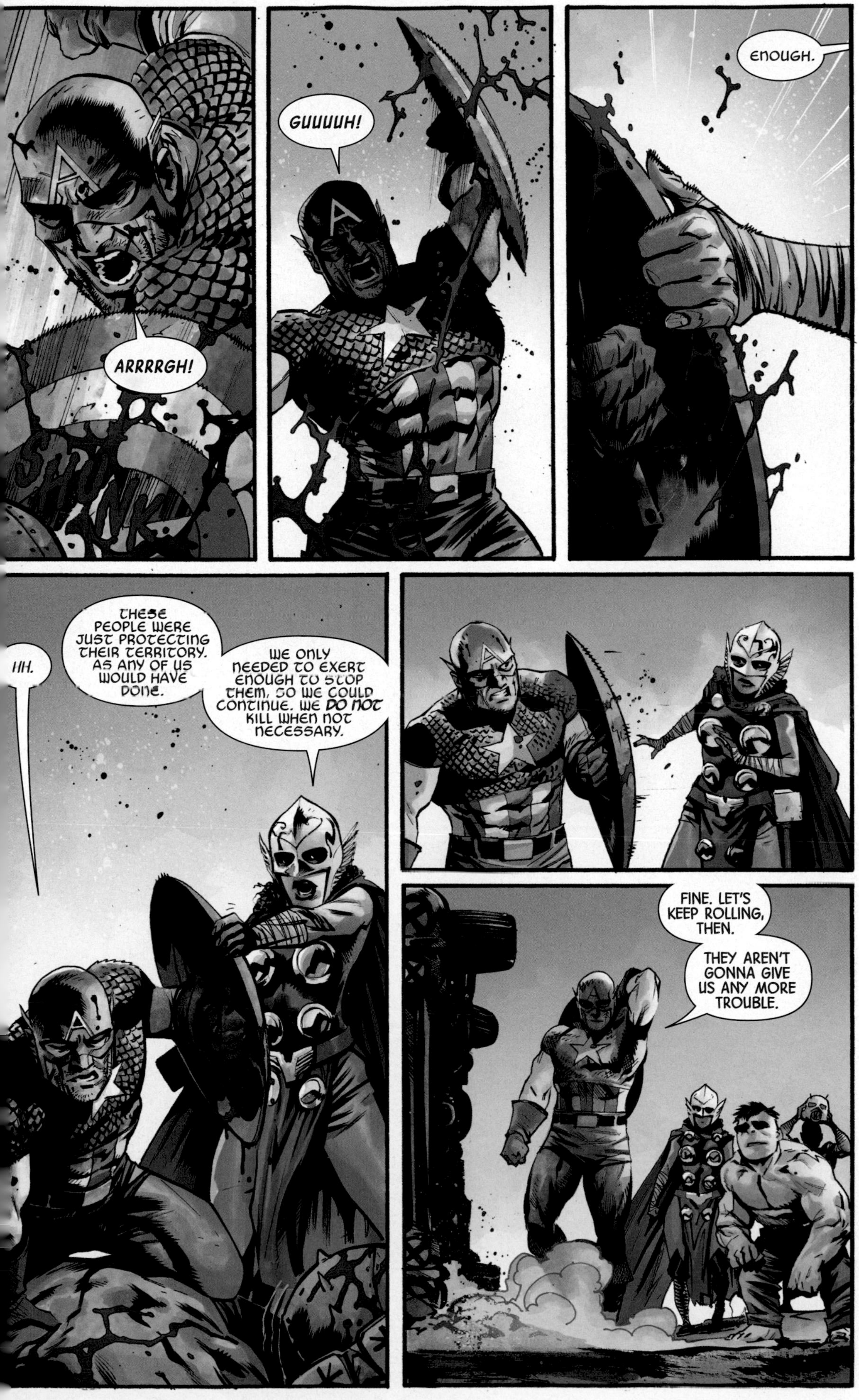
ARRRRGH!
SHUNK
GUUUUH!
ENOUGH.
HH.
THESE PEOPLE WERE JUST PROTECTING THEIR TERRITORY. AS ANY OF US WOULD HAVE DONE.
WE ONLY NEEDED TO EXERT ENOUGH TO STOP THEM, SO WE COULD CONTINUE. WE DO NOT KILL WHEN NOT NECESSARY.
FINE. LET'S KEEP ROLLING, THEN.
THEY AREN'T GONNA GIVE US ANY MORE TROUBLE.

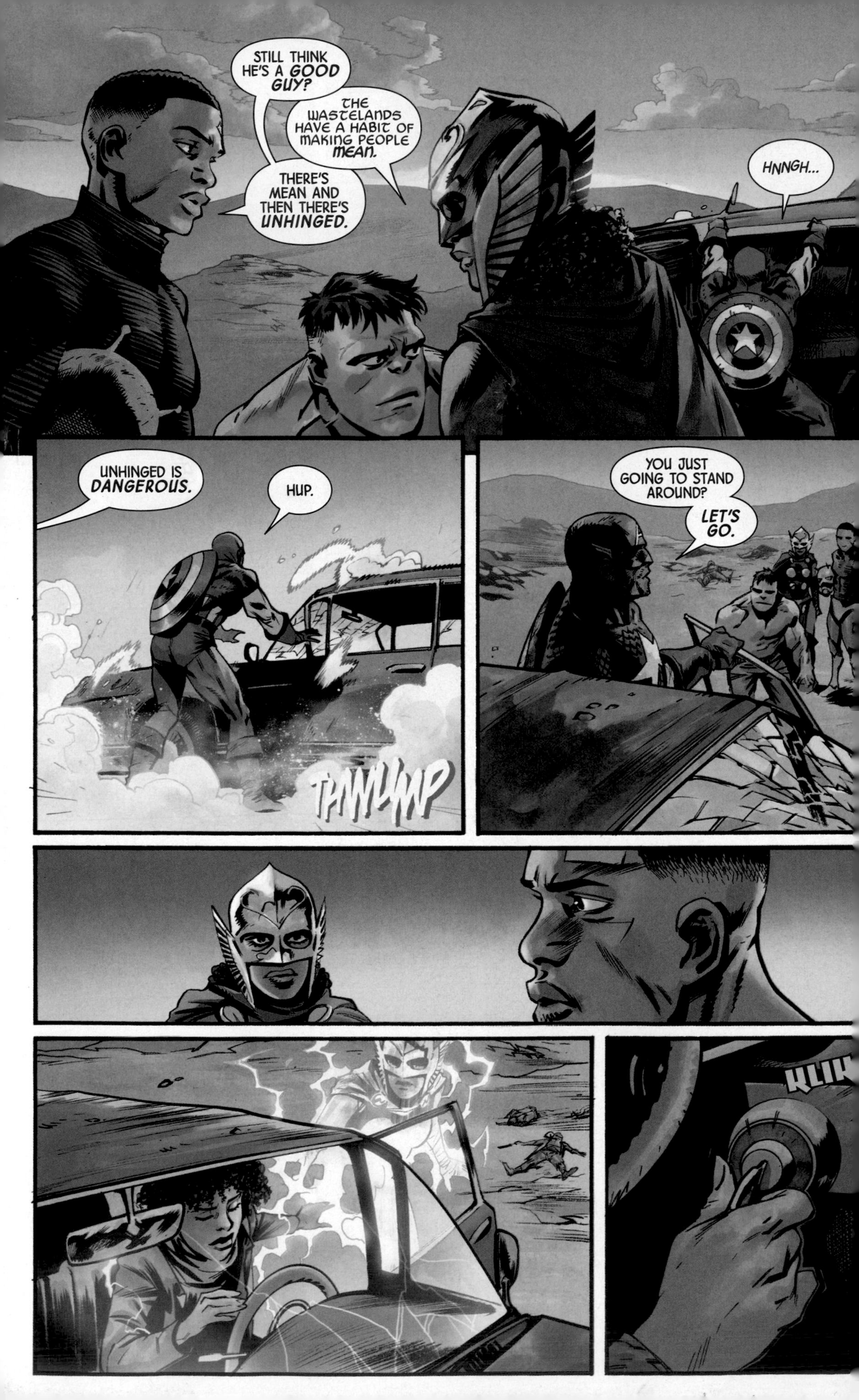

STILL THINK HE'S A GOOD GUY?
THE WASTELANDS HAVE A HABIT OF MAKING PEOPLE MEAN.
THERE'S MEAN AND THEN THERE'S UNHINGED.
HNNGH...
UNHINGED IS DANGEROUS.
HUP.
THWUMP
YOU JUST GOING TO STAND AROUND?
LET'S GO.
KLIK

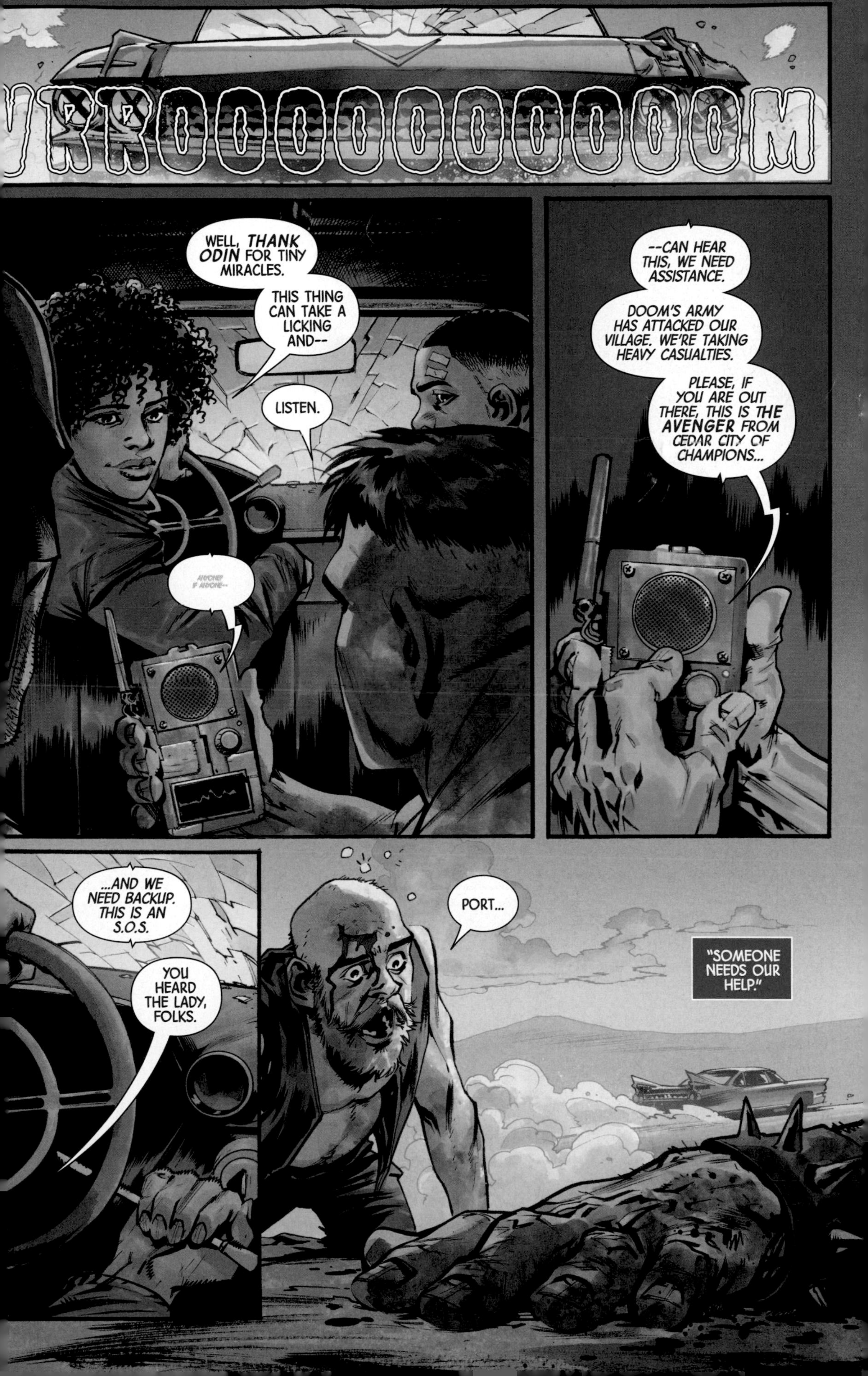
VRROOOOOOOOOOOM
WELL, THANK ODIN FOR TINY MIRACLES.
THIS THING CAN TAKE A LICKING AND--
LISTEN.
ANYONE? IF ANYONE--
--CAN HEAR THIS, WE NEED ASSISTANCE.
DOOM'S ARMY HAS ATTACKED OUR VILLAGE. WE'RE TAKING HEAVY CASUALTIES.
PLEASE, IF YOU ARE OUT THERE, THIS IS THE AVENGER FROM CEDAR CITY OF CHAMPIONS...
...AND WE NEED BACKUP. THIS IS AN S.O.S.
YOU HEARD THE LADY, FOLKS.
PORT...
"SOMEONE NEEDS OUR HELP."

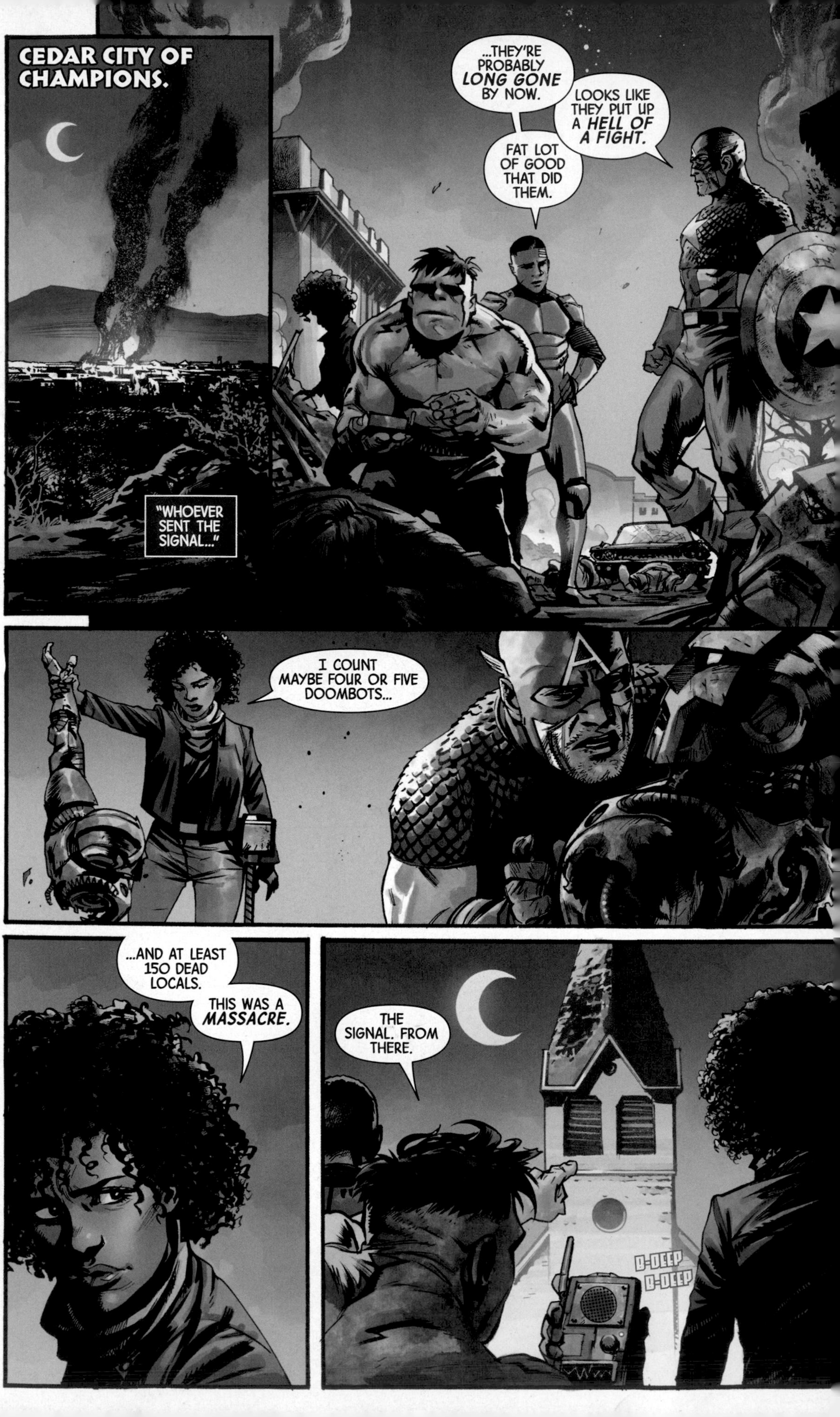
CEDAR CITY OF CHAMPIONS.
"WHOEVER SENT THE SIGNAL..."
...THEY'RE PROBABLY LONG GONE BY NOW.
FAT LOT OF GOOD THAT DID THEM.
LOOKS LIKE THEY PUT UP A HELL OF A FIGHT.
I COUNT MAYBE FOUR OR FIVE DOOMBOTS...
...AND AT LEAST 150 DEAD LOCALS.
THIS WAS A MASSACRE.
THE SIGNAL. FROM THERE.
B-DEEP
B-DEEP

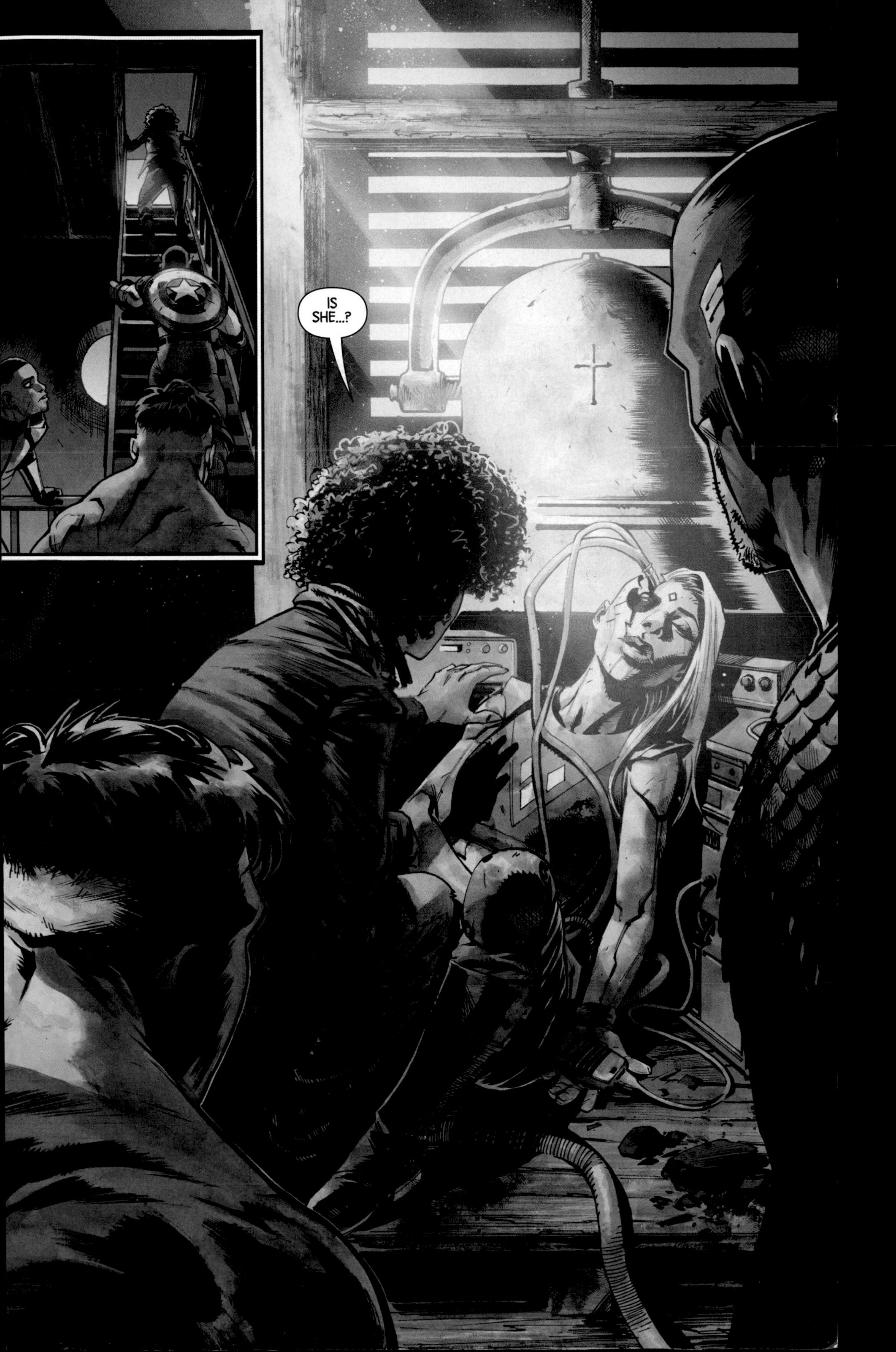
IS SHE...?

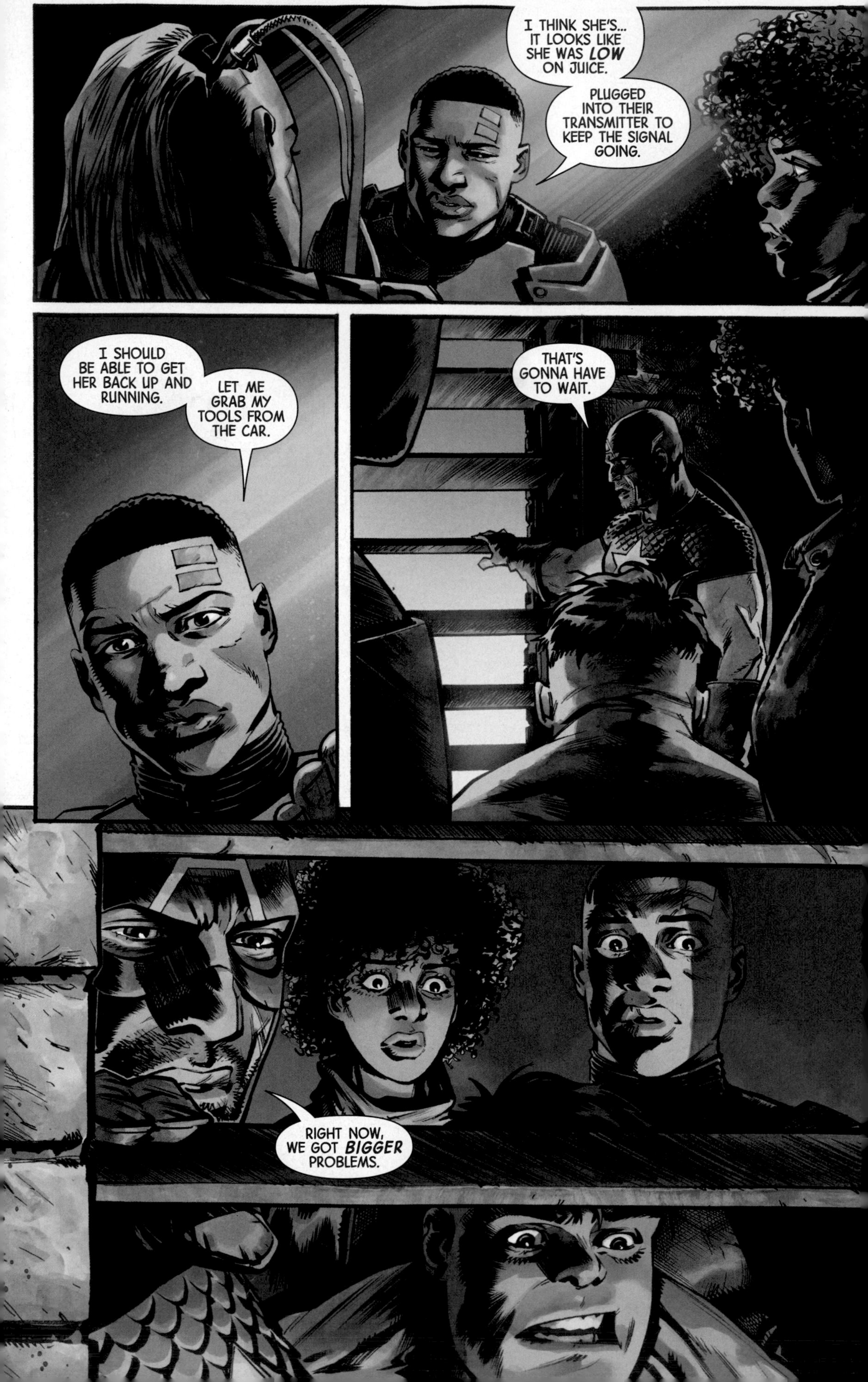
I THINK SHE'S... IT LOOKS LIKE SHE WAS LOW ON JUICE.
PLUGGED INTO THEIR TRANSMITTER TO KEEP THE SIGNAL GOING.
I SHOULD BE ABLE TO GET HER BACK UP AND RUNNING.
LET ME GRAB MY TOOLS FROM THE CAR.
THAT'S GONNA HAVE TO WAIT.
RIGHT NOW, WE GOT BIGGER PROBLEMS.

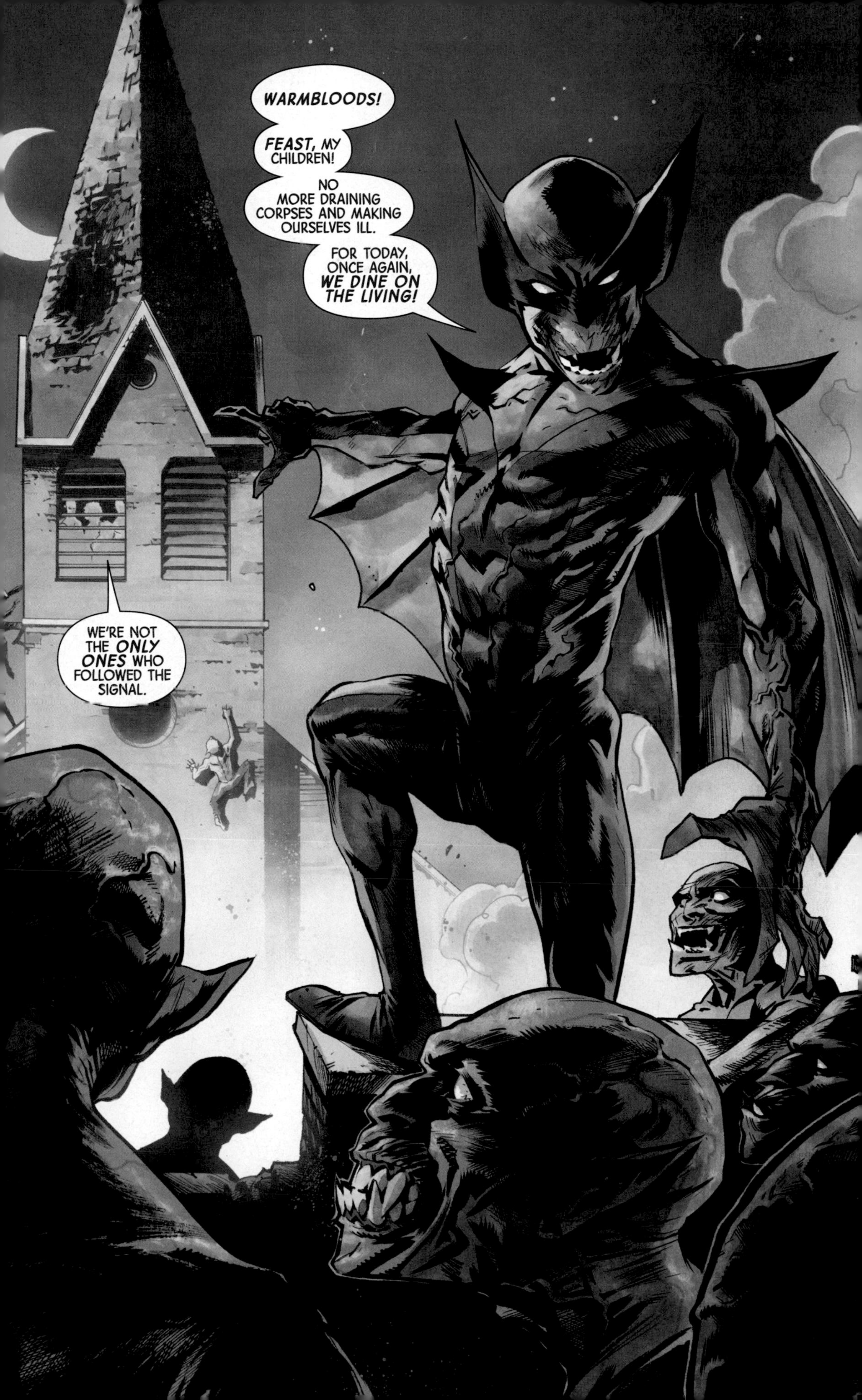
WARMBLOODS!
FEAST, MY CHILDREN!
NO MORE DRAINING CORPSES AND MAKING OURSELVES ILL.
FOR TODAY, ONCE AGAIN, WE DINE ON THE LIVING!
WE'RE NOT THE ONLY ONES WHO FOLLOWED THE SIGNAL.

3.

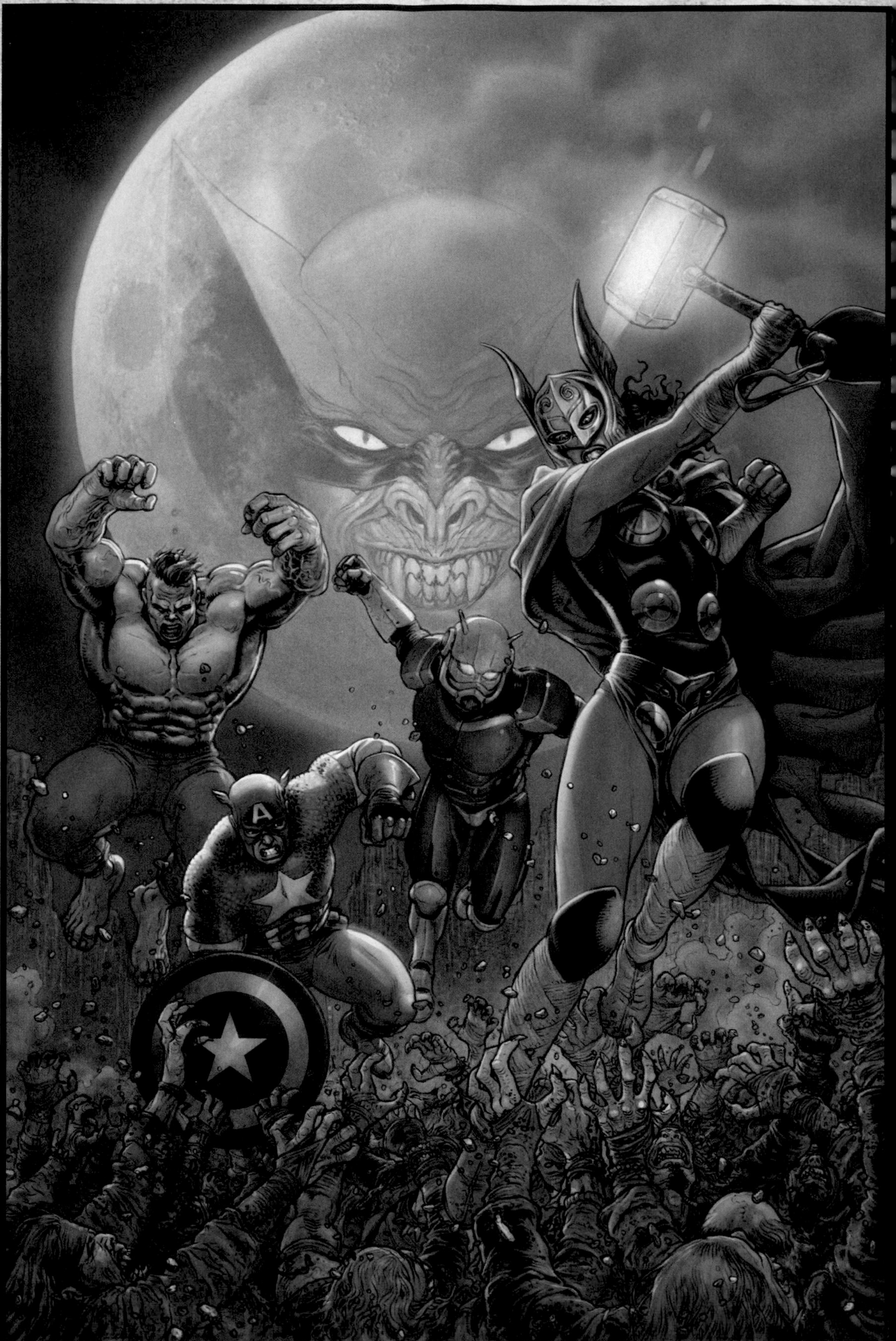

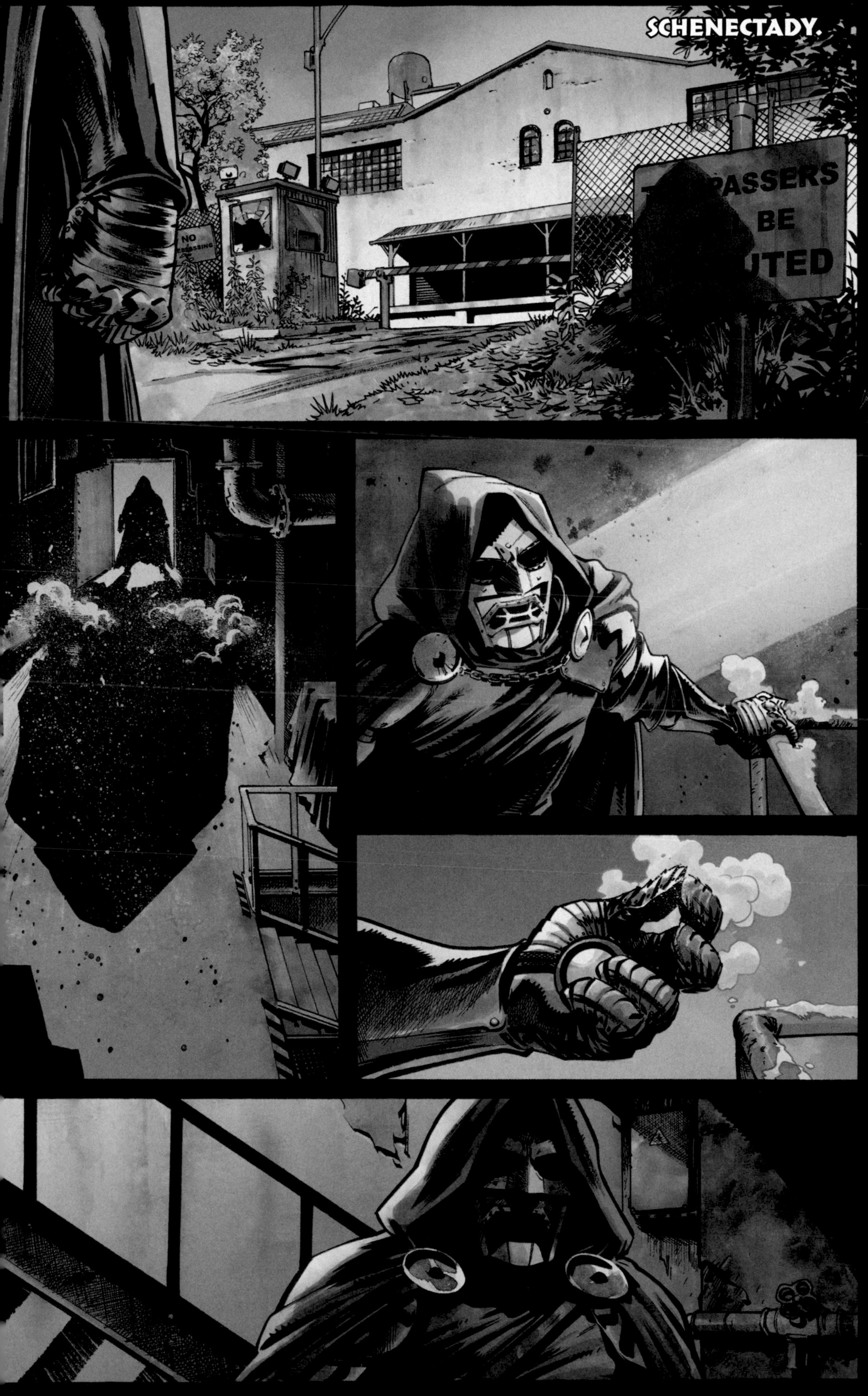
SCHENECTADY.
NO TRESPASSING
PASSERS
BE
UTED

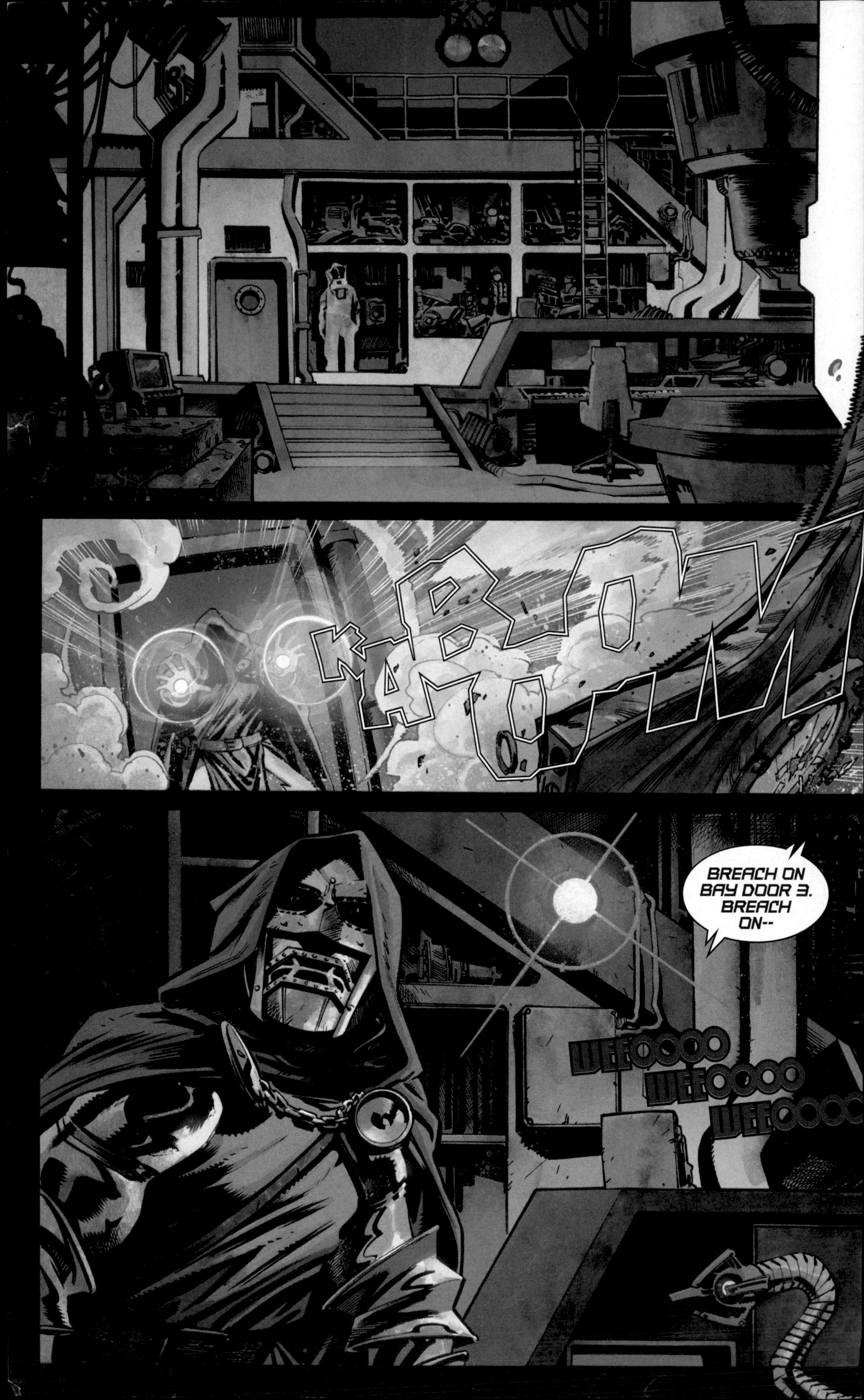
KA-BOOM
BREACH ON BAY DOOR 3. BREACH ON--
WEEOOOO WEEOOOO WEEOOOO

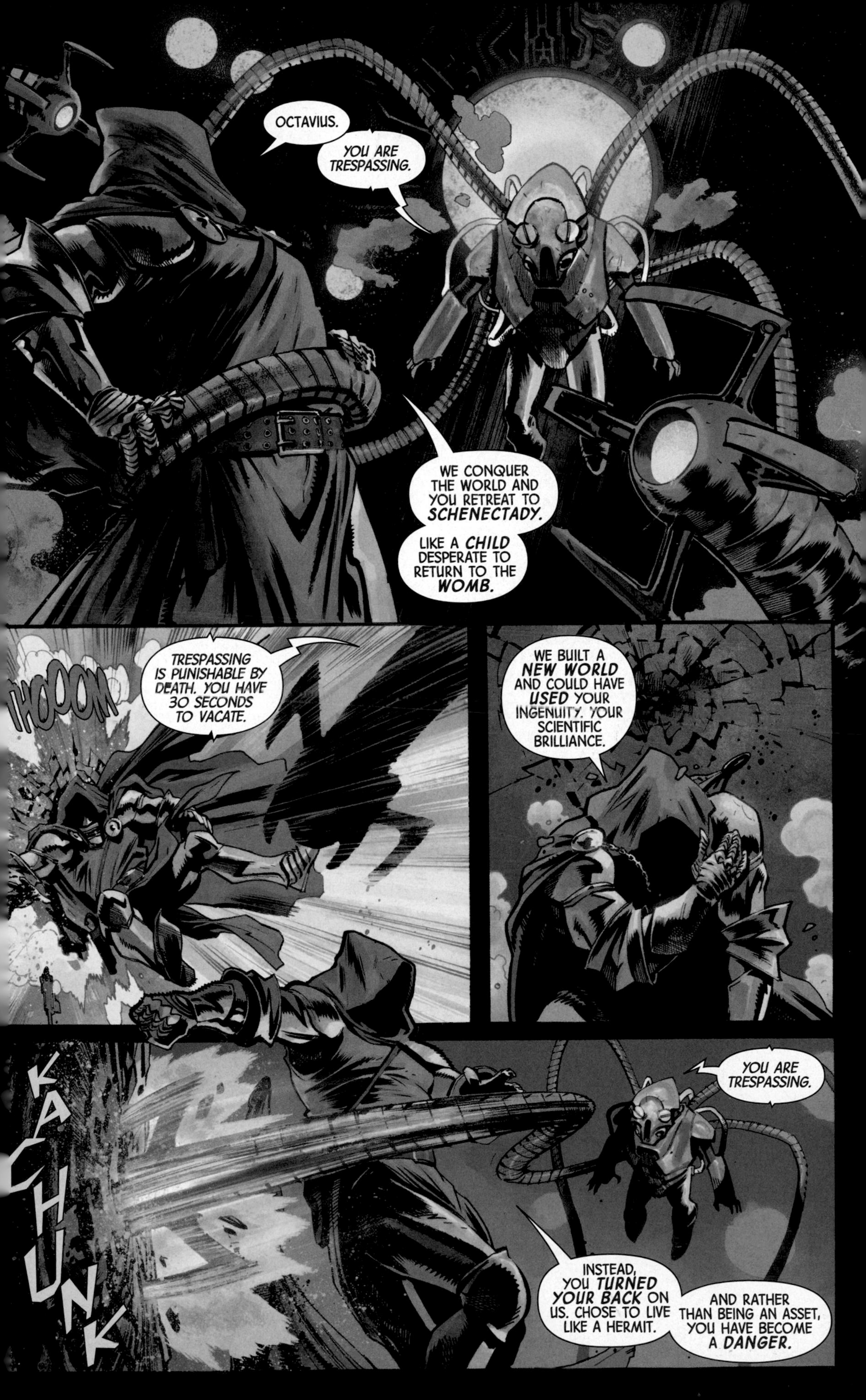
OCTAVIUS.
YOU ARE TRESPASSING.
WE CONQUER THE WORLD AND YOU RETREAT TO SCHENECTADY.
LIKE A CHILD DESPERATE TO RETURN TO THE WOMB.
THOOOM
TRESPASSING IS PUNISHABLE BY DEATH. YOU HAVE 30 SECONDS TO VACATE.
WE BUILT A NEW WORLD AND COULD HAVE USED YOUR INGENUITY. YOUR SCIENTIFIC BRILLIANCE.
KACHUNK
YOU ARE TRESPASSING.
INSTEAD, YOU TURNED YOUR BACK ON US. CHOSE TO LIVE LIKE A HERMIT.
AND RATHER THAN BEING AN ASSET, YOU HAVE BECOME A DANGER.

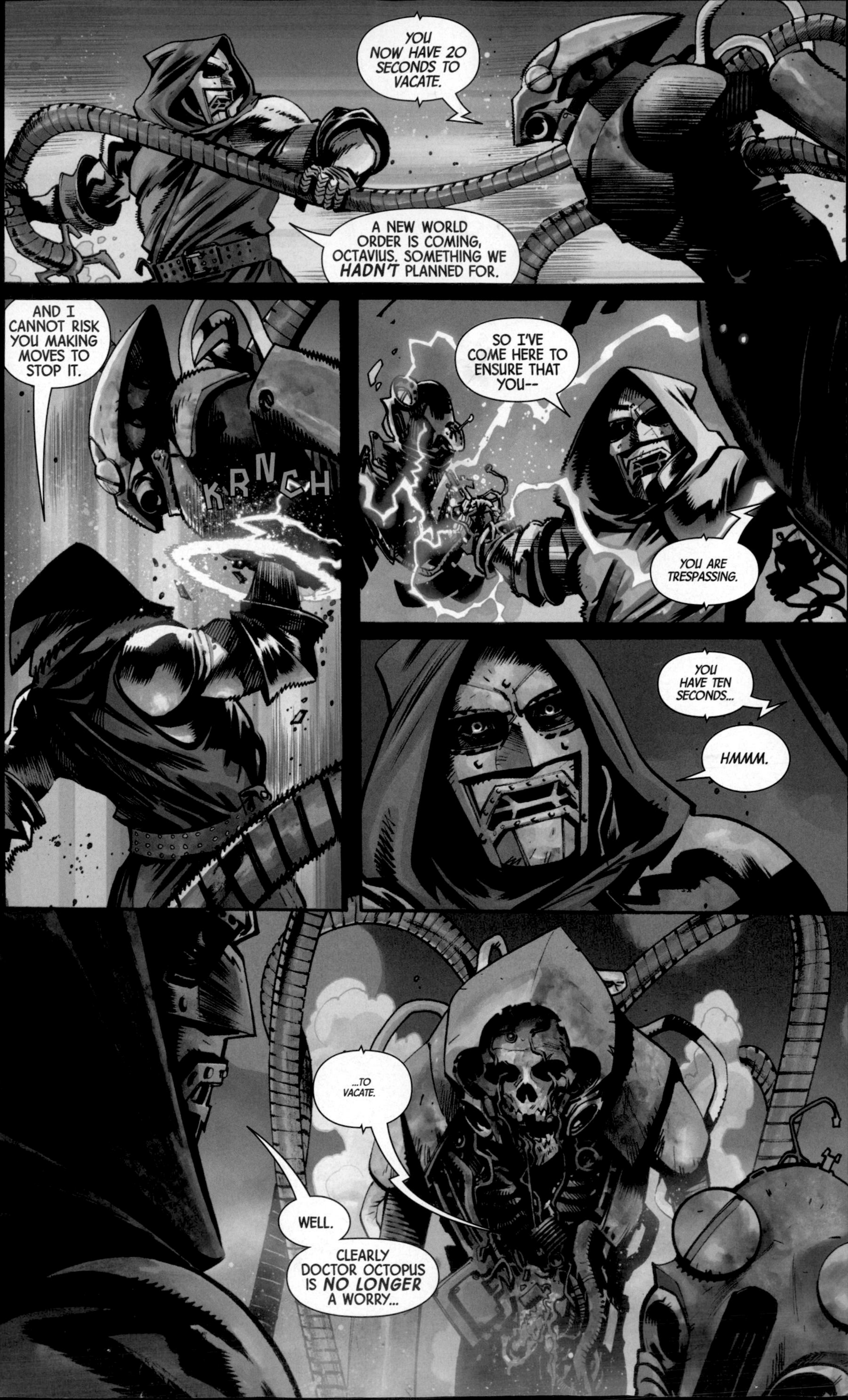
YOU NOW HAVE 20 SECONDS TO VACATE.
A NEW WORLD ORDER IS COMING, OCTAVIUS. SOMETHING WE ***HADN'T*** PLANNED FOR.
AND I CANNOT RISK YOU MAKING MOVES TO STOP IT.
KRNCH
SO I'VE COME HERE TO ENSURE THAT YOU--
YOU ARE TRESPASSING.
YOU HAVE TEN SECONDS...
HMMM.
...TO VACATE.
WELL.
CLEARLY DOCTOR OCTOPUS IS ***NO LONGER*** A WORRY...

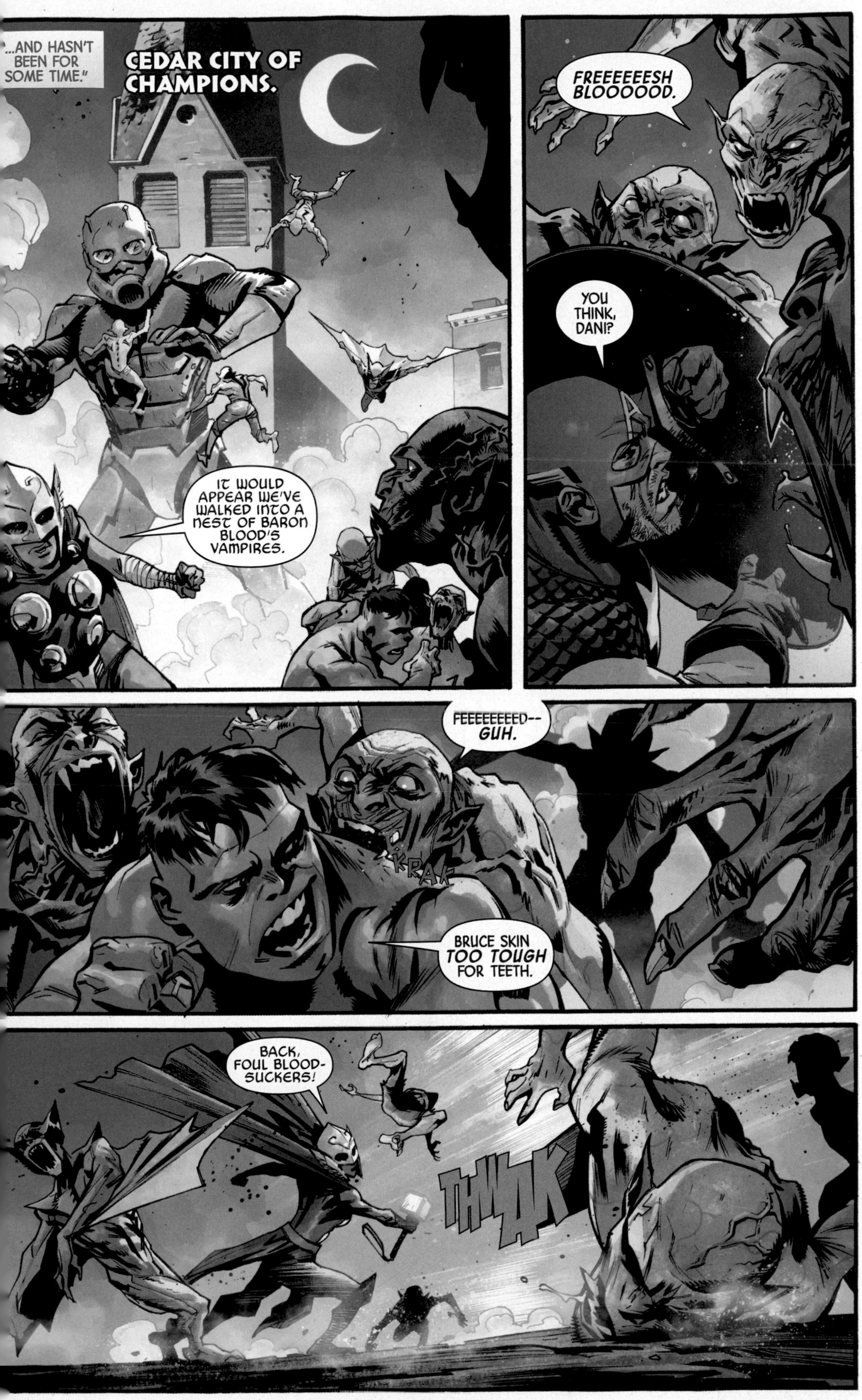

"...AND HASN'T BEEN FOR SOME TIME."
CEDAR CITY OF CHAMPIONS.
IT WOULD APPEAR WE'VE WALKED INTO A NEST OF BARON BLOOD'S VAMPIRES.
FREEEEEESH BLOOOOOD.
YOU THINK, DANI?
FEEEEEEEED-- GUH.
KRAK
BRUCE SKIN TOO TOUGH FOR TEETH.
BACK, FOUL BLOOD-SUCKERS!
THWAK

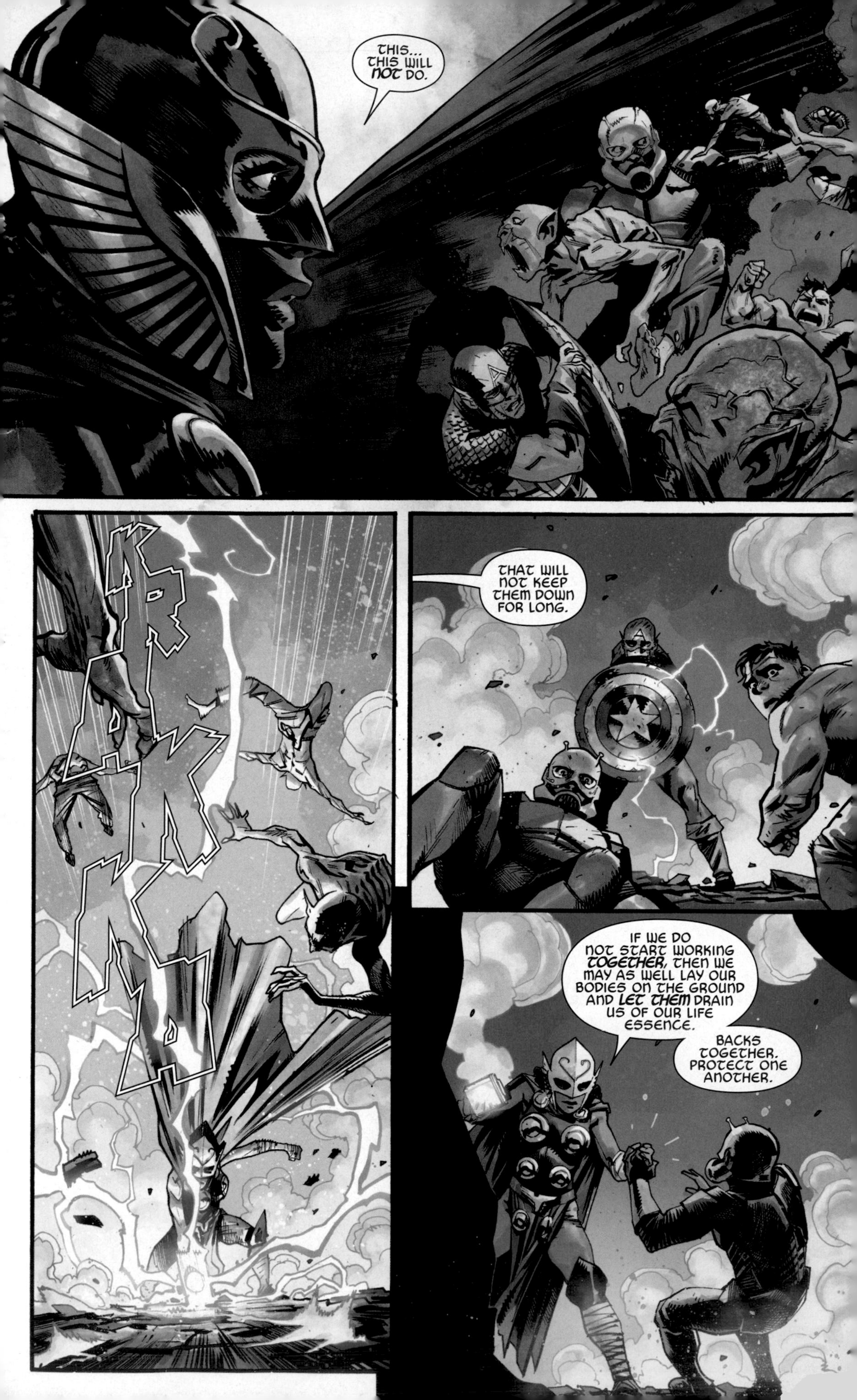
THIS... THIS WILL NOT DO.
KRAKA
THAT WILL NOT KEEP THEM DOWN FOR LONG.
IF WE DO NOT START WORKING TOGETHER, THEN WE MAY AS WELL LAY OUR BODIES ON THE GROUND AND LET THEM DRAIN US OF OUR LIFE ESSENCE.
BACKS TOGETHER. PROTECT ONE ANOTHER.

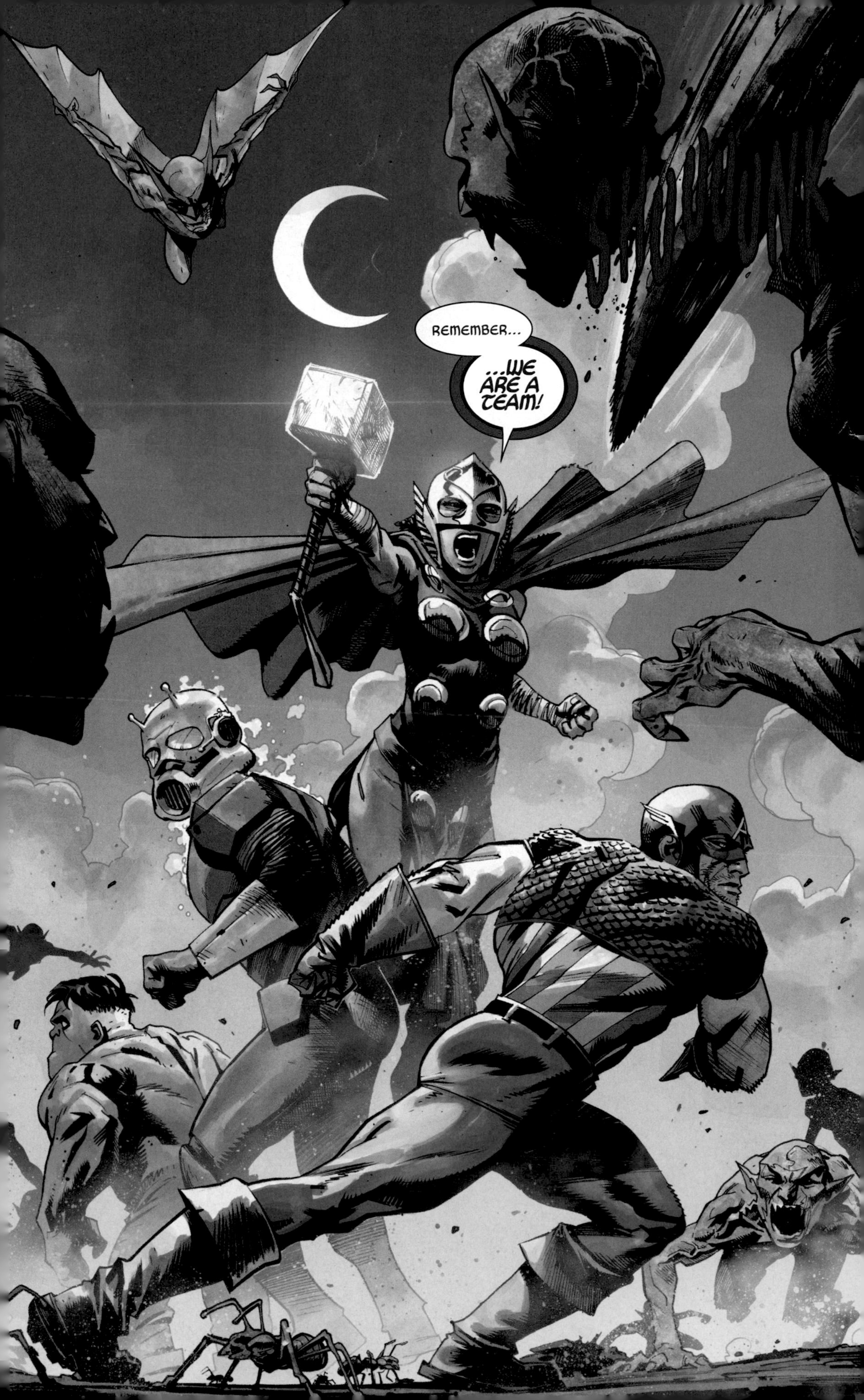
REMEMBER...
...WE ARE A TEAM!

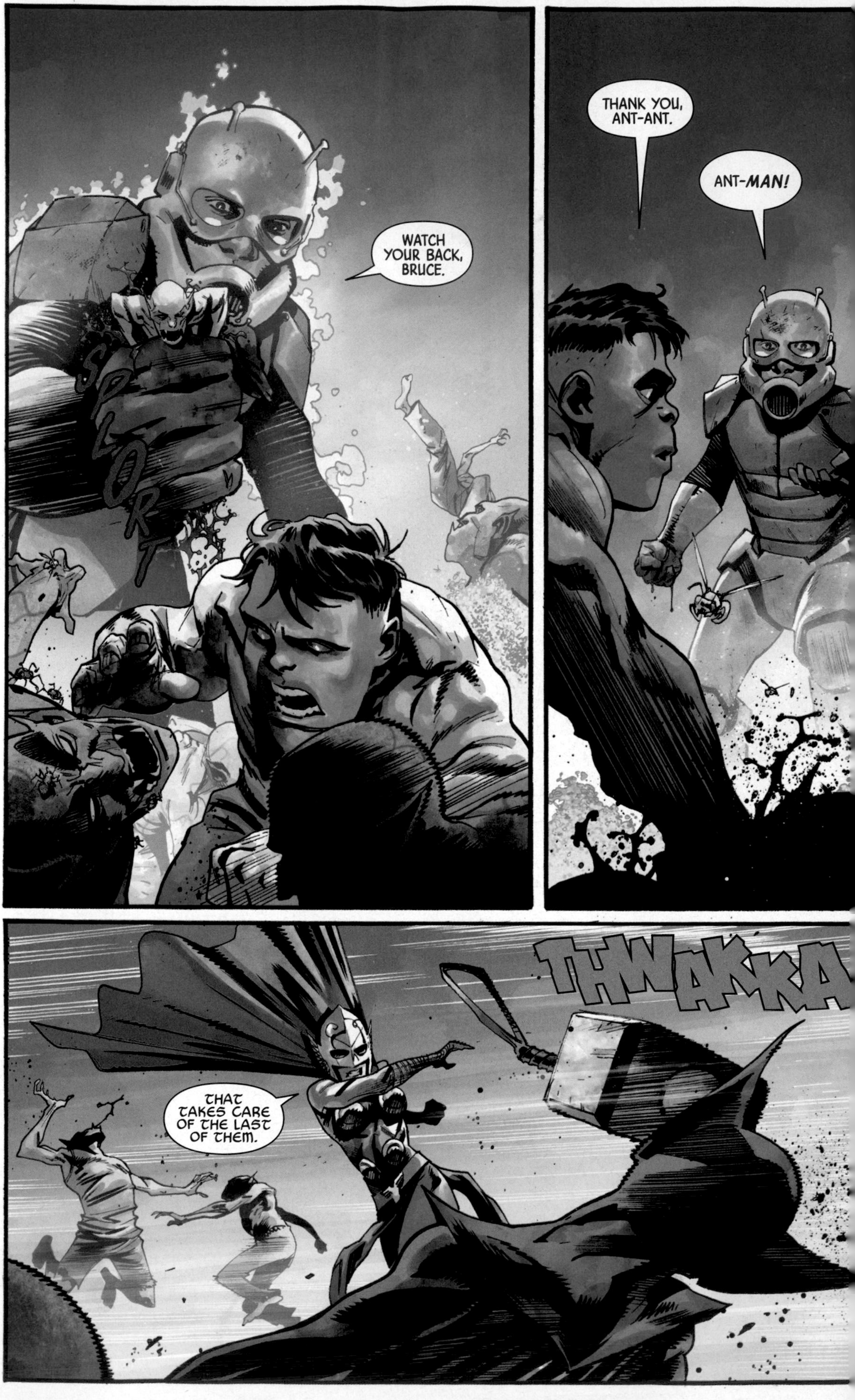
WATCH YOUR BACK, BRUCE.
SPLORT
THANK YOU, ANT-ANT.
ANT-MAN!
THWAKKA
THAT TAKES CARE OF THE LAST OF THEM.

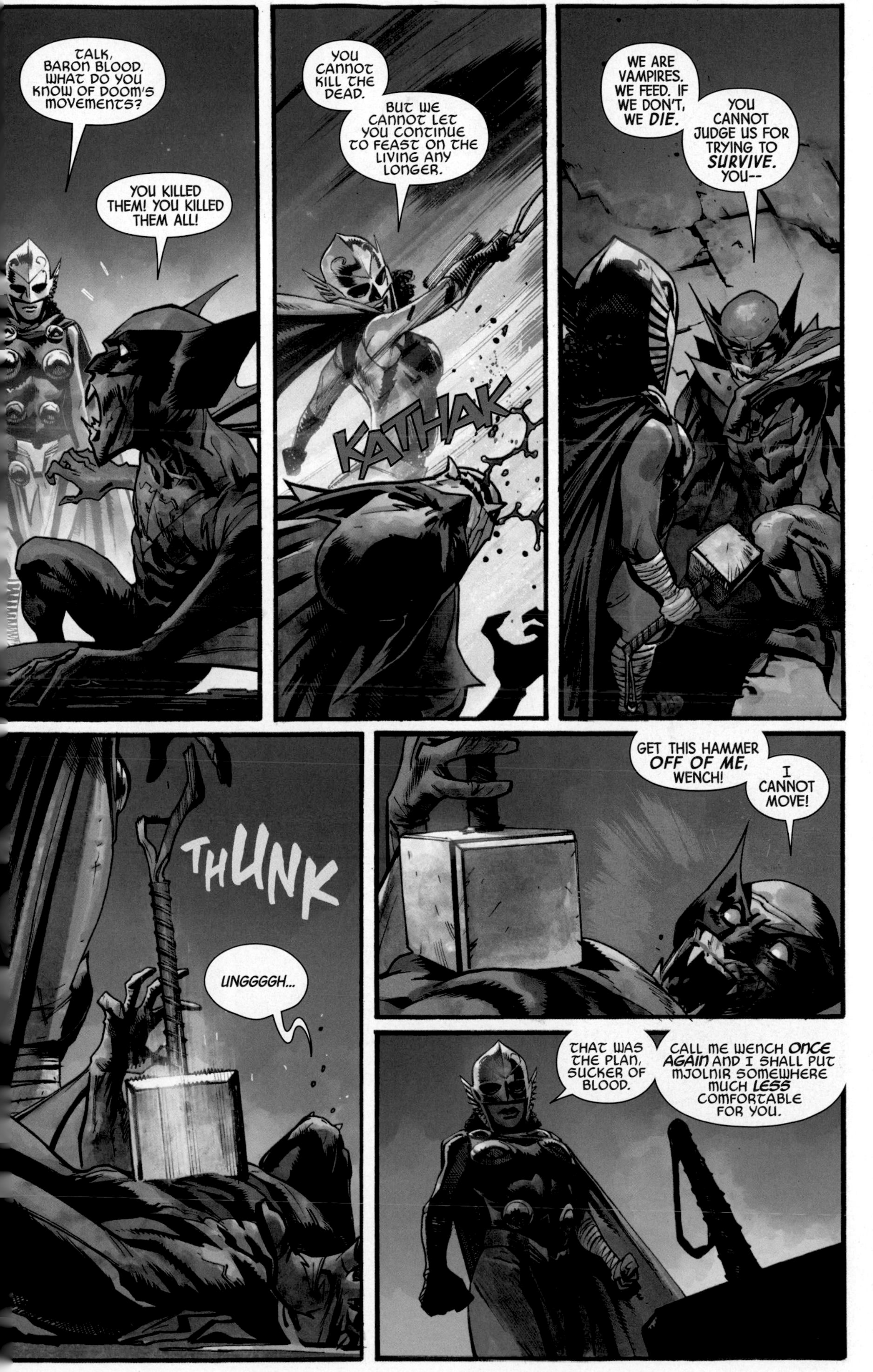
TALK, BARON BLOOD. WHAT DO YOU KNOW OF DOOM'S MOVEMENTS?
YOU KILLED THEM! YOU KILLED THEM ALL!
YOU CANNOT KILL THE DEAD.
BUT WE CANNOT LET YOU CONTINUE TO FEAST ON THE LIVING ANY LONGER.
KATHAK
WE ARE VAMPIRES. WE FEED. IF WE DON'T, WE DIE.
YOU CANNOT JUDGE US FOR TRYING TO SURVIVE. YOU--
THUNK
UNGGGGH...
GET THIS HAMMER OFF OF ME, WENCH!
I CANNOT MOVE!
THAT WAS THE PLAN, SUCKER OF BLOOD.
CALL ME WENCH ONCE AGAIN AND I SHALL PUT MJOLNIR SOMEWHERE MUCH LESS COMFORTABLE FOR YOU.

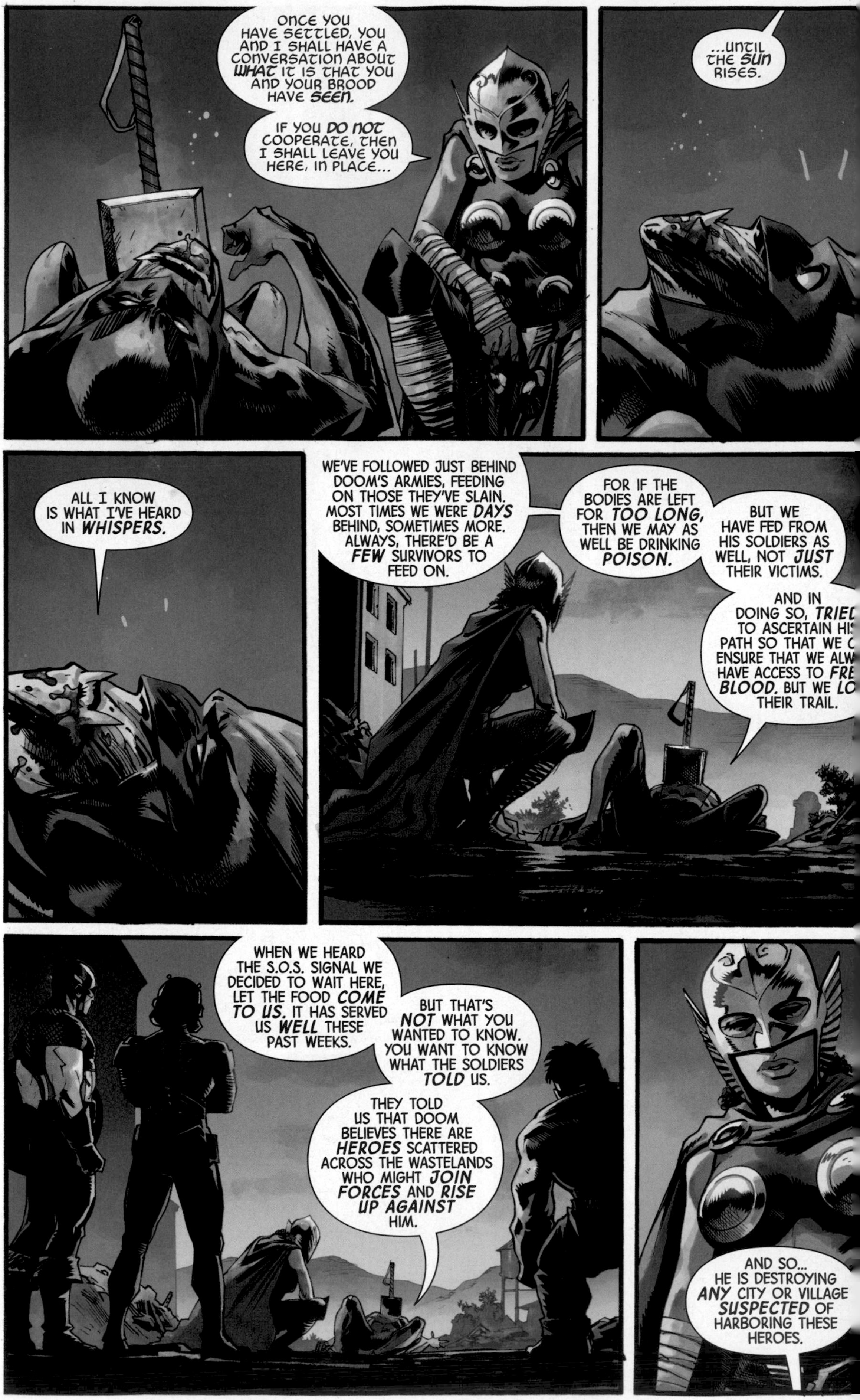
ONCE YOU HAVE SETTLED, YOU AND I SHALL HAVE A CONVERSATION ABOUT *WHAT* IT IS THAT YOU AND YOUR BROOD HAVE *SEEN.*
IF YOU *DO NOT* COOPERATE, THEN I SHALL LEAVE YOU HERE, IN PLACE...
...UNTIL THE *SUN* RISES.
ALL I KNOW IS WHAT I'VE HEARD IN *WHISPERS.*
WE'VE FOLLOWED JUST BEHIND DOOM'S ARMIES, FEEDING ON THOSE THEY'VE SLAIN. MOST TIMES WE WERE *DAYS* BEHIND, SOMETIMES MORE. ALWAYS, THERE'D BE A *FEW* SURVIVORS TO FEED ON.
FOR IF THE BODIES ARE LEFT FOR *TOO LONG,* THEN WE MAY AS WELL BE DRINKING *POISON.*
BUT WE HAVE FED FROM HIS SOLDIERS AS WELL, NOT *JUST* THEIR VICTIMS.
AND IN DOING SO, TRIE TO ASCERTAIN HI PATH SO THAT WE ENSURE THAT WE AL HAVE ACCESS TO FR *BLOOD.* BUT WE L THEIR TRAIL.
WHEN WE HEARD THE S.O.S. SIGNAL WE DECIDED TO WAIT HERE, LET THE FOOD *COME TO US.* IT HAS SERVED US *WELL* THESE PAST WEEKS.
BUT THAT'S *NOT* WHAT YOU WANTED TO KNOW. YOU WANT TO KNOW WHAT THE SOLDIERS *TOLD* US.
THEY TOLD US THAT DOOM BELIEVES THERE ARE *HEROES* SCATTERED ACROSS THE WASTELANDS WHO MIGHT *JOIN FORCES* AND *RISE UP AGAINST* HIM.
AND SO... HE IS DESTROYING *ANY* CITY OR VILLAGE *SUSPECTED* OF HARBORING THESE HEROES.

LOOKING AT THE GROUP OF YOU...

...IT SEEMS THAT PERHAPS HIS WORRIES WERE *JUSTIFIED.*

WHERE IS DOOM?

WHERE'S HE HEADED NEXT?

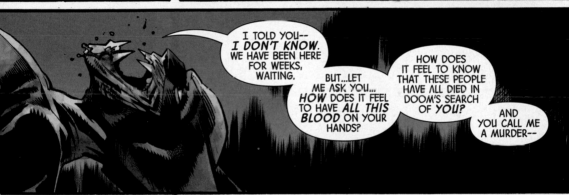

I TOLD YOU-- *I DON'T KNOW.* WE HAVE BEEN HERE FOR WEEKS, WAITING.

BUT...LET ME ASK YOU... *HOW* DOES IT FEEL TO HAVE *ALL THIS BLOOD* ON YOUR HANDS?

HOW DOES IT FEEL TO KNOW THAT THESE PEOPLE HAVE ALL DIED IN DOOM'S SEARCH OF *YOU?*

AND YOU CALL ME A MURDER--

SHUNK

GRANT! WHAT THE HEL WAS THAT?

WE GOT WHAT WE NEEDED FROM HIM.

LETTING HIM TALK ANY MORE WOULD BE WASTING OUR TIME.

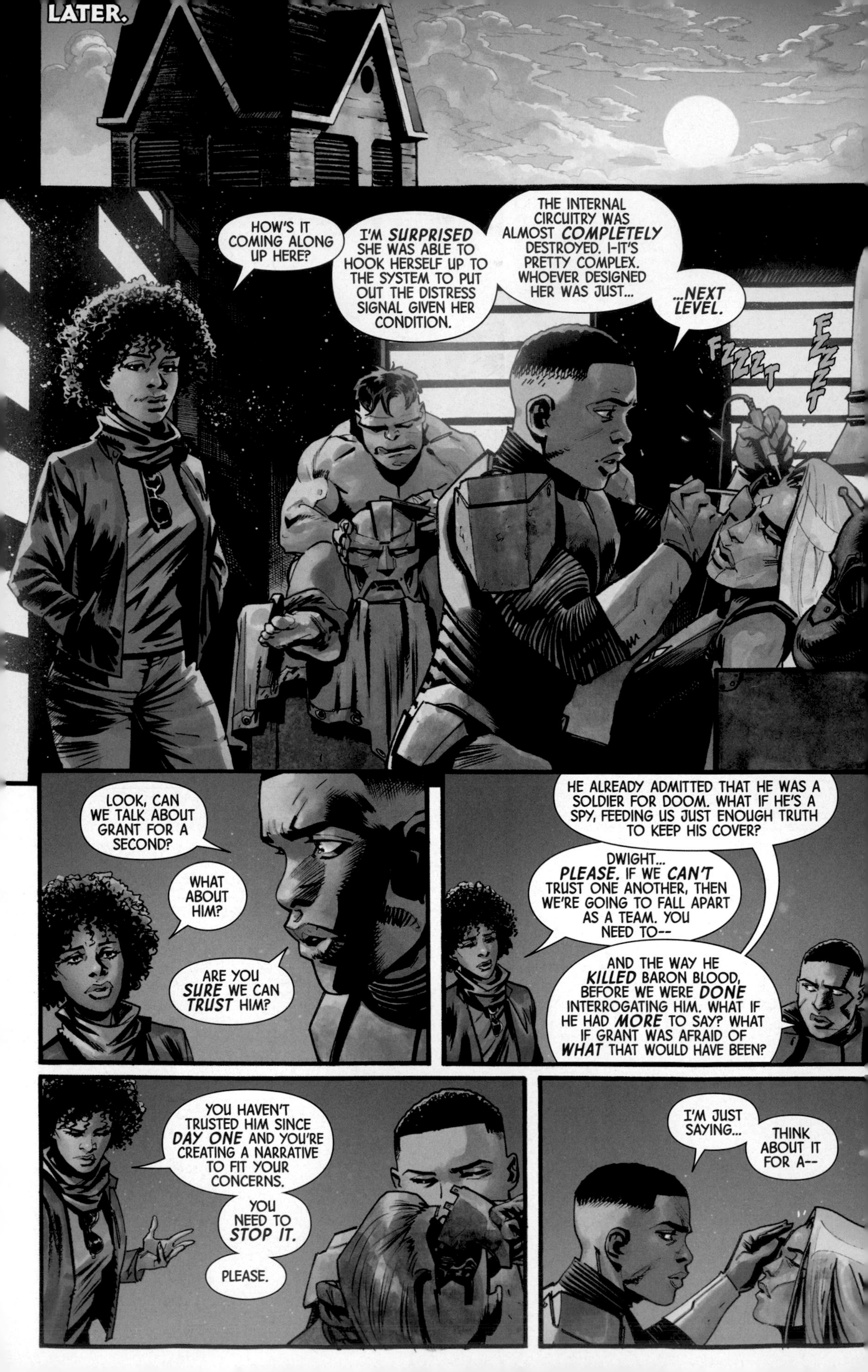
LATER.
HOW'S IT COMING ALONG UP HERE?
I'M SURPRISED SHE WAS ABLE TO HOOK HERSELF UP TO THE SYSTEM TO PUT OUT THE DISTRESS SIGNAL GIVEN HER CONDITION.
THE INTERNAL CIRCUITRY WAS ALMOST COMPLETELY DESTROYED. I-IT'S PRETTY COMPLEX. WHOEVER DESIGNED HER WAS JUST...
...NEXT LEVEL.
FZZZT
FZZZT
LOOK, CAN WE TALK ABOUT GRANT FOR A SECOND?
WHAT ABOUT HIM?
ARE YOU SURE WE CAN TRUST HIM?
HE ALREADY ADMITTED THAT HE WAS A SOLDIER FOR DOOM. WHAT IF HE'S A SPY, FEEDING US JUST ENOUGH TRUTH TO KEEP HIS COVER?
DWIGHT... PLEASE. IF WE CAN'T TRUST ONE ANOTHER, THEN WE'RE GOING TO FALL APART AS A TEAM. YOU NEED TO--
AND THE WAY HE KILLED BARON BLOOD, BEFORE WE WERE DONE INTERROGATING HIM. WHAT IF HE HAD MORE TO SAY? WHAT IF GRANT WAS AFRAID OF WHAT THAT WOULD HAVE BEEN?
YOU HAVEN'T TRUSTED HIM SINCE DAY ONE AND YOU'RE CREATING A NARRATIVE TO FIT YOUR CONCERNS.
YOU NEED TO STOP IT.
PLEASE.
I'M JUST SAYING...
THINK ABOUT IT FOR A--

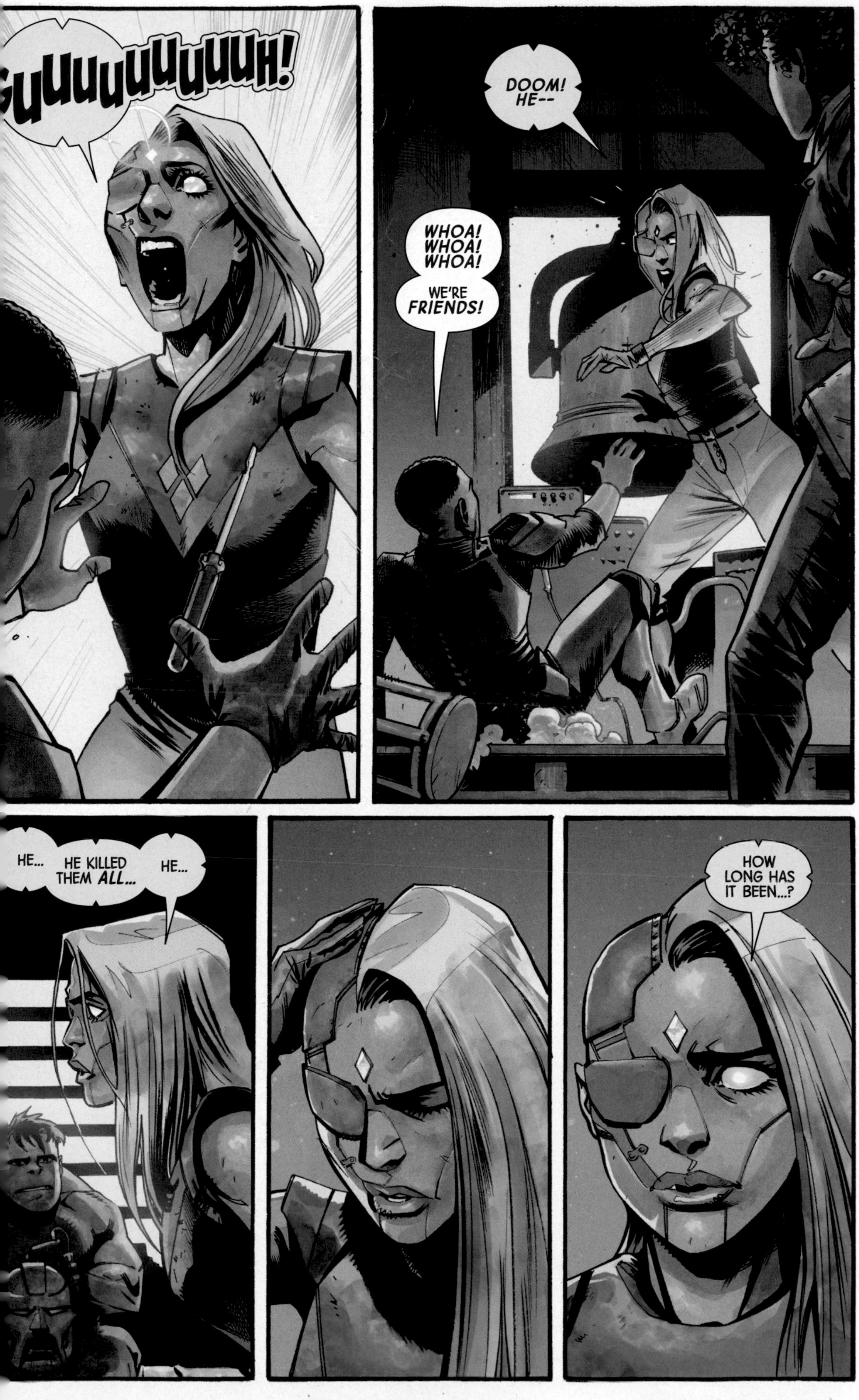
GUUUUUUUUUH!
DOOM! HE--
WHOA! WHOA! WHOA!
WE'RE FRIENDS!
HE...
HE KILLED THEM ALL...
HE...
HOW LONG HAS IT BEEN...?

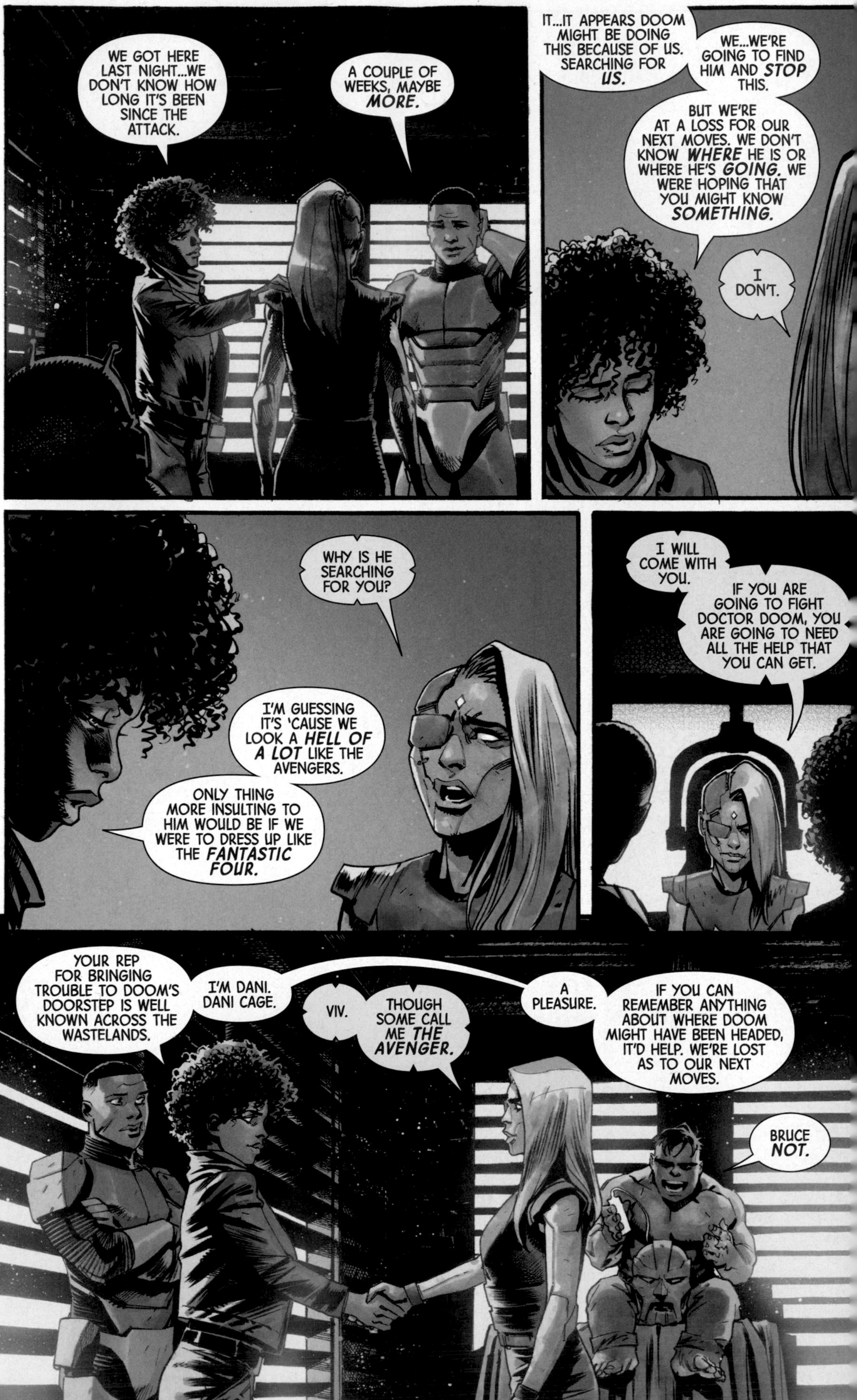
WE GOT HERE LAST NIGHT...WE DON'T KNOW HOW LONG IT'S BEEN SINCE THE ATTACK.
A COUPLE OF WEEKS, MAYBE MORE.
IT...IT APPEARS DOOM MIGHT BE DOING THIS BECAUSE OF US. SEARCHING FOR US.
WE...WE'RE GOING TO FIND HIM AND STOP THIS.
BUT WE'RE AT A LOSS FOR OUR NEXT MOVES. WE DON'T KNOW WHERE HE IS OR WHERE HE'S GOING. WE WERE HOPING THAT YOU MIGHT KNOW SOMETHING.
I DON'T.
WHY IS HE SEARCHING FOR YOU?
I'M GUESSING IT'S 'CAUSE WE LOOK A HELL OF A LOT LIKE THE AVENGERS.
ONLY THING MORE INSULTING TO HIM WOULD BE IF WE WERE TO DRESS UP LIKE THE FANTASTIC FOUR.
I WILL COME WITH YOU.
IF YOU ARE GOING TO FIGHT DOCTOR DOOM, YOU ARE GOING TO NEED ALL THE HELP THAT YOU CAN GET.
YOUR REP FOR BRINGING TROUBLE TO DOOM'S DOORSTEP IS WELL KNOWN ACROSS THE WASTELANDS.
I'M DANI. DANI CAGE.
VIV.
THOUGH SOME CALL ME THE AVENGER.
A PLEASURE.
IF YOU CAN REMEMBER ANYTHING ABOUT WHERE DOOM MIGHT HAVE BEEN HEADED, IT'D HELP. WE'RE LOST AS TO OUR NEXT MOVES.
BRUCE NOT.

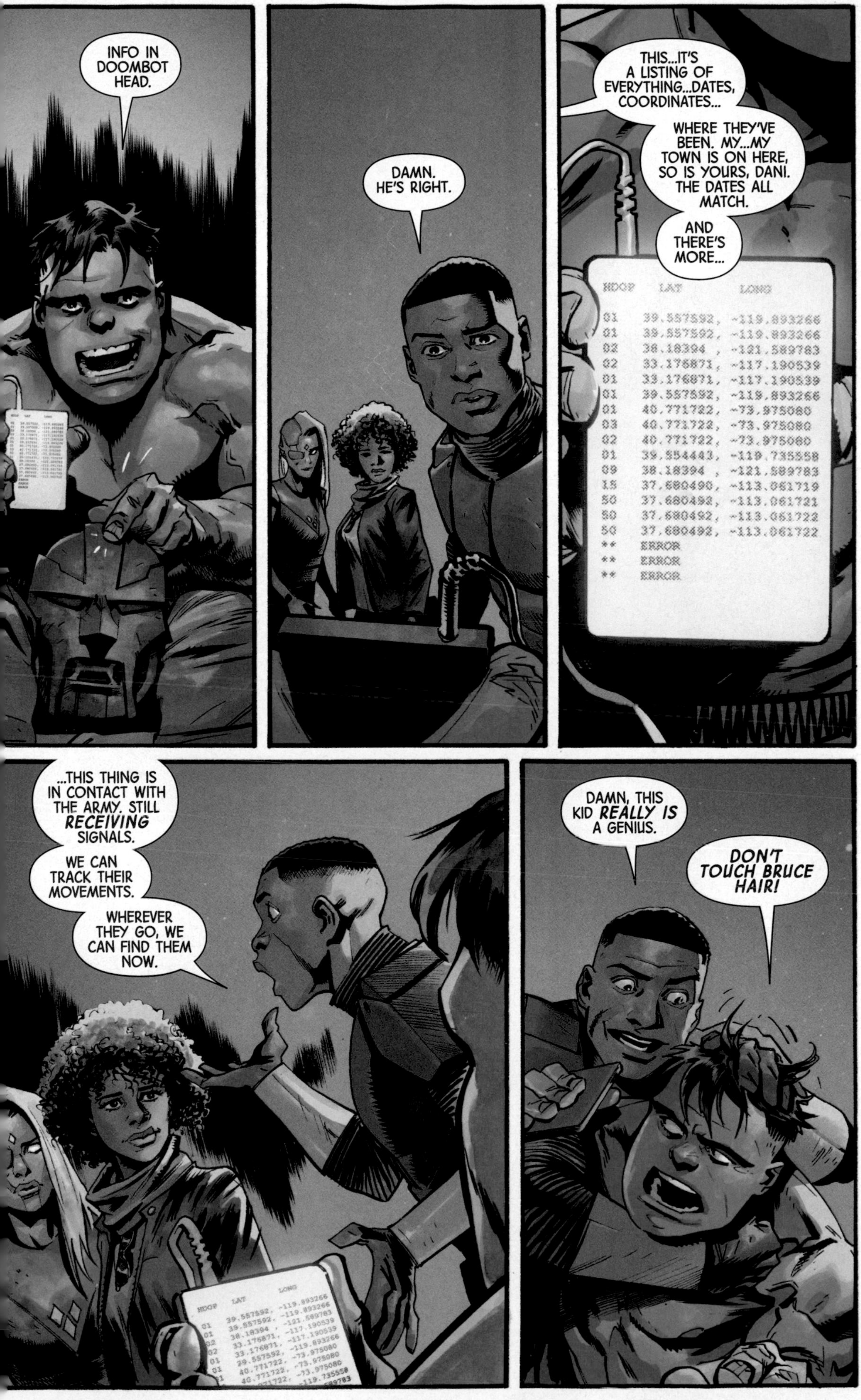
INFO IN DOOMBOT HEAD.
DAMN. HE'S RIGHT.
THIS...IT'S A LISTING OF EVERYTHING...DATES, COORDINATES...
WHERE THEY'VE BEEN. MY...MY TOWN IS ON HERE, SO IS YOURS, DANI. THE DATES ALL MATCH.
AND THERE'S MORE...
HDOP LAT LONG
01 39.557592, -119.893266
01 39.557592, -119.893266
02 38.18394 , -121.589783
02 33.176871, -117.190539
01 33.176871, -117.190539
01 39.557592, -119.893266
01 40.771722, -73.975080
03 40.771722, -73.975080
02 40.771722, -73.975080
01 39.554443, -119.735558
09 38.18394 , -121.589783
15 37.680490, -113.061719
50 37.680492, -113.061721
50 37,680492, -113.061722
50 37,680492, -113.061722
** ERROR
** ERROR
** ERROR
...THIS THING IS IN CONTACT WITH THE ARMY. STILL RECEIVING SIGNALS.
WE CAN TRACK THEIR MOVEMENTS.
WHEREVER THEY GO, WE CAN FIND THEM NOW.
DAMN, THIS KID REALLY IS A GENIUS.
DON'T TOUCH BRUCE HAIR!

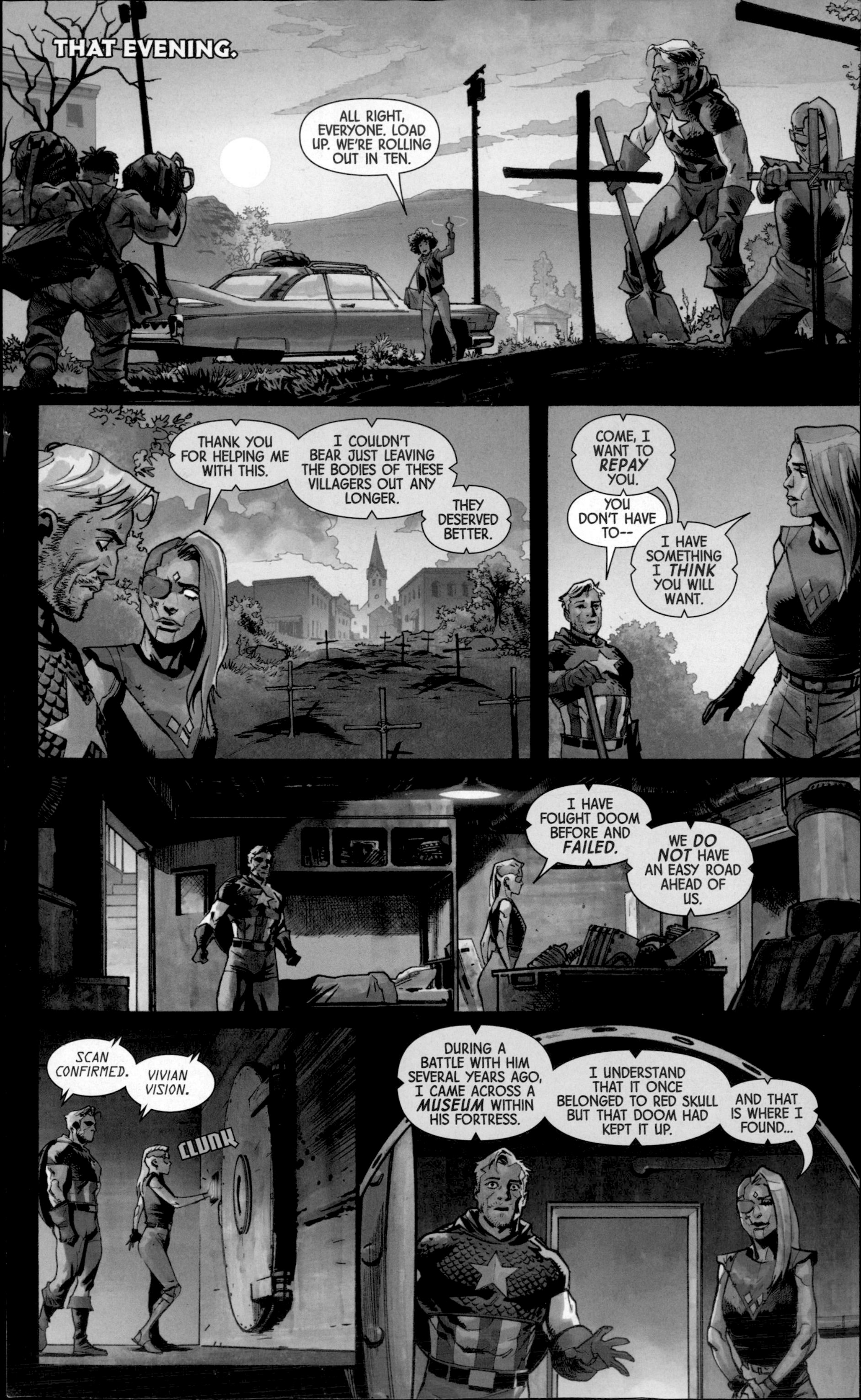
THAT EVENING.
ALL RIGHT, EVERYONE. LOAD UP. WE'RE ROLLING OUT IN TEN.
THANK YOU FOR HELPING ME WITH THIS.
I COULDN'T BEAR JUST LEAVING THE BODIES OF THESE VILLAGERS OUT ANY LONGER.
THEY DESERVED BETTER.
COME, I WANT TO REPAY YOU.
YOU DON'T HAVE TO--
I HAVE SOMETHING I THINK YOU WILL WANT.
I HAVE FOUGHT DOOM BEFORE AND FAILED.
WE DO NOT HAVE AN EASY ROAD AHEAD OF US.
SCAN CONFIRMED.
VIVIAN VISION.
CLUNK
DURING A BATTLE WITH HIM SEVERAL YEARS AGO, I CAME ACROSS A MUSEUM WITHIN HIS FORTRESS.
I UNDERSTAND THAT IT ONCE BELONGED TO RED SKULL BUT THAT DOOM HAD KEPT IT UP.
AND THAT IS WHERE I FOUND...

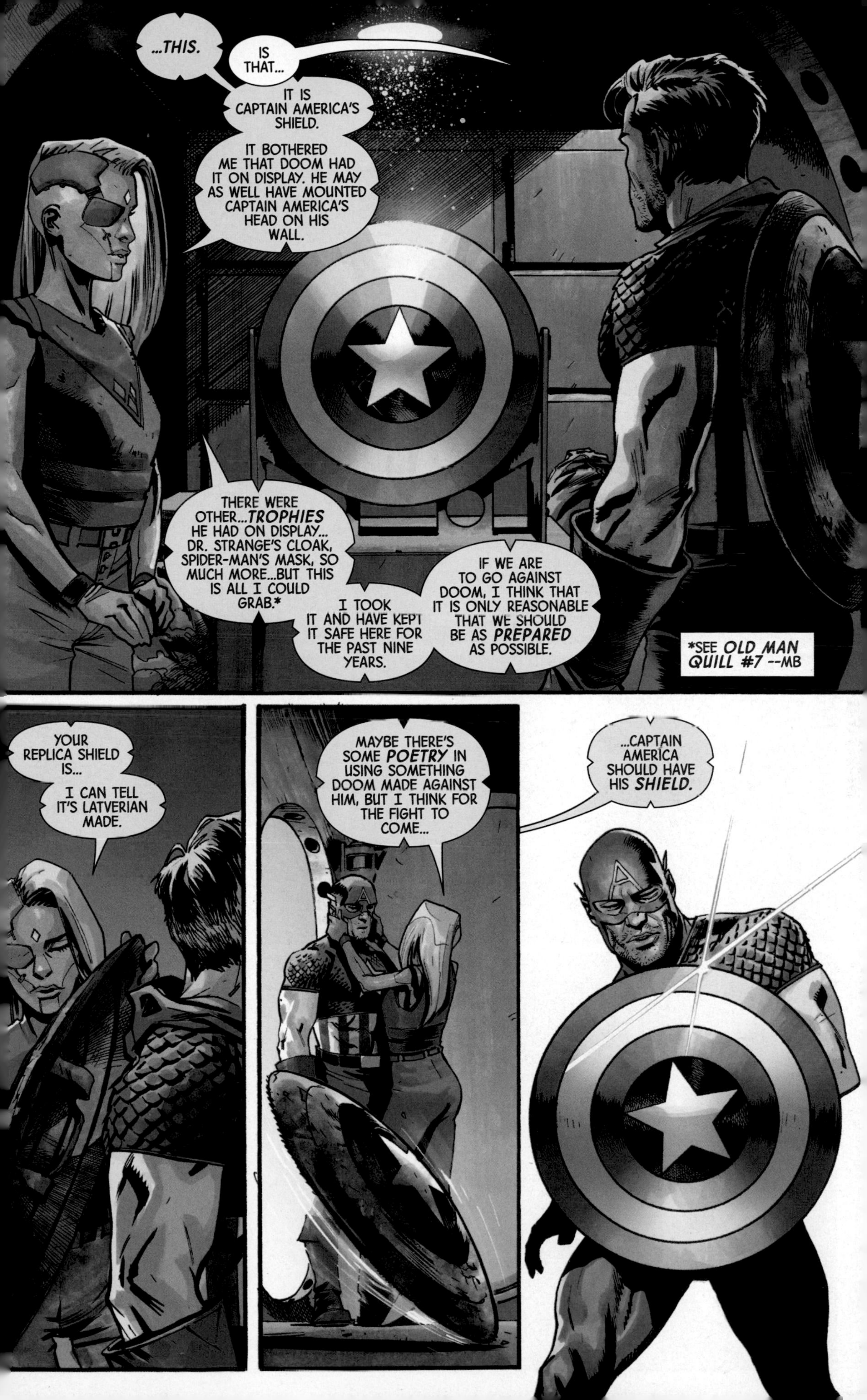

...THIS.
IS THAT...
IT IS CAPTAIN AMERICA'S SHIELD.
IT BOTHERED ME THAT DOOM HAD IT ON DISPLAY. HE MAY AS WELL HAVE MOUNTED CAPTAIN AMERICA'S HEAD ON HIS WALL.
THERE WERE OTHER...TROPHIES HE HAD ON DISPLAY... DR. STRANGE'S CLOAK, SPIDER-MAN'S MASK, SO MUCH MORE...BUT THIS IS ALL I COULD GRAB.*
I TOOK IT AND HAVE KEPT IT SAFE HERE FOR THE PAST NINE YEARS.
IF WE ARE TO GO AGAINST DOOM, I THINK THAT IT IS ONLY REASONABLE THAT WE SHOULD BE AS PREPARED AS POSSIBLE.
*SEE OLD MAN QUILL #7 --MB
YOUR REPLICA SHIELD IS...
I CAN TELL IT'S LATVERIAN MADE.
MAYBE THERE'S SOME POETRY IN USING SOMETHING DOOM MADE AGAINST HIM, BUT I THINK FOR THE FIGHT TO COME...
...CAPTAIN AMERICA SHOULD HAVE HIS SHIELD.

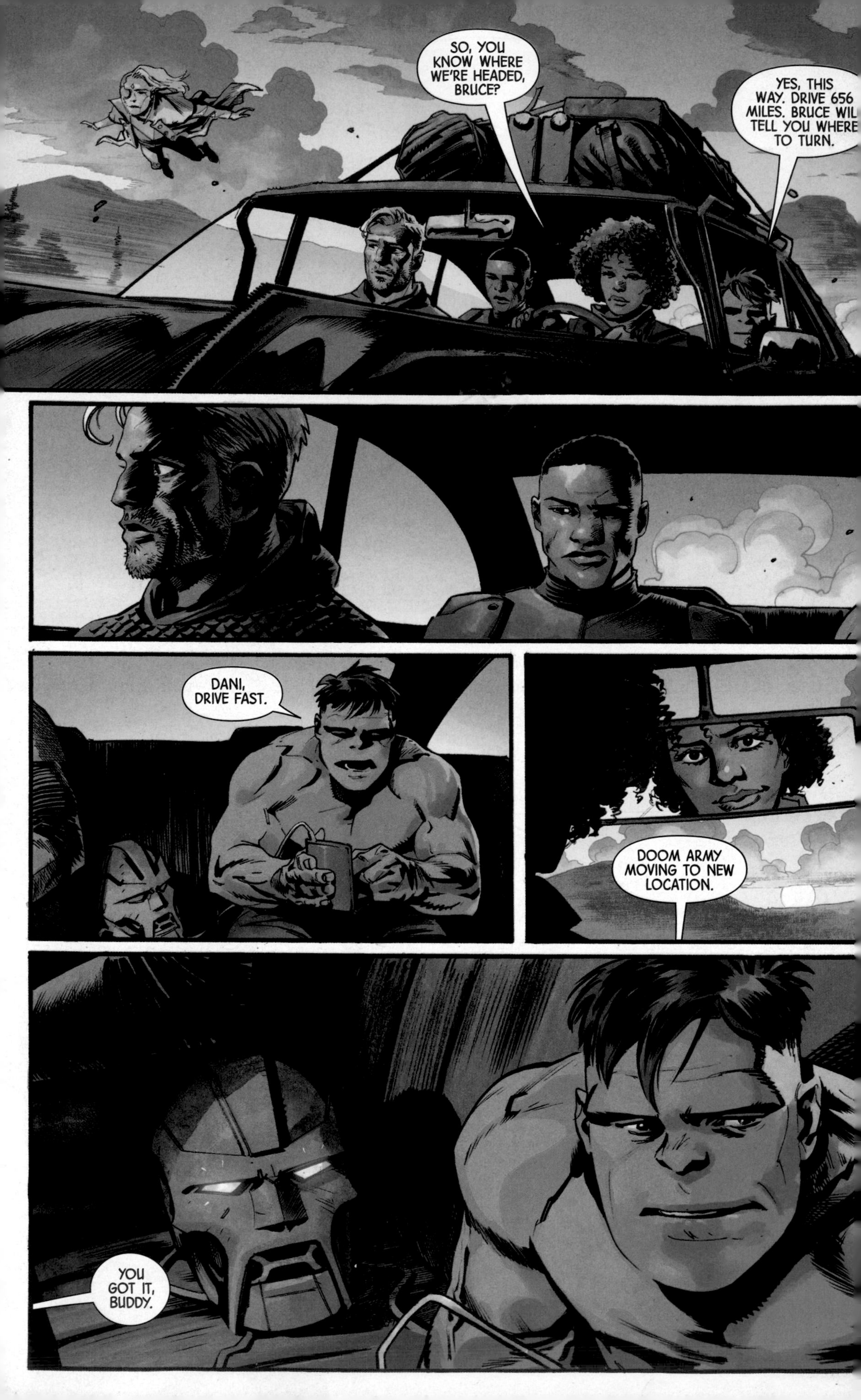
SO, YOU KNOW WHERE WE'RE HEADED, BRUCE?
YES, THIS WAY. DRIVE 656 MILES. BRUCE WIL TELL YOU WHERE TO TURN.
DANI, DRIVE FAST.
DOOM ARMY MOVING TO NEW LOCATION.
YOU GOT IT, BUDDY.

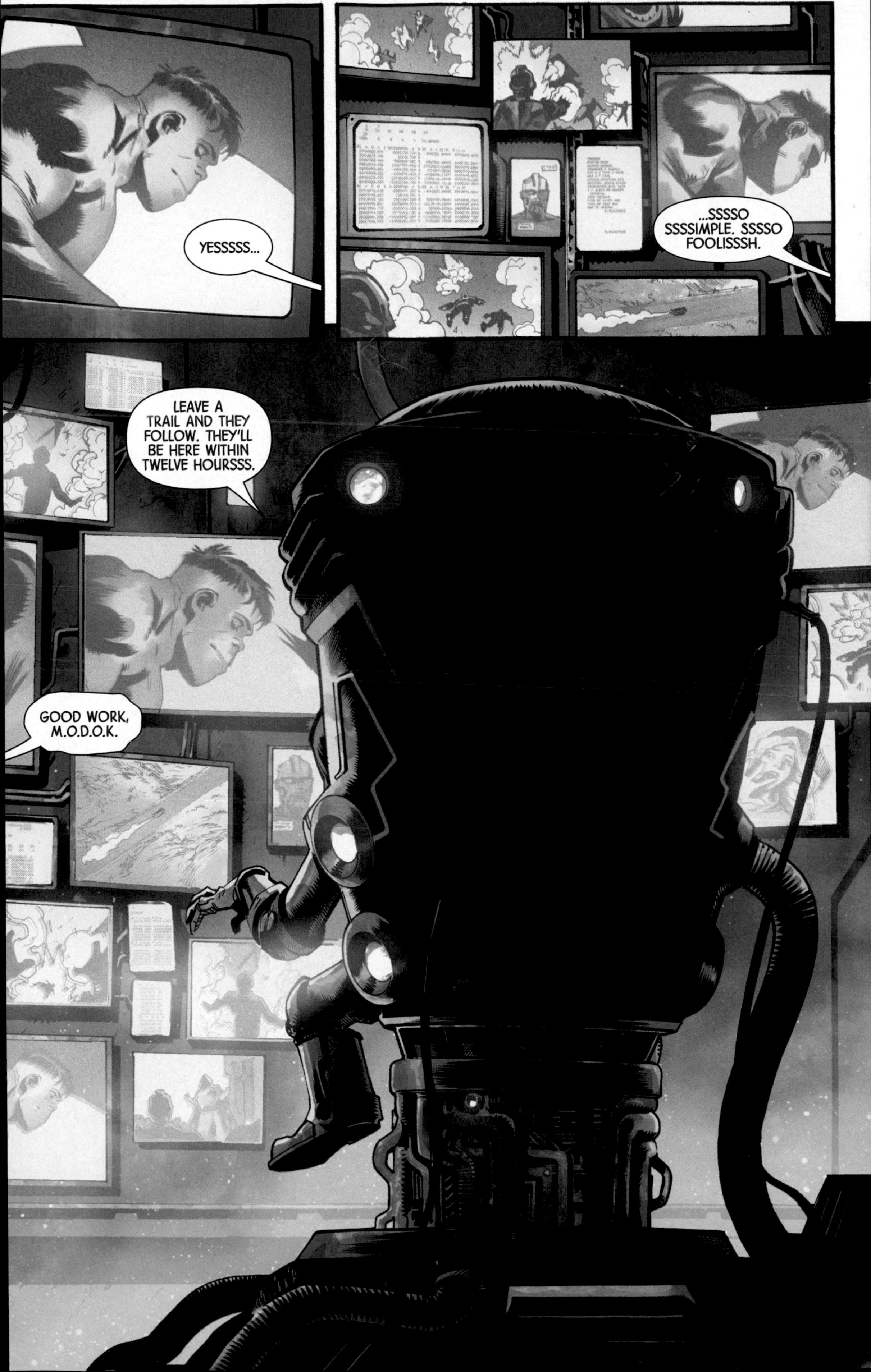
YESSSSS...
...SSSSO SSSSIMPLE. SSSSO FOOLISSSH.
LEAVE A TRAIL AND THEY FOLLOW. THEY'LL BE HERE WITHIN TWELVE HOURSSS.
GOOD WORK, M.O.D.O.K.

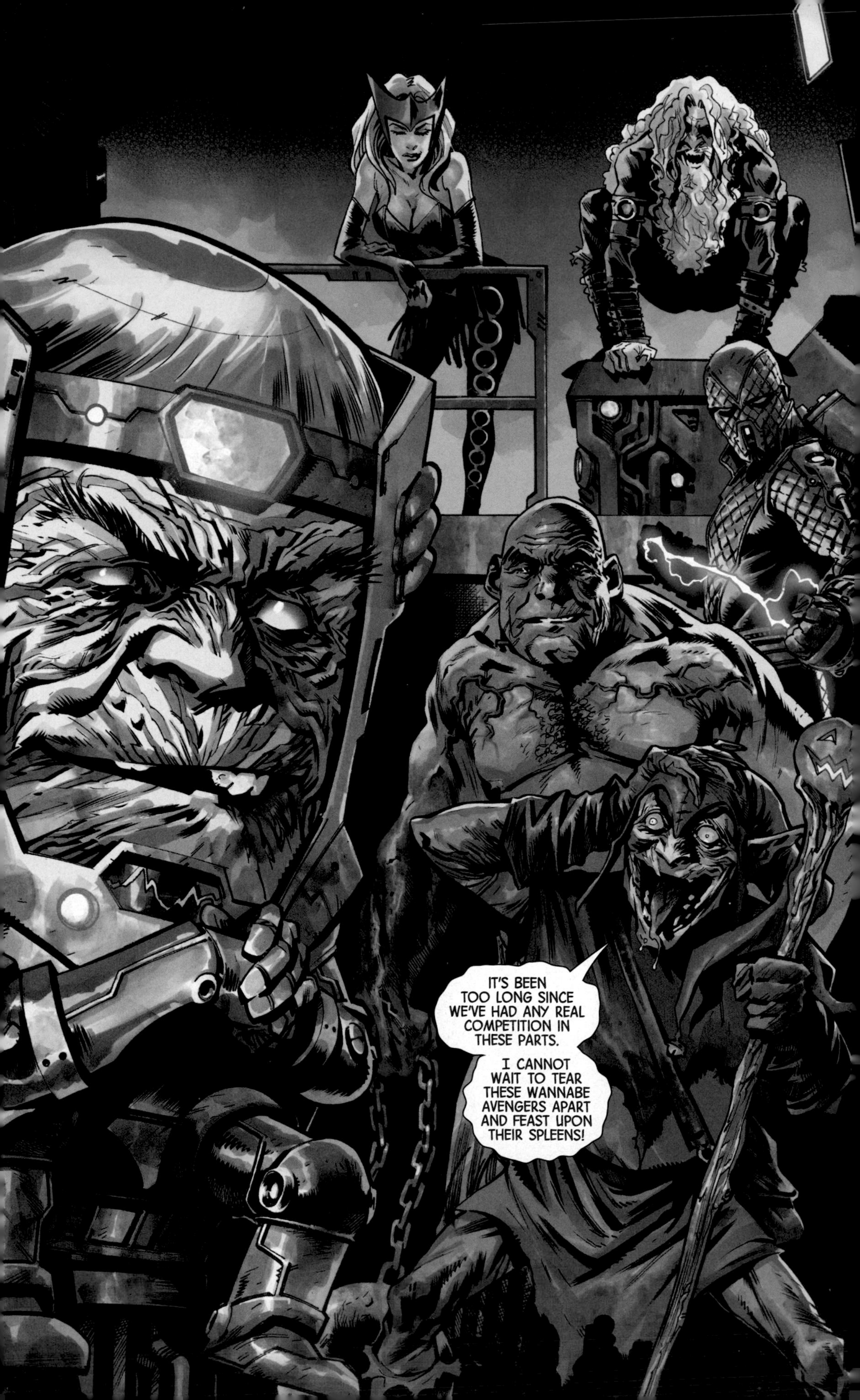
IT'S BEEN TOO LONG SINCE WE'VE HAD ANY REAL COMPETITION IN THESE PARTS.
I CANNOT WAIT TO TEAR THESE WANNABE AVENGERS APART AND FEAST UPON THEIR SPLEENS!

4.

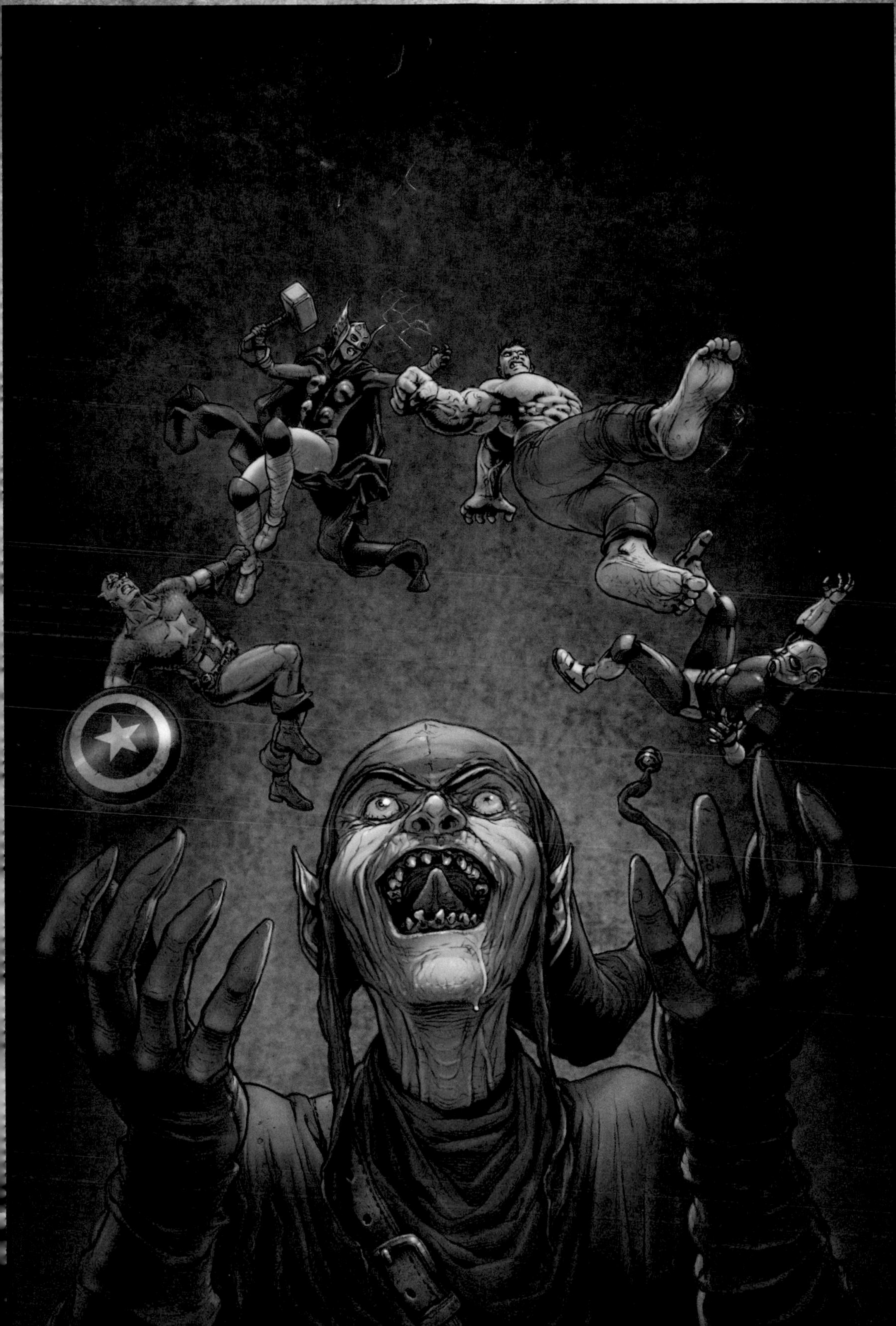

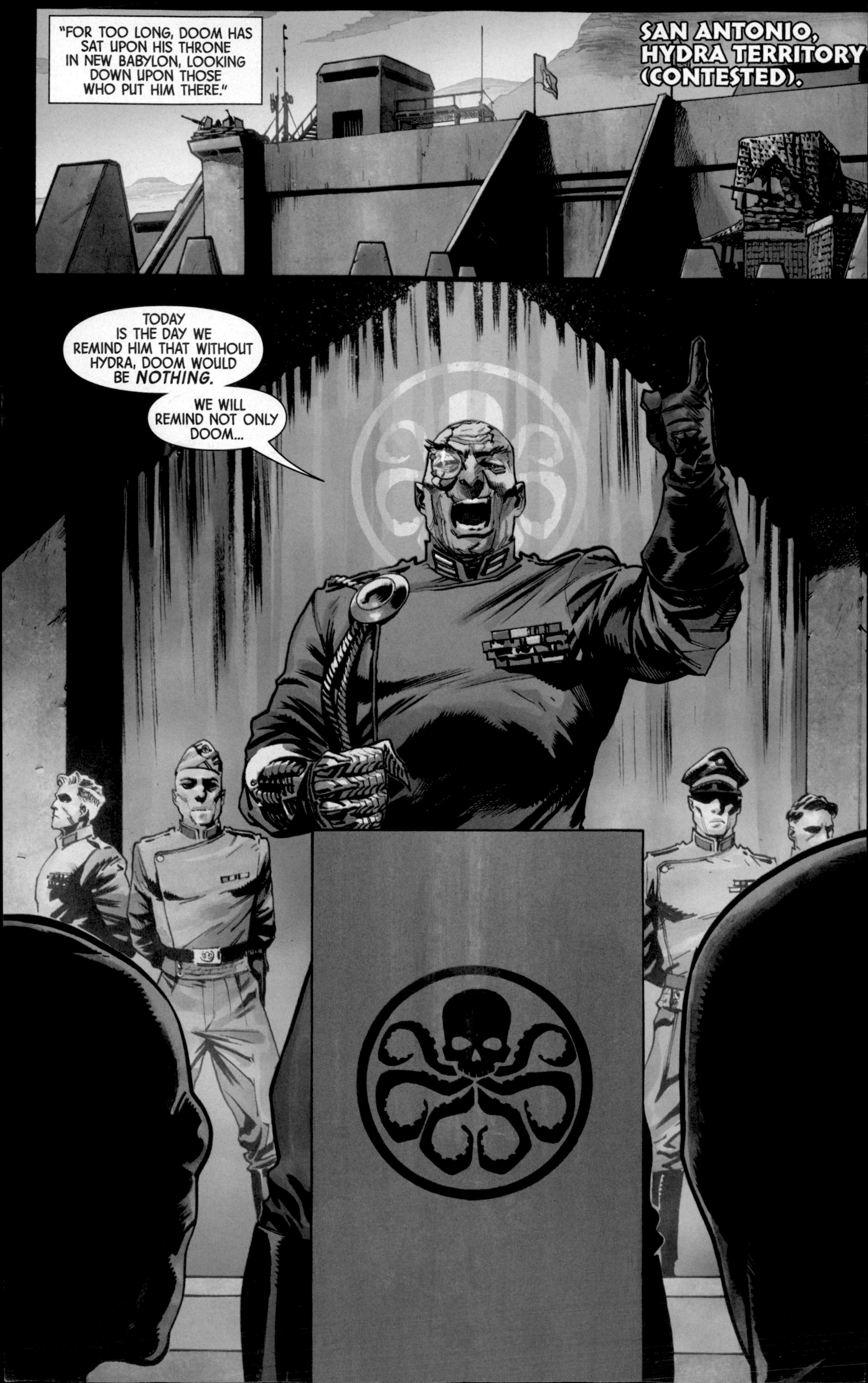
"FOR TOO LONG, DOOM HAS SAT UPON HIS THRONE IN NEW BABYLON, LOOKING DOWN UPON THOSE WHO PUT HIM THERE."
SAN ANTONIO, HYDRA TERRITORY (CONTESTED).
TODAY IS THE DAY WE REMIND HIM THAT WITHOUT HYDRA, DOOM WOULD BE NOTHING.
WE WILL REMIND NOT ONLY DOOM...

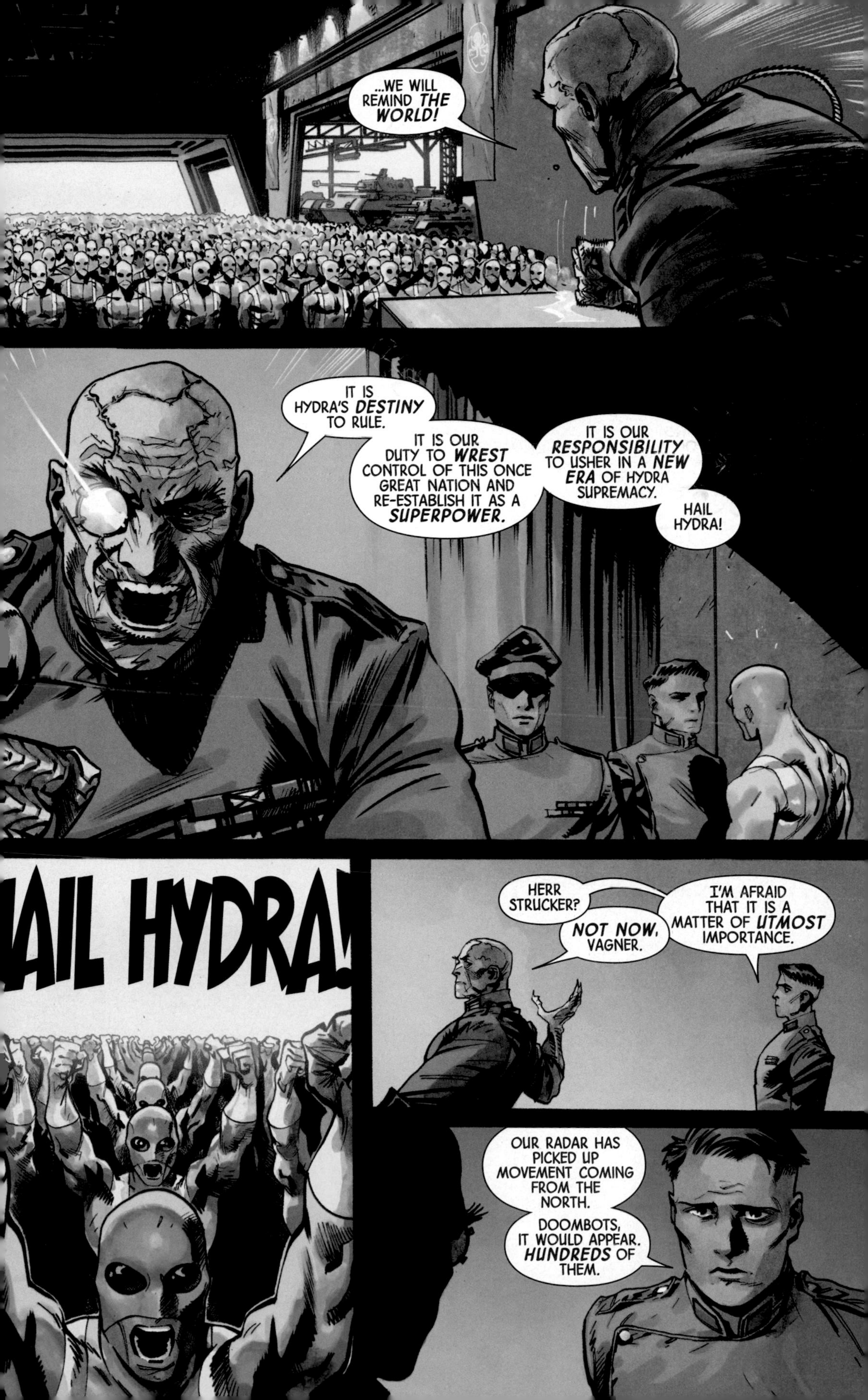
...WE WILL REMIND THE WORLD!
IT IS HYDRA'S DESTINY TO RULE.
IT IS OUR DUTY TO WREST CONTROL OF THIS ONCE GREAT NATION AND RE-ESTABLISH IT AS A SUPERPOWER.
IT IS OUR RESPONSIBILITY TO USHER IN A NEW ERA OF HYDRA SUPREMACY.
HAIL HYDRA!
AIL HYDRA!
HERR STRUCKER?
I'M AFRAID THAT IT IS A MATTER OF UTMOST IMPORTANCE.
NOT NOW, VAGNER.
OUR RADAR HAS PICKED UP MOVEMENT COMING FROM THE NORTH.
DOOMBOTS, IT WOULD APPEAR. HUNDREDS OF THEM.

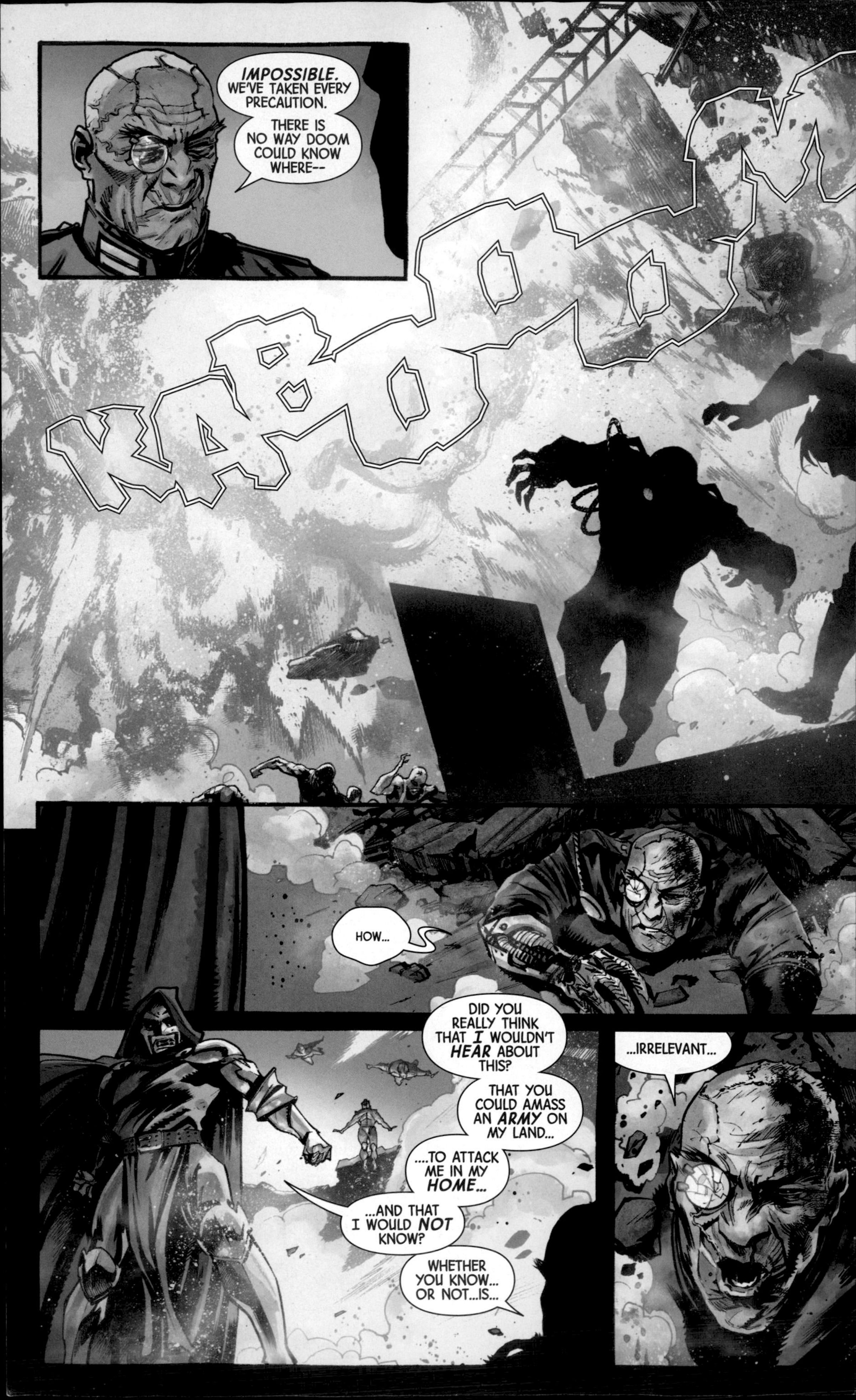

IMPOSSIBLE. WE'VE TAKEN EVERY PRECAUTION.
THERE IS NO WAY DOOM COULD KNOW WHERE--
KABOOOM
HOW...
DID YOU REALLY THINK THAT I WOULDN'T HEAR ABOUT THIS?
THAT YOU COULD AMASS AN ARMY ON MY LAND...
....TO ATTACK ME IN MY HOME...
...AND THAT I WOULD NOT KNOW?
WHETHER YOU KNOW... OR NOT...IS...
...IRRELEVANT...

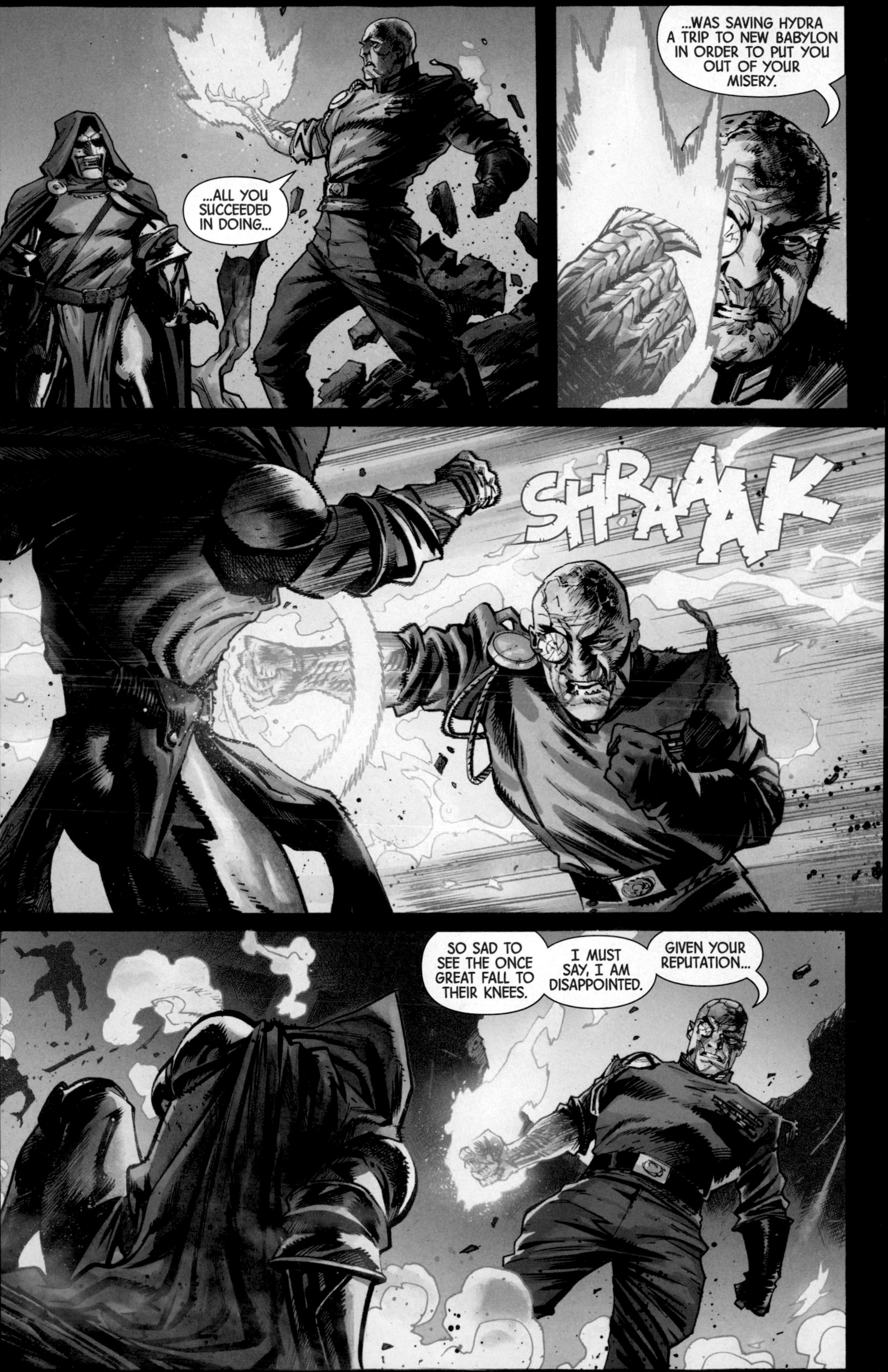
...ALL YOU SUCCEEDED IN DOING...
...WAS SAVING HYDRA A TRIP TO NEW BABYLON IN ORDER TO PUT YOU OUT OF YOUR MISERY.
SHRAAAK
GIVEN YOUR REPUTATION...
I MUST SAY, I AM DISAPPOINTED.
SO SAD TO SEE THE ONCE GREAT FALL TO THEIR KNEES.

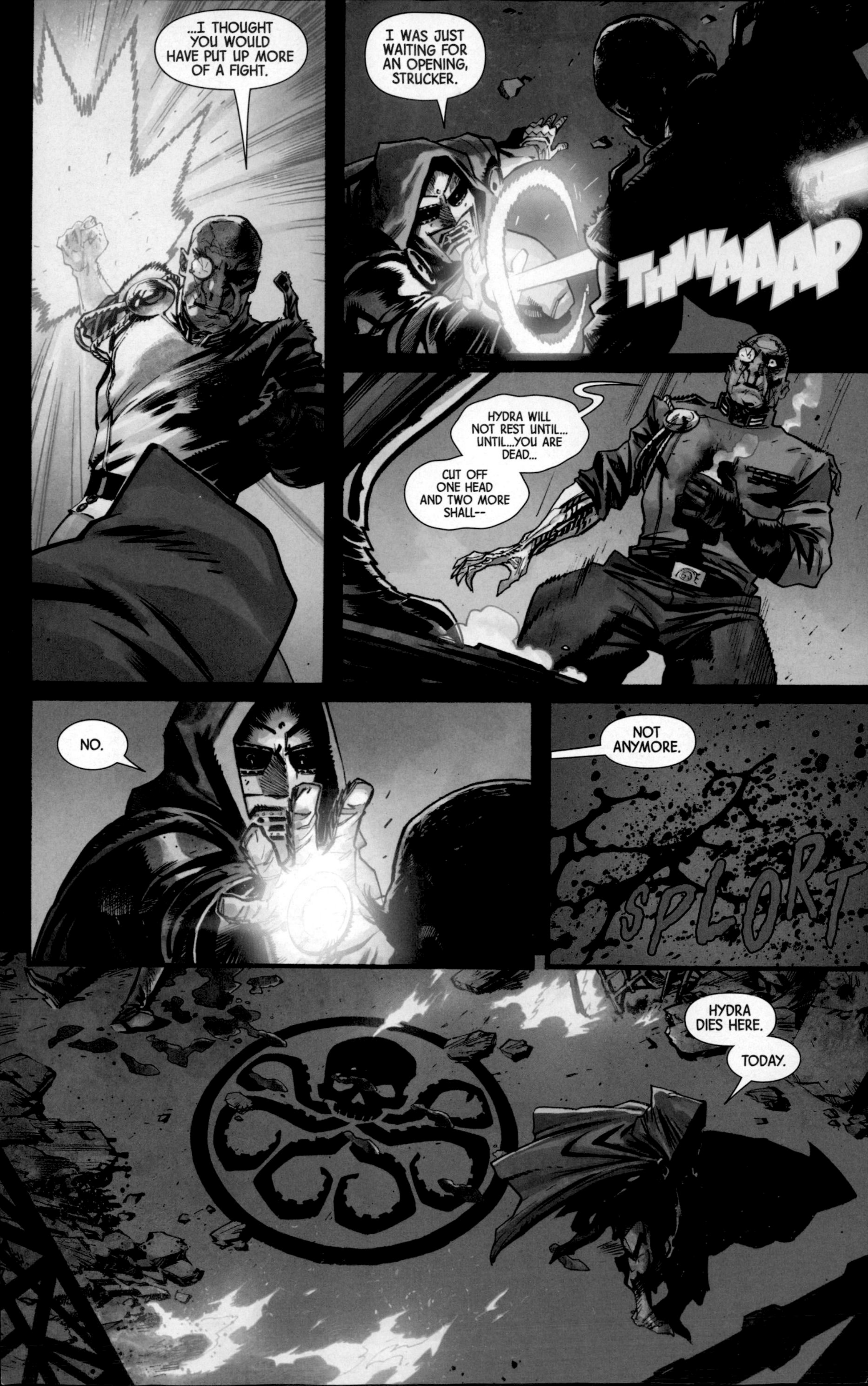
...I THOUGHT YOU WOULD HAVE PUT UP MORE OF A FIGHT.
I WAS JUST WAITING FOR AN OPENING, STRUCKER.
THWAAAP
HYDRA WILL NOT REST UNTIL... UNTIL...YOU ARE DEAD...
CUT OFF ONE HEAD AND TWO MORE SHALL--
NO.
NOT ANYMORE.
SPLORT
HYDRA DIES HERE.
TODAY.

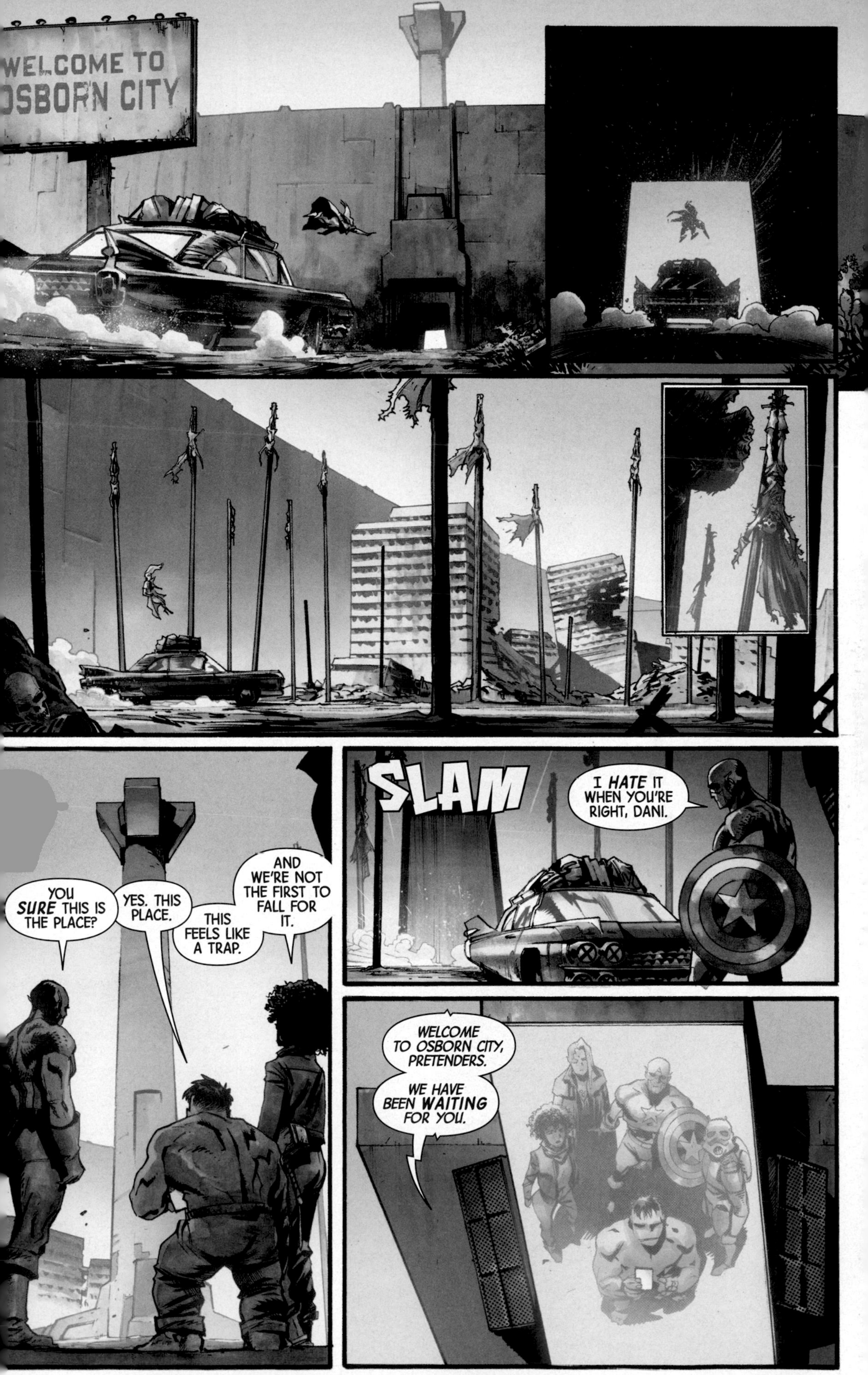
WELCOME TO OSBORN CITY
YOU SURE THIS IS THE PLACE?
YES. THIS PLACE.
THIS FEELS LIKE A TRAP.
AND WE'RE NOT THE FIRST TO FALL FOR IT.
SLAM
I HATE IT WHEN YOU'RE RIGHT, DANI.
WELCOME TO OSBORN CITY, PRETENDERS.
WE HAVE BEEN WAITING FOR YOU.

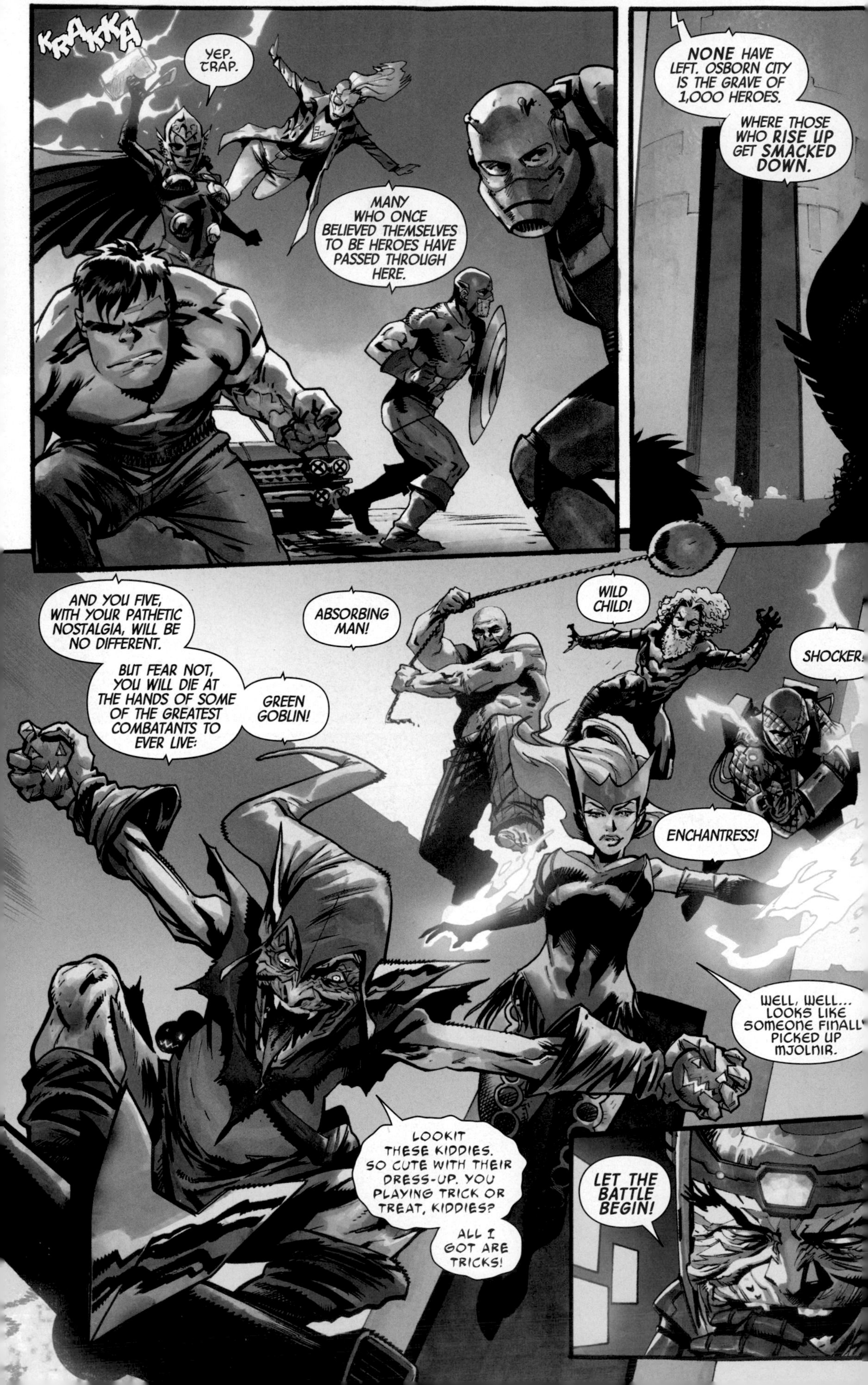
KRAKKA
YEP. TRAP.
MANY WHO ONCE BELIEVED THEMSELVES TO BE HEROES HAVE PASSED THROUGH HERE.
NONE HAVE LEFT. OSBORN CITY IS THE GRAVE OF 1,000 HEROES.
WHERE THOSE WHO RISE UP GET SMACKED DOWN.
AND YOU FIVE, WITH YOUR PATHETIC NOSTALGIA, WILL BE NO DIFFERENT.
BUT FEAR NOT, YOU WILL DIE AT THE HANDS OF SOME OF THE GREATEST COMBATANTS TO EVER LIVE:
GREEN GOBLIN!
ABSORBING MAN!
WILD CHILD!
SHOCKER!
ENCHANTRESS!
WELL, WELL... LOOKS LIKE SOMEONE FINALL PICKED UP MJOLNIR.
LOOKIT THESE KIDDIES. SO CUTE WITH THEIR DRESS-UP. YOU PLAYING TRICK OR TREAT, KIDDIES?
ALL I GOT ARE TRICKS!
LET THE BATTLE BEGIN!

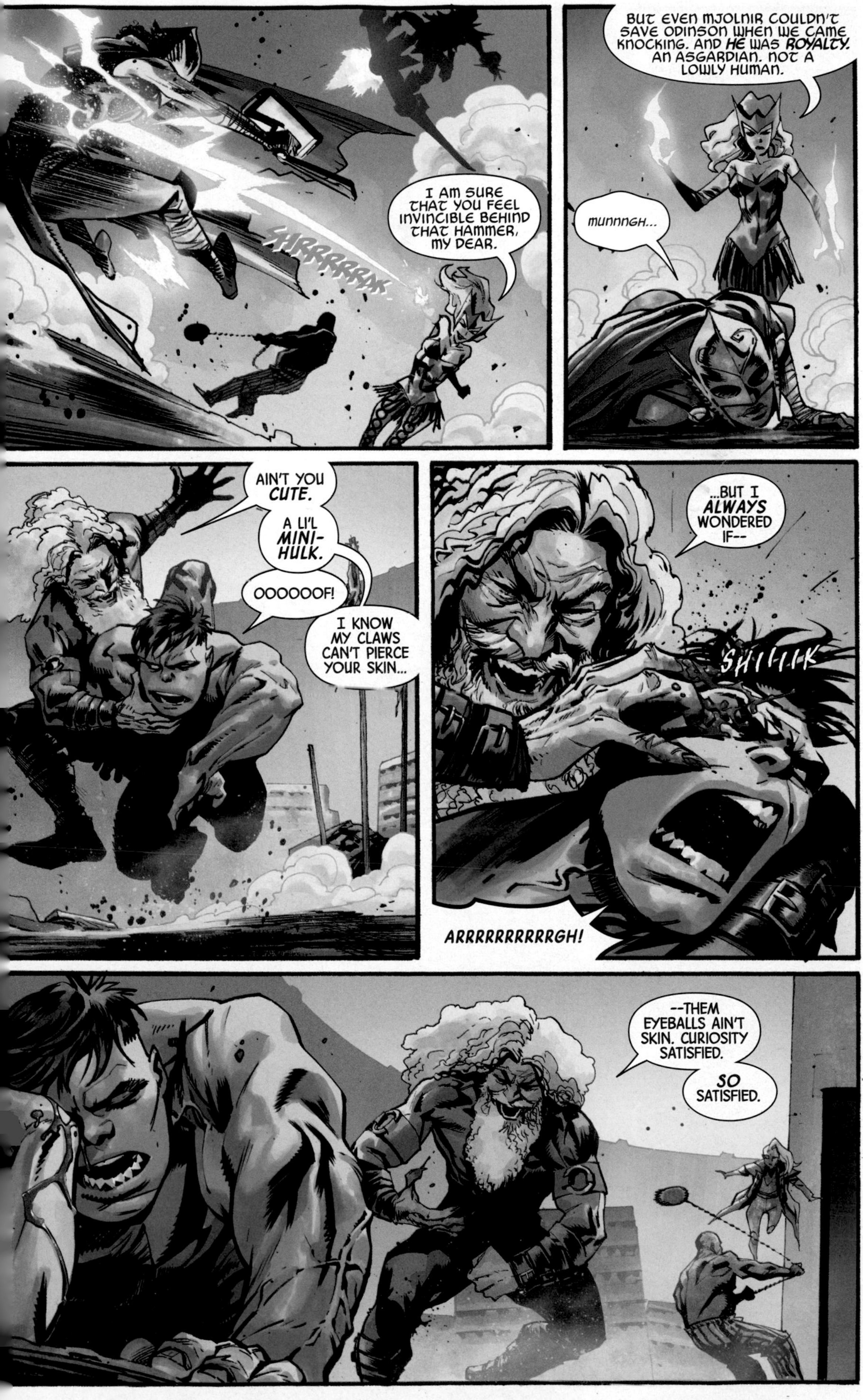
SHRRRRRRK
I AM SURE THAT YOU FEEL INVINCIBLE BEHIND THAT HAMMER, MY DEAR.
BUT EVEN MJOLNIR COULDN'T SAVE ODINSON WHEN WE CAME KNOCKING. AND HE WAS ROYALTY. AN ASGARDIAN. NOT A LOWLY HUMAN.
MUNNNGH...
AIN'T YOU CUTE.
A LI'L MINI-HULK.
OOOOOOF!
I KNOW MY CLAWS CAN'T PIERCE YOUR SKIN...
...BUT I ALWAYS WONDERED IF--
SHIIIIK
ARRRRRRRRRRGH!
--THEM EYEBALLS AIN'T SKIN. CURIOSITY SATISFIED.
SO SATISFIED.

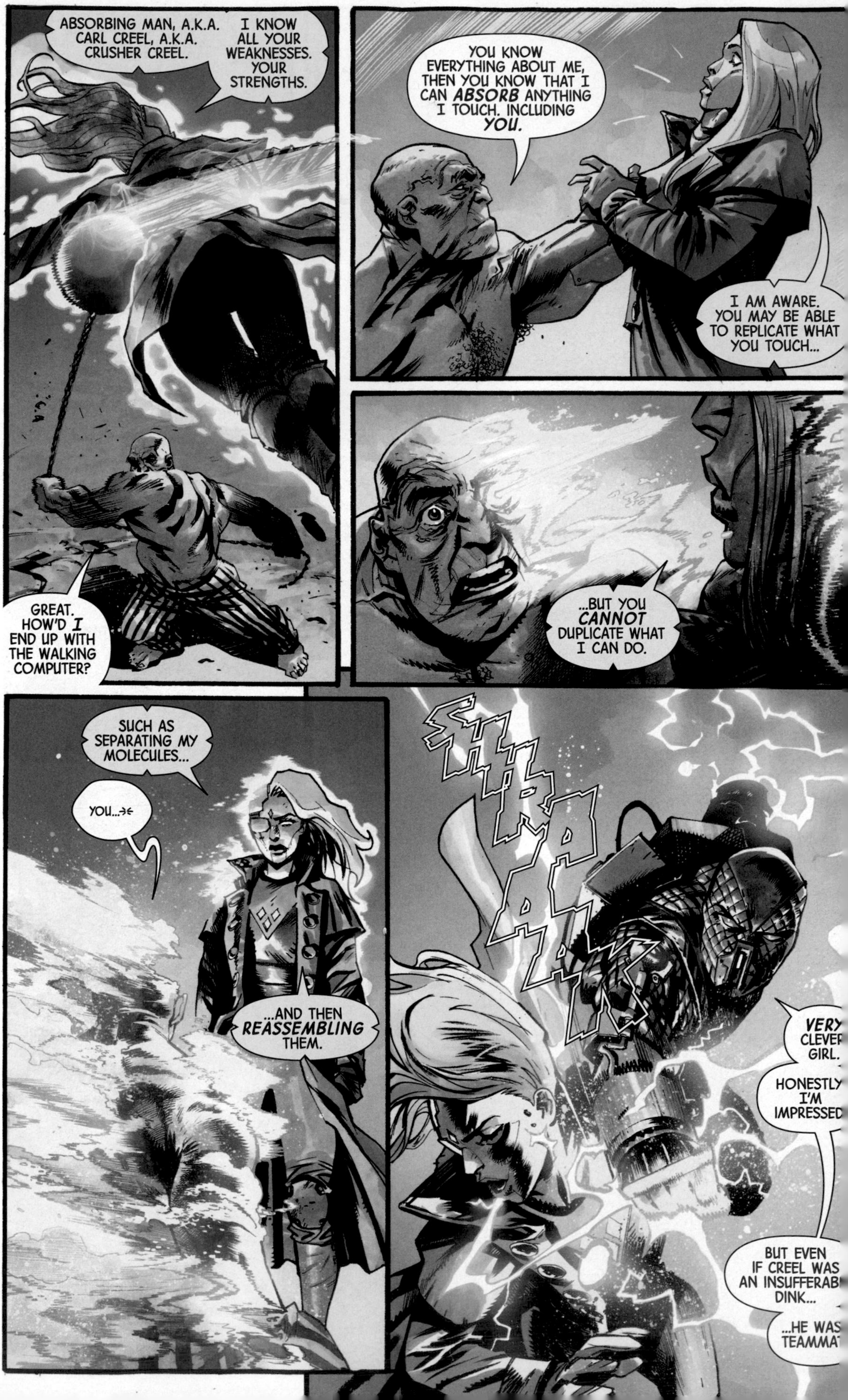
ABSORBING MAN, A.K.A. CARL CREEL, A.K.A. CRUSHER CREEL.
I KNOW ALL YOUR WEAKNESSES. YOUR STRENGTHS.
GREAT. HOW'D I END UP WITH THE WALKING COMPUTER?
YOU KNOW EVERYTHING ABOUT ME, THEN YOU KNOW THAT I CAN ABSORB ANYTHING I TOUCH. INCLUDING YOU.
I AM AWARE. YOU MAY BE ABLE TO REPLICATE WHAT YOU TOUCH...
...BUT YOU CANNOT DUPLICATE WHAT I CAN DO.
SUCH AS SEPARATING MY MOLECULES...
YOU...
...AND THEN REÄSSEMBLING THEM.
VERY CLEVER GIRL.
HONESTLY I'M IMPRESSED
BUT EVEN IF CREEL WAS AN INSUFFERAB DINK...
...HE WAS TEAMMAT

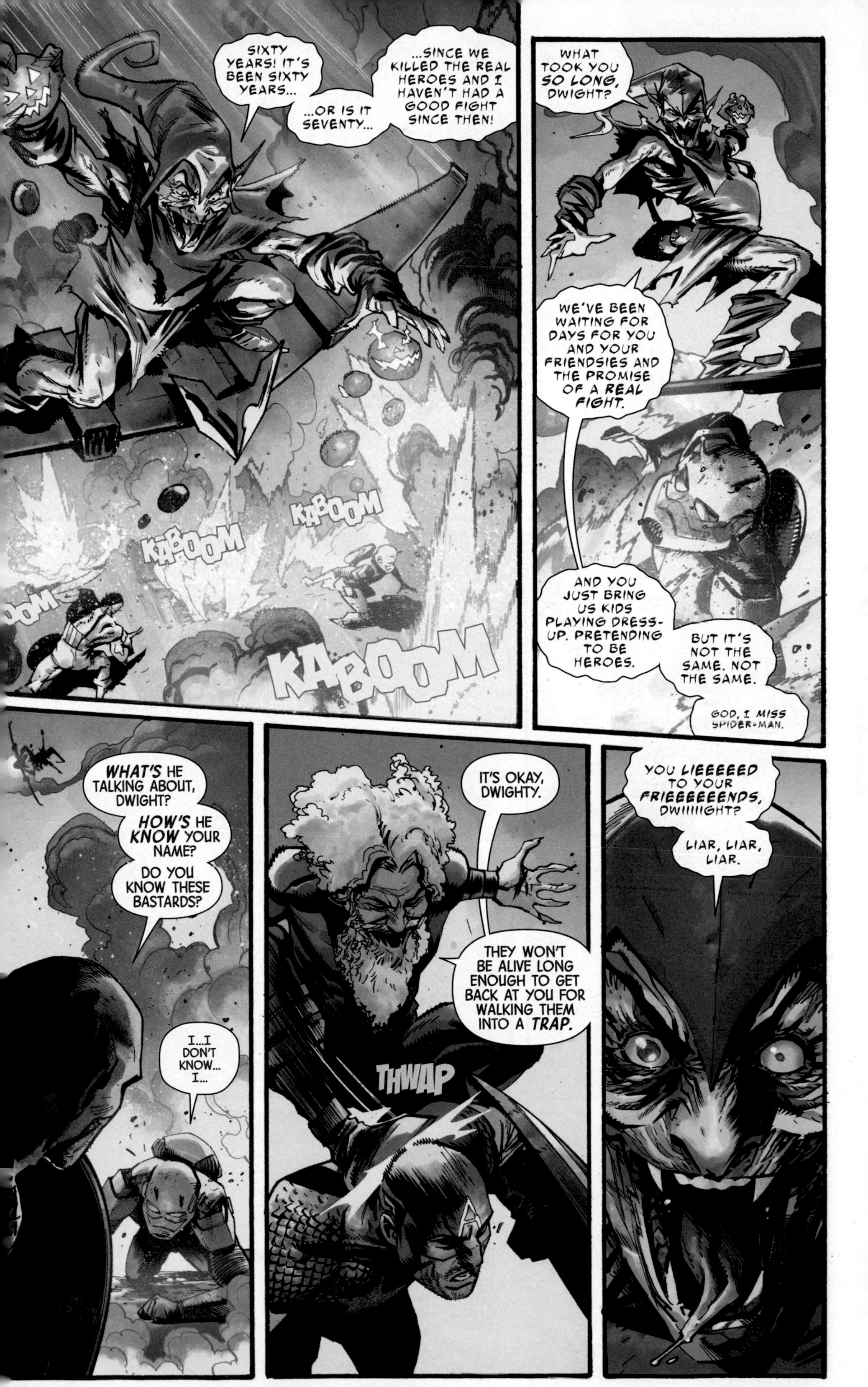
SIXTY YEARS! IT'S BEEN SIXTY YEARS...
...OR IS IT SEVENTY...
...SINCE WE KILLED THE REAL HEROES AND I HAVEN'T HAD A GOOD FIGHT SINCE THEN!
KABOOM
KABOOM
KABOOM
WHAT TOOK YOU SO LONG, DWIGHT?
WE'VE BEEN WAITING FOR DAYS FOR YOU AND YOUR FRIENDSIES AND THE PROMISE OF A REAL FIGHT.
AND YOU JUST BRING US KIDS PLAYING DRESS-UP. PRETENDING TO BE HEROES.
BUT IT'S NOT THE SAME. NOT THE SAME.
GOD, I MISS SPIDER-MAN.
WHAT'S HE TALKING ABOUT, DWIGHT?
HOW'S HE KNOW YOUR NAME?
DO YOU KNOW THESE BASTARDS?
I...I DON'T KNOW... I...
IT'S OKAY, DWIGHTY.
THEY WON'T BE ALIVE LONG ENOUGH TO GET BACK AT YOU FOR WALKING THEM INTO A TRAP.
THWAP
YOU LIEEEEED TO YOUR FRIEEEEEEENDS, DWIIIIIGHT?
LIAR, LIAR, LIAR.

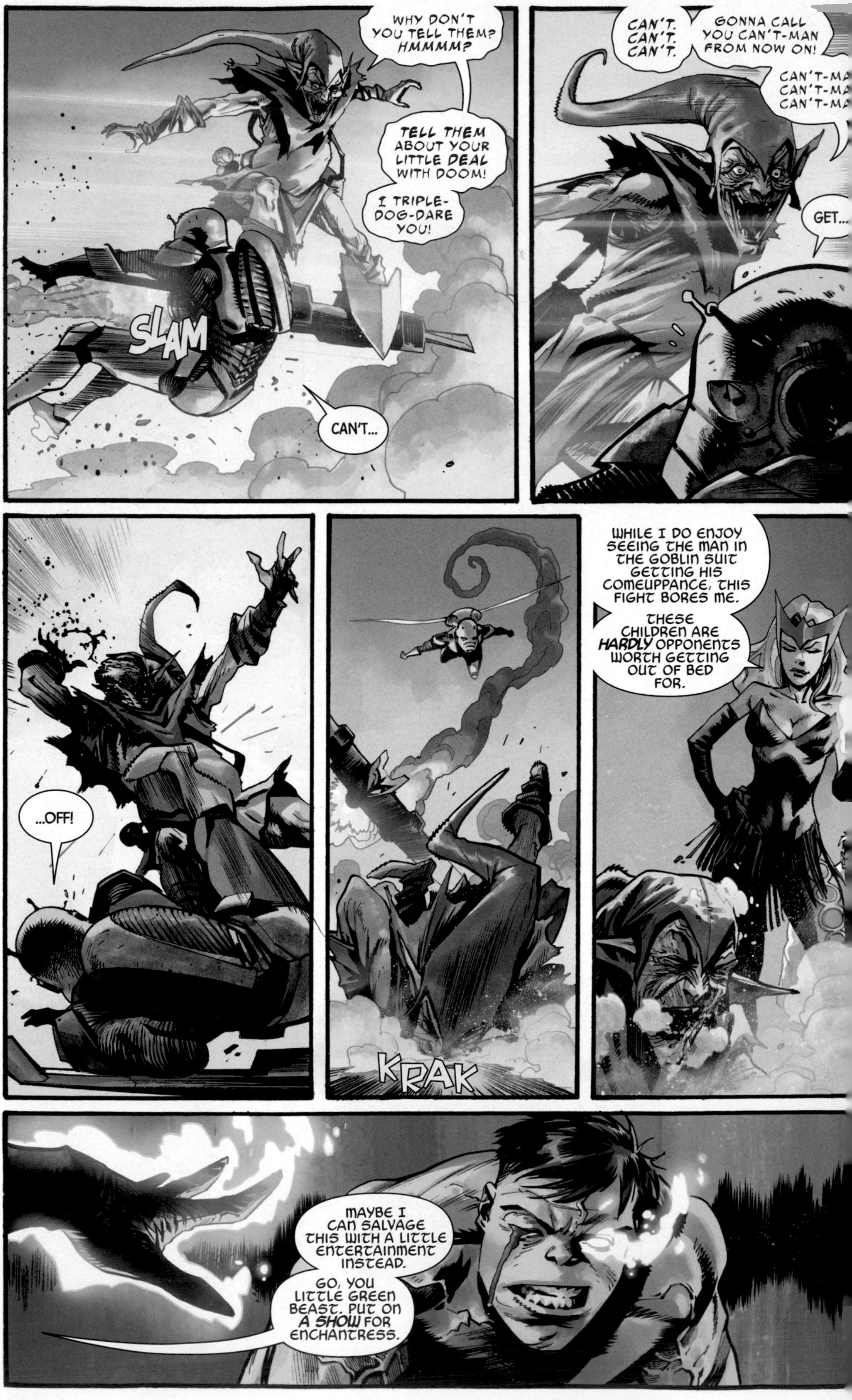
WHY DON'T YOU TELL THEM? HMMMM?
TELL THEM ABOUT YOUR LITTLE DEAL WITH DOOM!
I TRIPLE-DOG-DARE YOU!
SLAM
CAN'T...
CAN'T. CAN'T. CAN'T.
GONNA CALL YOU CAN'T-MAN FROM NOW ON!
GET...
...OFF!
KRAK
WHILE I DO ENJOY SEEING THE MAN IN THE GOBLIN SUIT GETTING HIS COMEUPPANCE, THIS FIGHT BORES ME.
THESE CHILDREN ARE HARDLY OPPONENTS WORTH GETTING OUT OF BED FOR.
MAYBE I CAN SALVAGE THIS WITH A LITTLE ENTERTAINMENT INSTEAD.
GO, YOU LITTLE GREEN BEAST. PUT ON A SHOW FOR ENCHANTRESS.

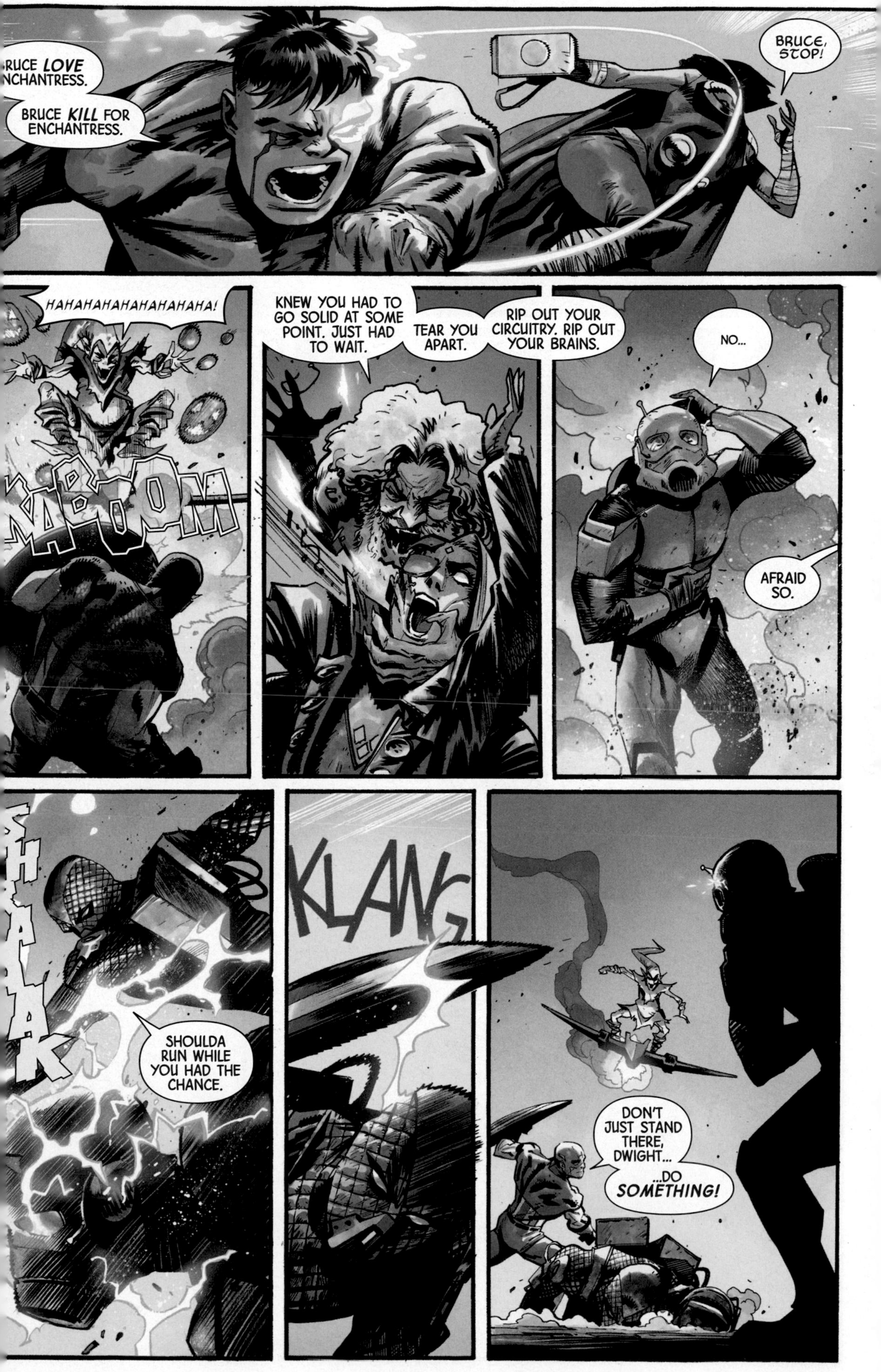
BRUCE LOVE ENCHANTRESS.
BRUCE KILL FOR ENCHANTRESS.
BRUCE, STOP!
HAHAHAHAHAHAHAHAHA!
KABOOM
KNEW YOU HAD TO GO SOLID AT SOME POINT. JUST HAD TO WAIT.
TEAR YOU APART.
RIP OUT YOUR CIRCUITRY. RIP OUT YOUR BRAINS.
NO...
AFRAID SO.
SHAPAK
SHOULDA RUN WHILE YOU HAD THE CHANCE.
KLANG
DON'T JUST STAND THERE, DWIGHT...
...DO SOMETHING!

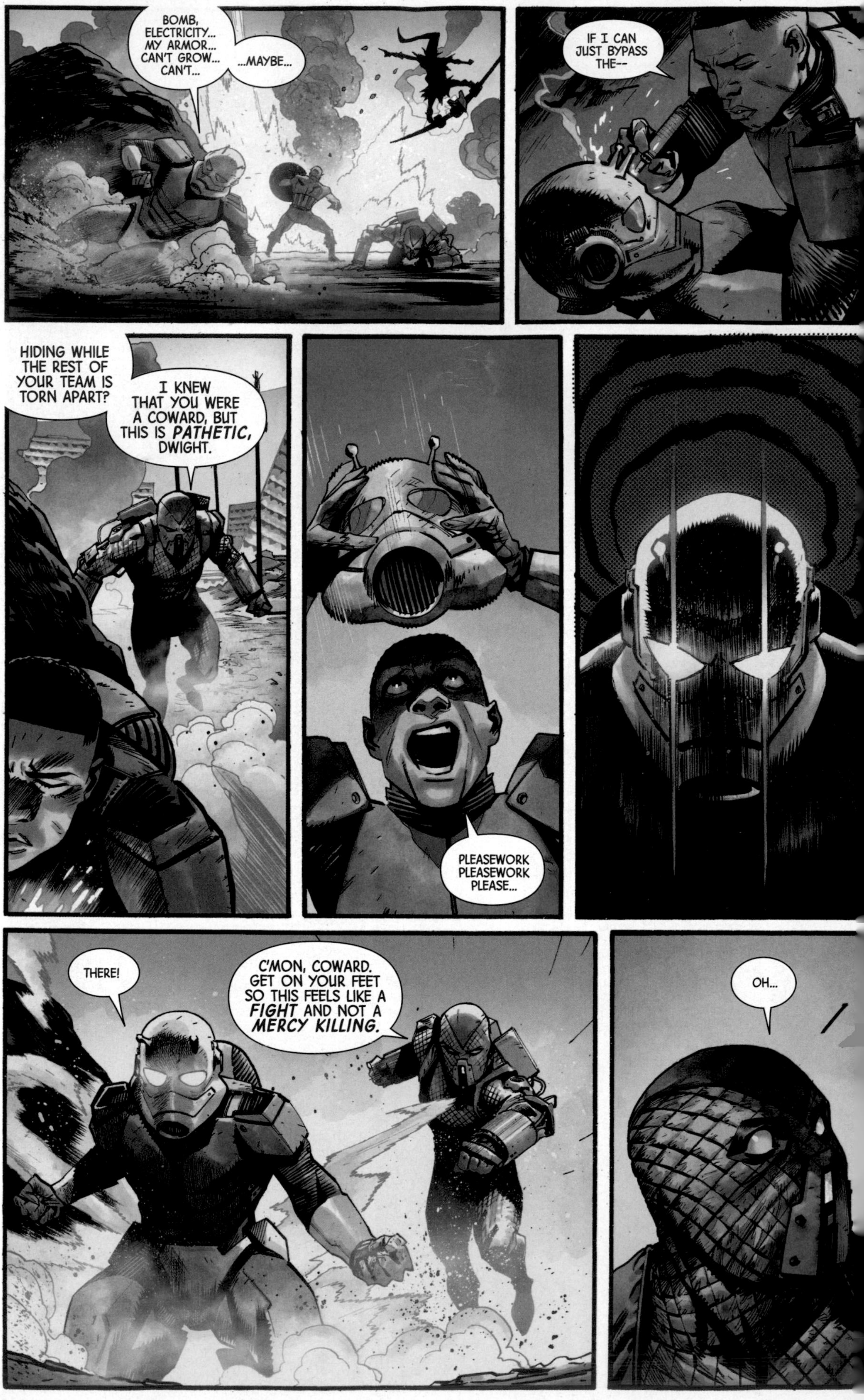
BOMB, ELECTRICITY... MY ARMOR... CAN'T GROW... CAN'T...
...MAYBE...
IF I CAN JUST BYPASS THE--
HIDING WHILE THE REST OF YOUR TEAM IS TORN APART?
I KNEW THAT YOU WERE A COWARD, BUT THIS IS PATHETIC, DWIGHT.
PLEASEWORK PLEASEWORK PLEASE...
THERE!
C'MON, COWARD. GET ON YOUR FEET SO THIS FEELS LIKE A FIGHT AND NOT A MERCY KILLING.
OH...

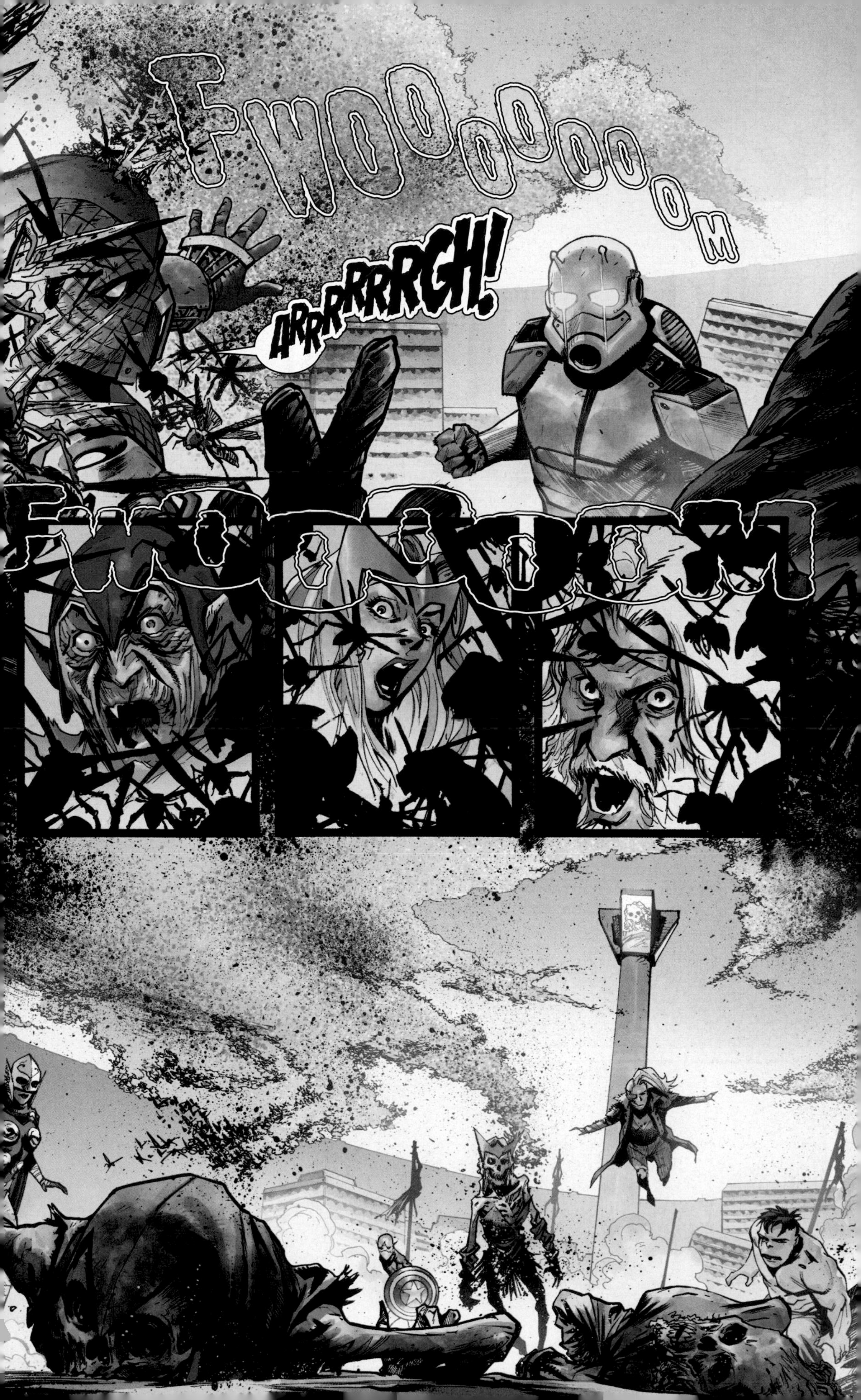
FWOOOOOOOOM
ARRRRRRRGH!
FWOOOOOOM

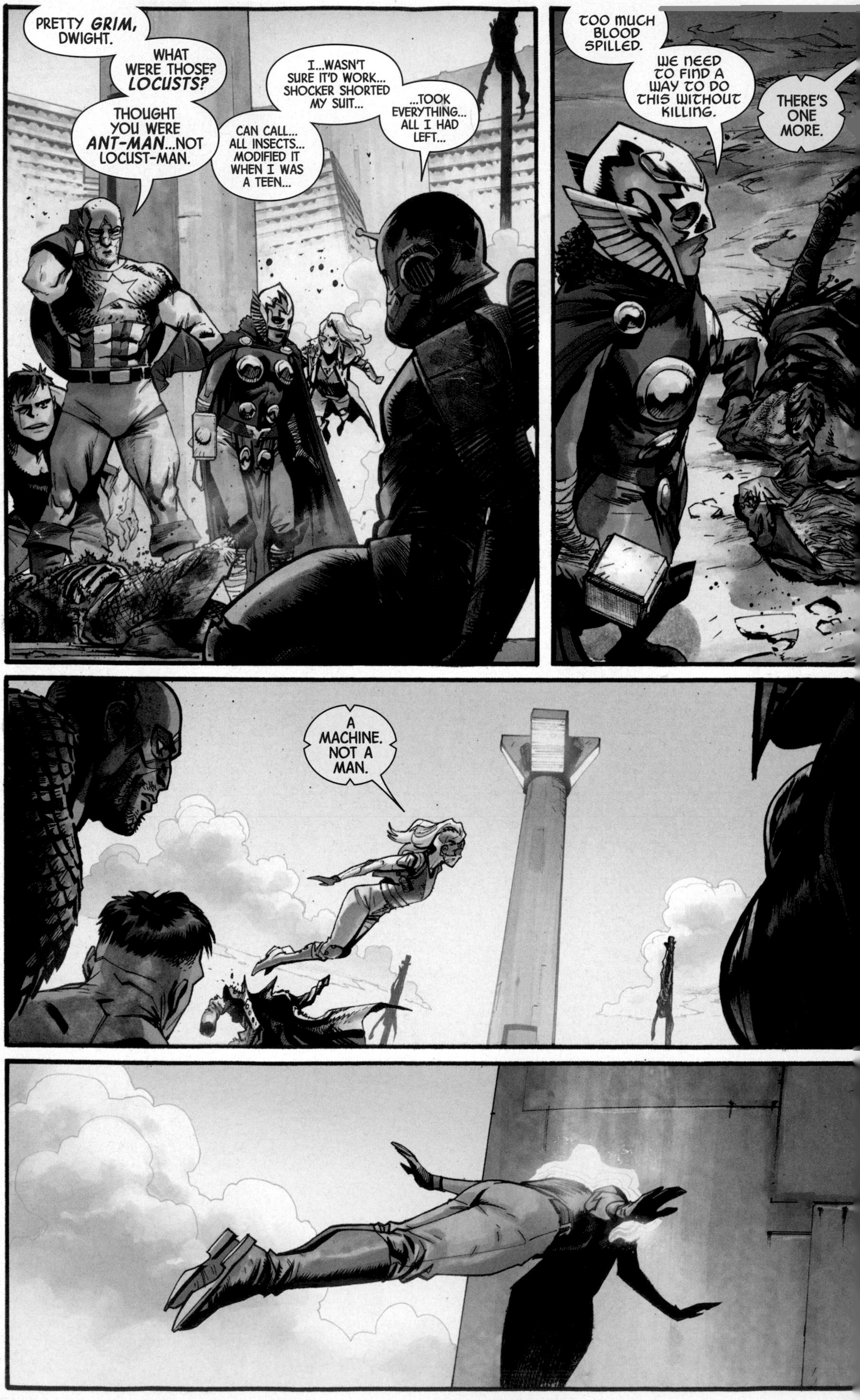
PRETTY GRIM, DWIGHT.
WHAT WERE THOSE? LOCUSTS?
THOUGHT YOU WERE ANT-MAN...NOT LOCUST-MAN.
I...WASN'T SURE IT'D WORK... SHOCKER SHORTED MY SUIT...
CAN CALL... ALL INSECTS... MODIFIED IT WHEN I WAS A TEEN...
...TOOK EVERYTHING... ALL I HAD LEFT...
TOO MUCH BLOOD SPILLED.
WE NEED TO FIND A WAY TO DO THIS WITHOUT KILLING.
THERE'S ONE MORE.
A MACHINE. NOT A MAN.

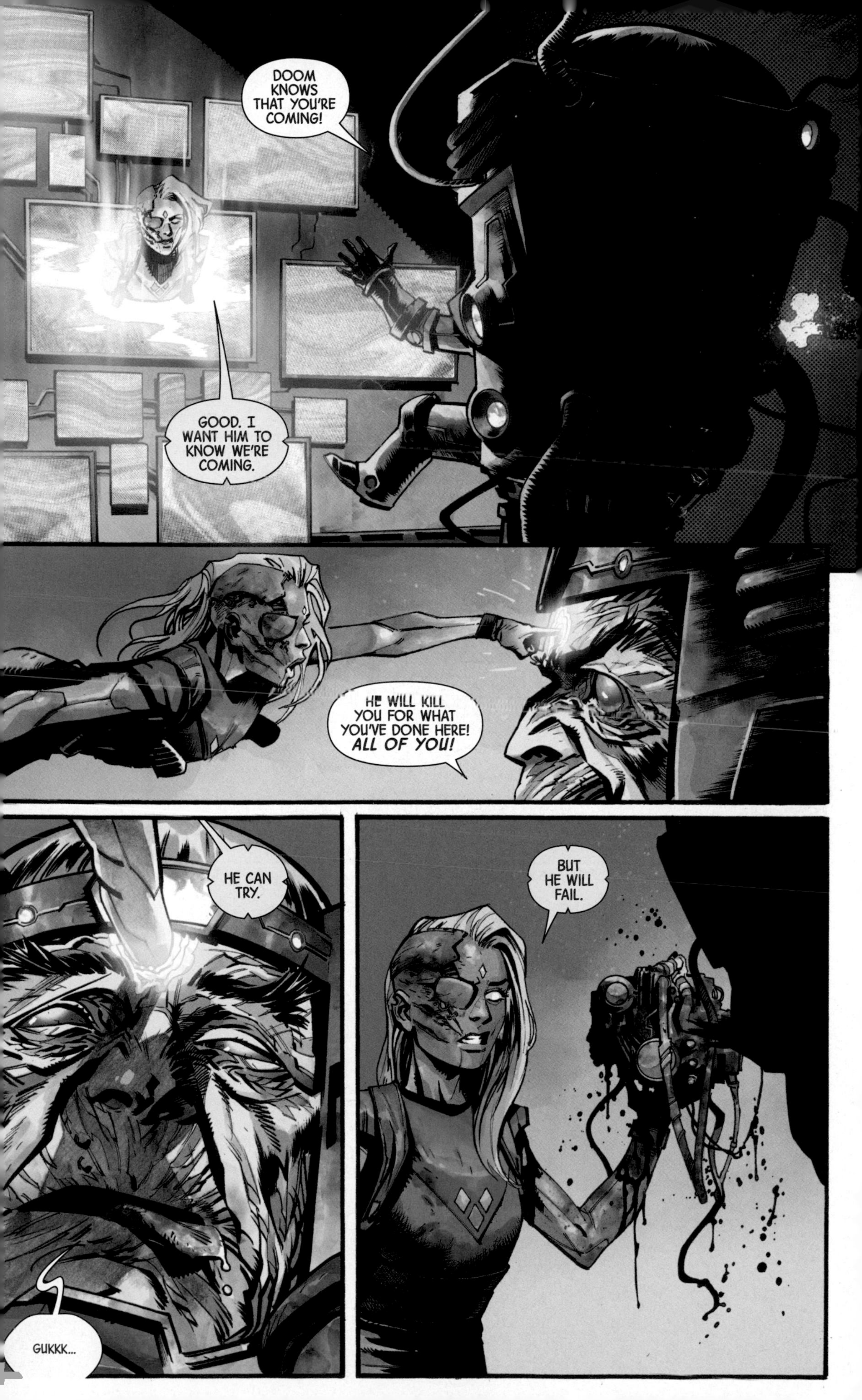
DOOM KNOWS THAT YOU'RE COMING!
GOOD. I WANT HIM TO KNOW WE'RE COMING.
HE WILL KILL YOU FOR WHAT YOU'VE DONE HERE! ALL OF YOU!
HE CAN TRY.
GUKKK...
BUT HE WILL FAIL.

DWIGHT...

WHAT THEY SAID... IS IT--?

IT'S TRUE.

I WAS THE ONE THAT PROGRAMMED THE LOCATION INTO THE DOOMBOT'S HEAD.

I KNEW BRUCE WOULD FIND IT AND BRING US HERE.

WHY?

BECAUSE I MADE A DEAL WITH DOOM.

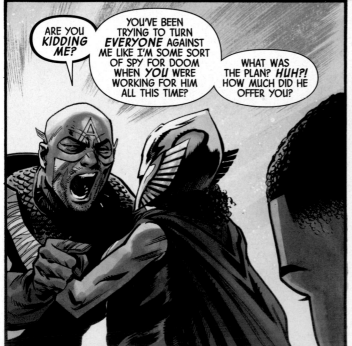

ARE YOU KIDDING ME?

YOU'VE BEEN TRYING TO TURN EVERYONE AGAINST ME LIKE I'M SOME SORT OF SPY FOR DOOM WHEN YOU WERE WORKING FOR HIM ALL THIS TIME?

WHAT WAS THE PLAN? HUH?! HOW MUCH DID HE OFFER YOU?

IT'S...

...NOT LIKE THAT.

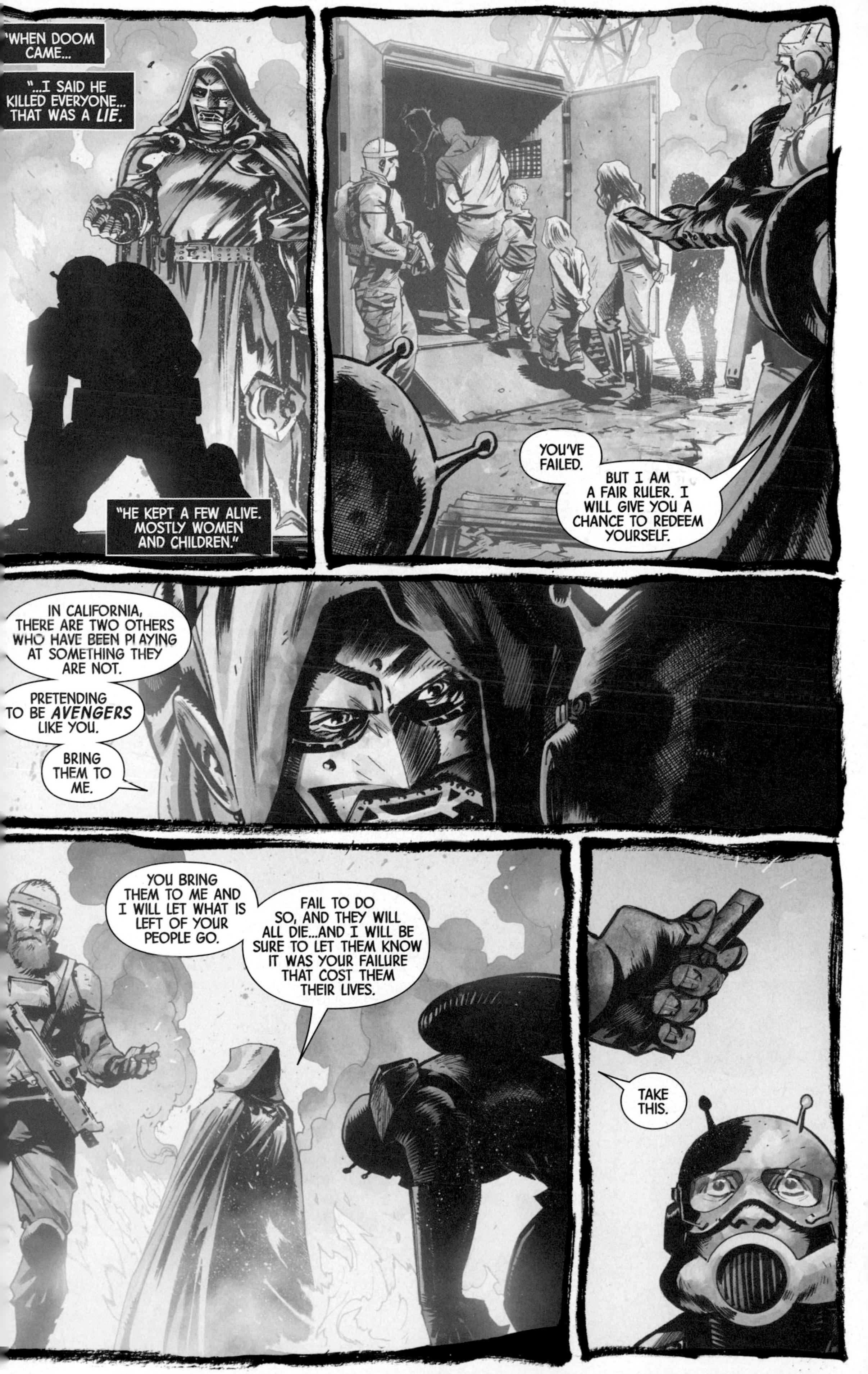
"WHEN DOOM CAME...
"...I SAID HE KILLED EVERYONE... THAT WAS A LIE.
"HE KEPT A FEW ALIVE. MOSTLY WOMEN AND CHILDREN."
YOU'VE FAILED.
BUT I AM A FAIR RULER. I WILL GIVE YOU A CHANCE TO REDEEM YOURSELF.
IN CALIFORNIA, THERE ARE TWO OTHERS WHO HAVE BEEN PLAYING AT SOMETHING THEY ARE NOT.
PRETENDING TO BE AVENGERS LIKE YOU.
BRING THEM TO ME.
YOU BRING THEM TO ME AND I WILL LET WHAT IS LEFT OF YOUR PEOPLE GO.
FAIL TO DO SO, AND THEY WILL ALL DIE...AND I WILL BE SURE TO LET THEM KNOW IT WAS YOUR FAILURE THAT COST THEM THEIR LIVES.
TAKE THIS.

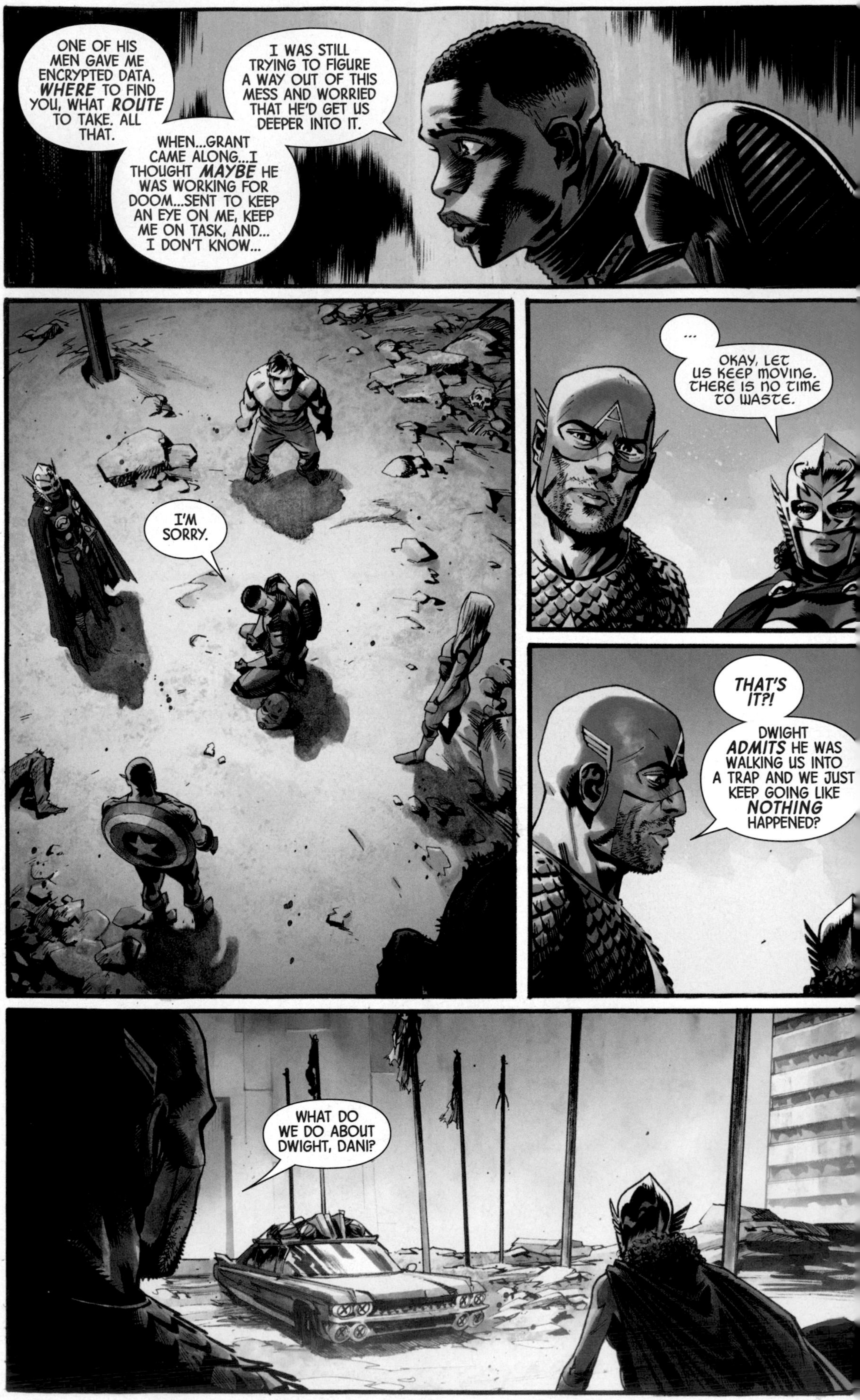
ONE OF HIS MEN GAVE ME ENCRYPTED DATA. WHERE TO FIND YOU, WHAT ROUTE TO TAKE. ALL THAT.
WHEN...GRANT CAME ALONG...I THOUGHT MAYBE HE WAS WORKING FOR DOOM...SENT TO KEEP AN EYE ON ME, KEEP ME ON TASK, AND... I DON'T KNOW...
I WAS STILL TRYING TO FIGURE A WAY OUT OF THIS MESS AND WORRIED THAT HE'D GET US DEEPER INTO IT.
I'M SORRY.
...
OKAY, LET US KEEP MOVING. THERE IS NO TIME TO WASTE.
THAT'S IT?!
DWIGHT ADMITS HE WAS WALKING US INTO A TRAP AND WE JUST KEEP GOING LIKE NOTHING HAPPENED?
WHAT DO WE DO ABOUT DWIGHT, DANI?

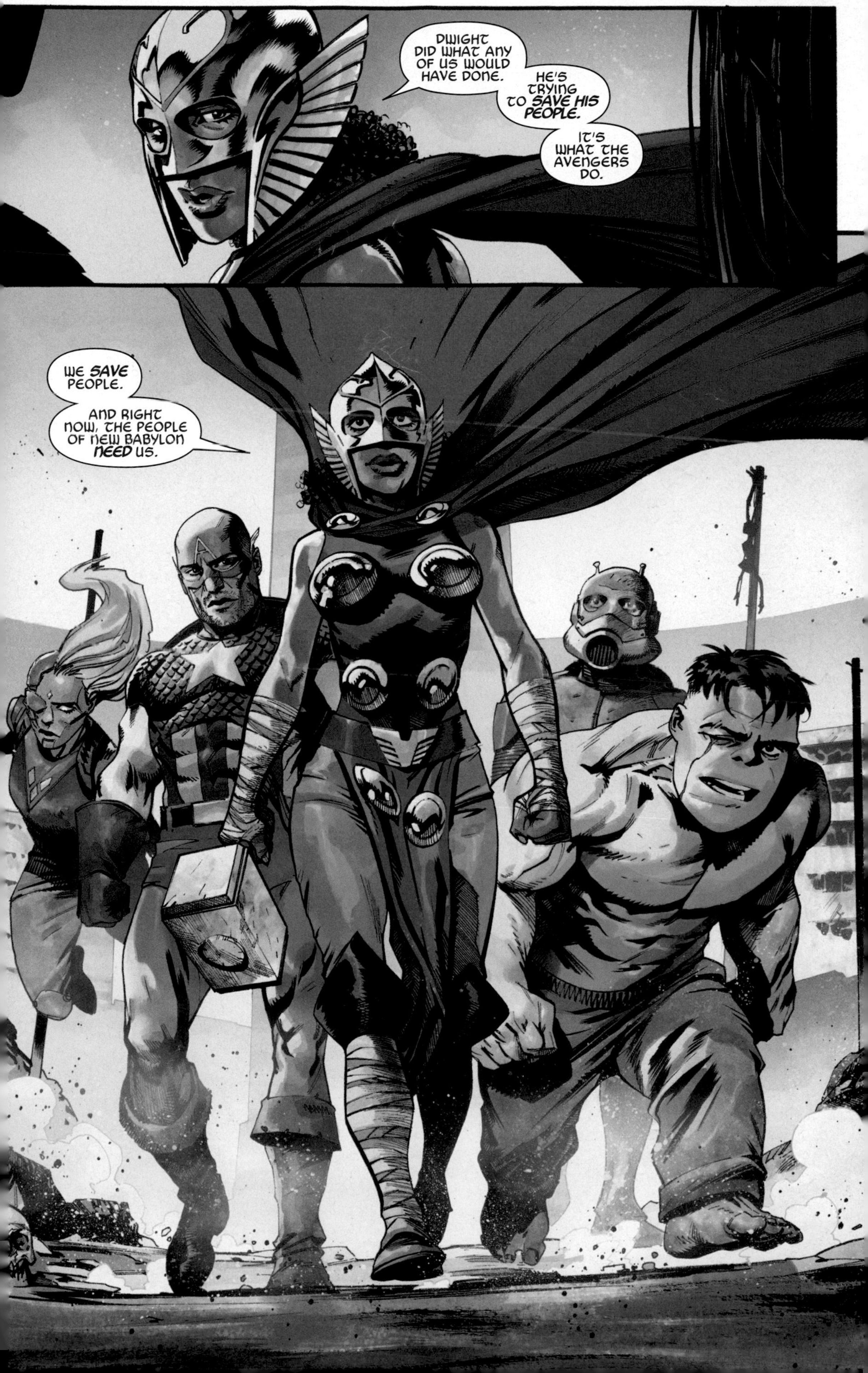

DWIGHT DID WHAT ANY OF US WOULD HAVE DONE.
HE'S TRYING TO **SAVE HIS PEOPLE.**
IT'S WHAT THE AVENGERS DO.
WE **SAVE** PEOPLE.
AND RIGHT NOW, THE PEOPLE OF NEW BABYLON **NEED** US.

5.

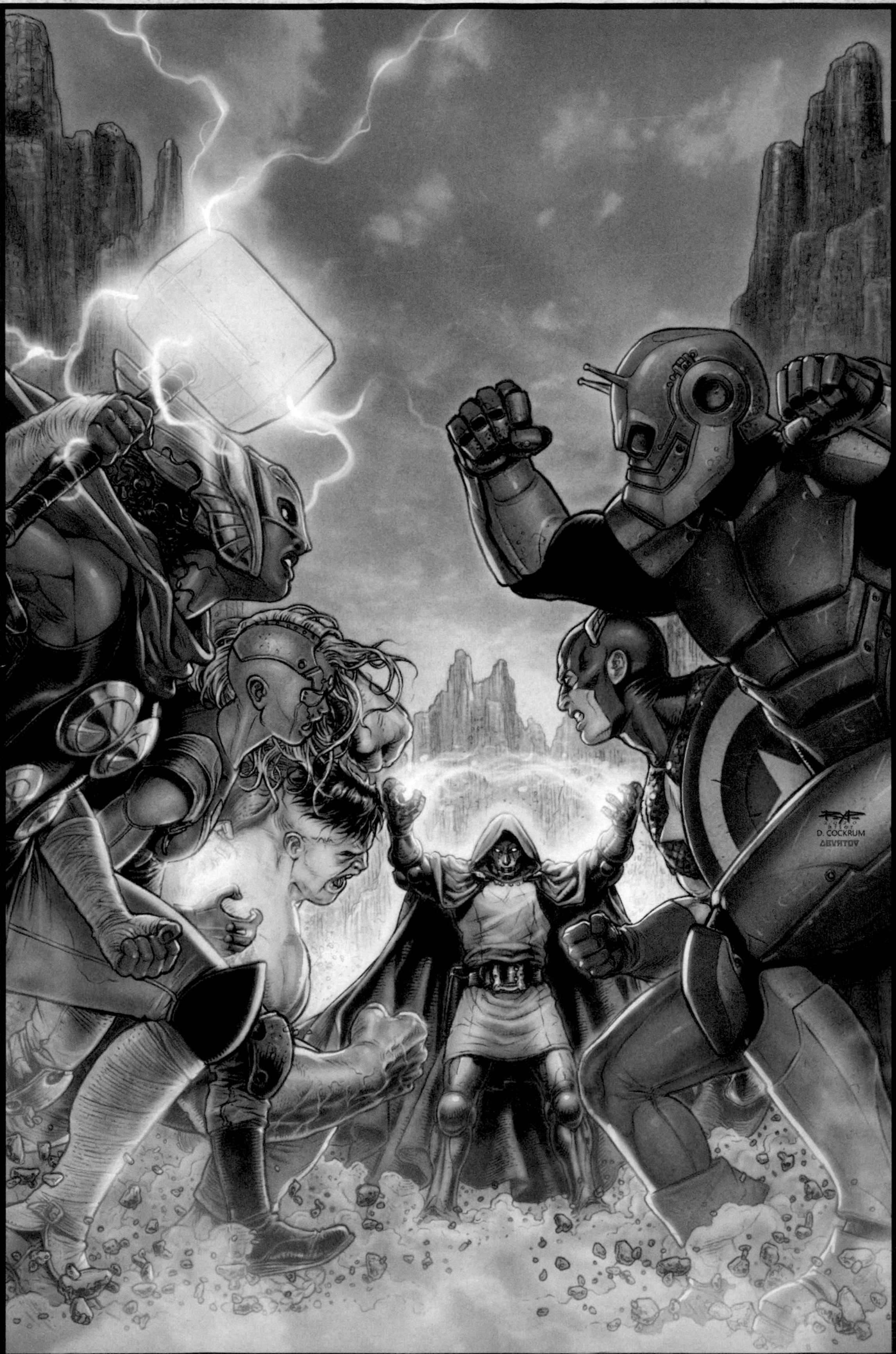
D. COCKRUM

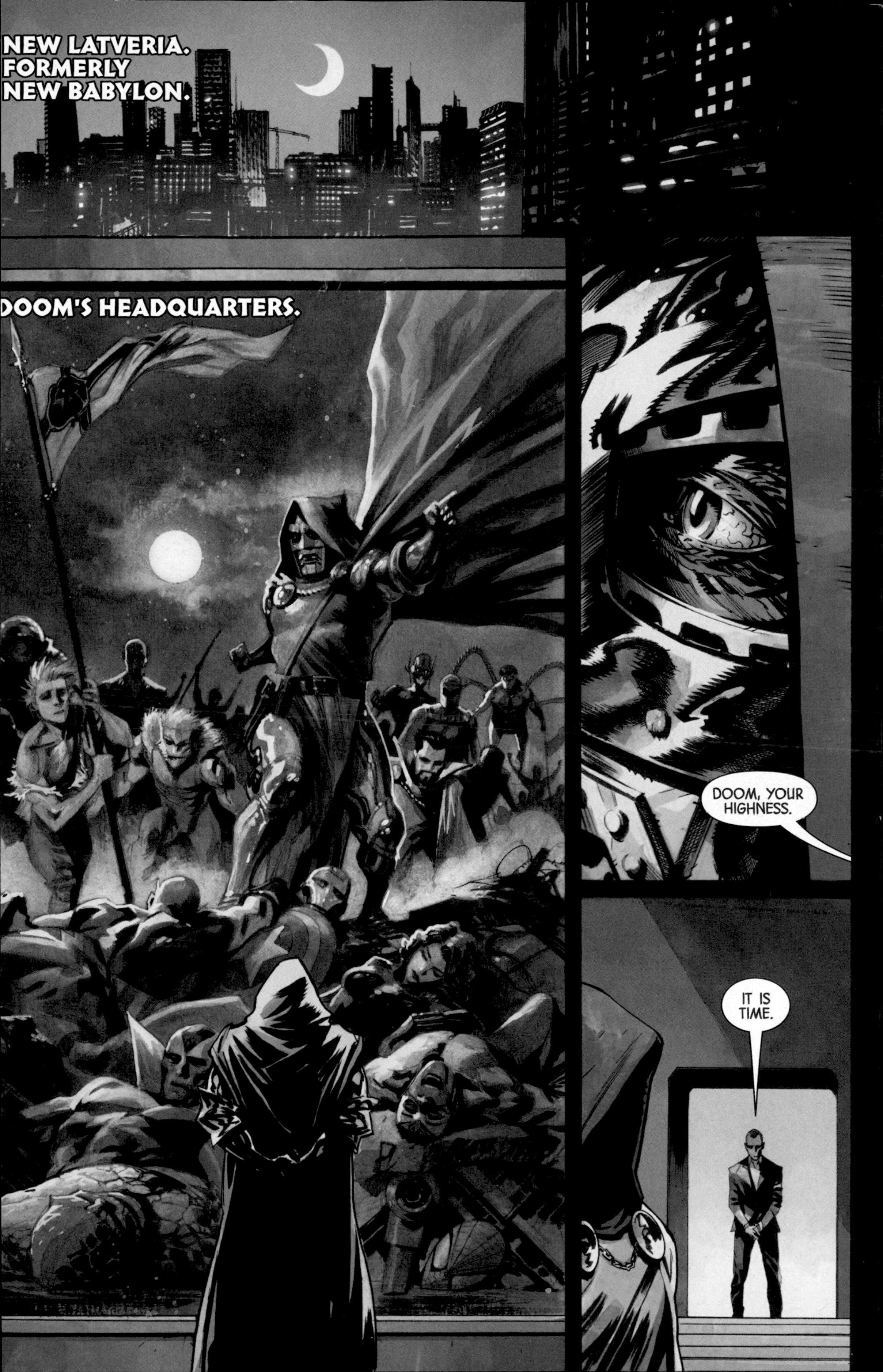
NEW LATVERIA. FORMERLY NEW BABYLON.
DOOM'S HEADQUARTERS.
DOOM, YOUR HIGHNESS.
IT IS TIME.

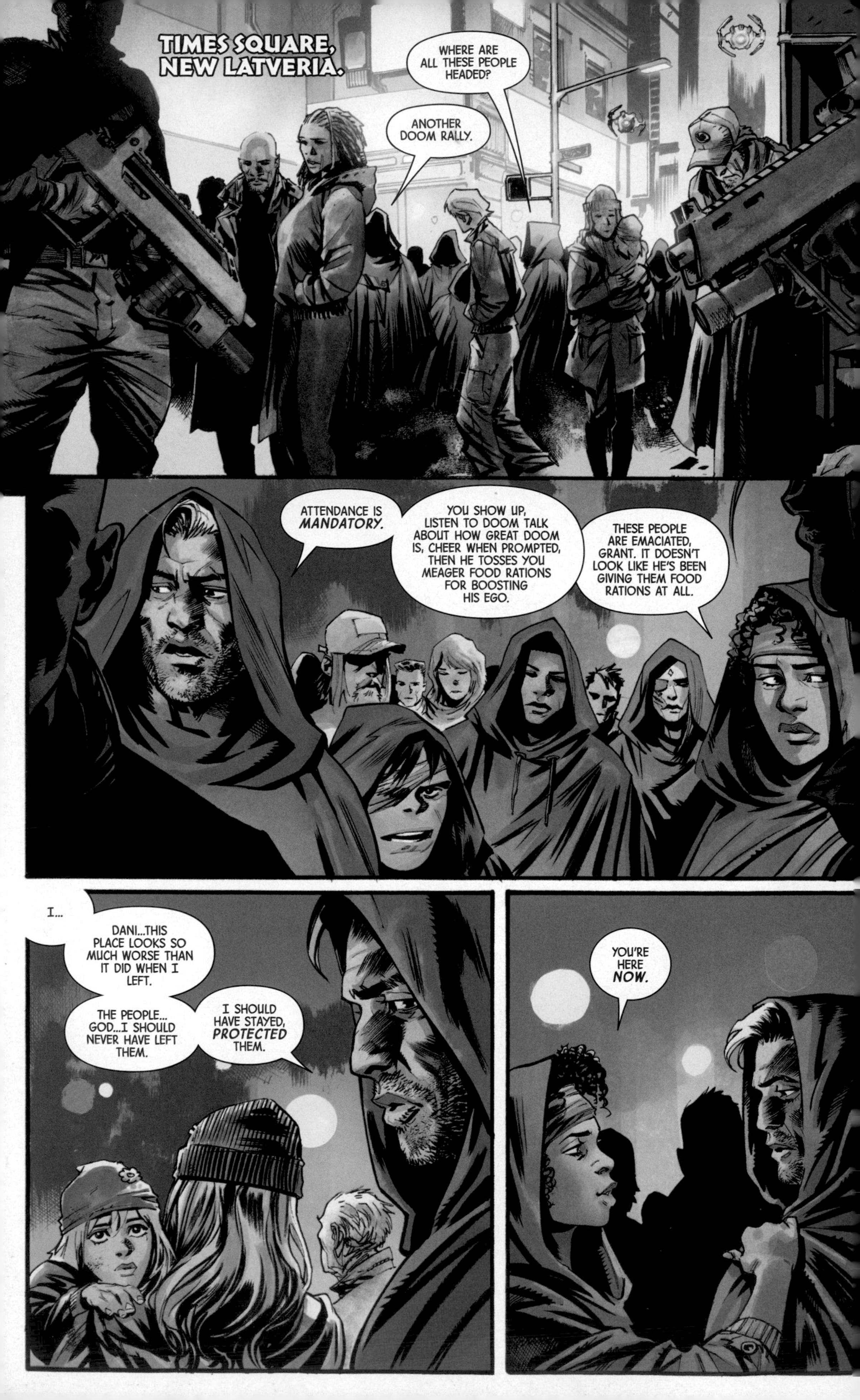

TIMES SQUARE, NEW LATVERIA.
WHERE ARE ALL THESE PEOPLE HEADED?
ANOTHER DOOM RALLY.
ATTENDANCE IS *MANDATORY.*
YOU SHOW UP, LISTEN TO DOOM TALK ABOUT HOW GREAT DOOM IS, CHEER WHEN PROMPTED, THEN HE TOSSES YOU MEAGER FOOD RATIONS FOR BOOSTING HIS EGO.
THESE PEOPLE ARE EMACIATED, GRANT. IT DOESN'T LOOK LIKE HE'S BEEN GIVING THEM FOOD RATIONS AT ALL.
I...
DANI...THIS PLACE LOOKS SO MUCH WORSE THAN IT DID WHEN I LEFT.
THE PEOPLE... GOD...I SHOULD NEVER HAVE LEFT THEM.
I SHOULD HAVE STAYED, *PROTECTED* THEM.
YOU'RE HERE *NOW.*

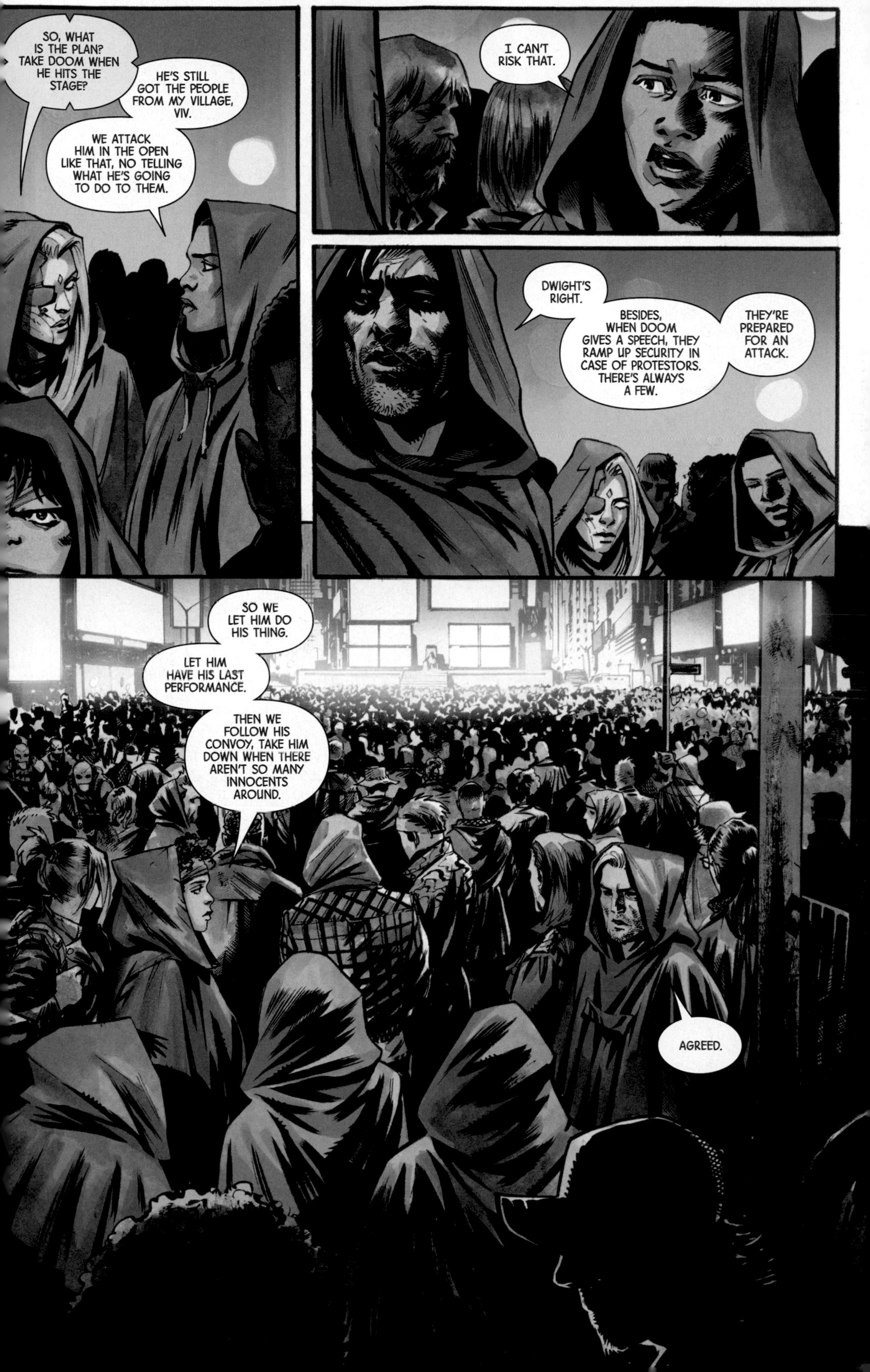
SO, WHAT IS THE PLAN? TAKE DOOM WHEN HE HITS THE STAGE?
HE'S STILL GOT THE PEOPLE FROM MY VILLAGE, VIV.
WE ATTACK HIM IN THE OPEN LIKE THAT, NO TELLING WHAT HE'S GOING TO DO TO THEM.
I CAN'T RISK THAT.
DWIGHT'S RIGHT.
BESIDES, WHEN DOOM GIVES A SPEECH, THEY RAMP UP SECURITY IN CASE OF PROTESTORS. THERE'S ALWAYS A FEW.
THEY'RE PREPARED FOR AN ATTACK.
SO WE LET HIM DO HIS THING.
LET HIM HAVE HIS LAST PERFORMANCE.
THEN WE FOLLOW HIS CONVOY, TAKE HIM DOWN WHEN THERE AREN'T SO MANY INNOCENTS AROUND.
AGREED.

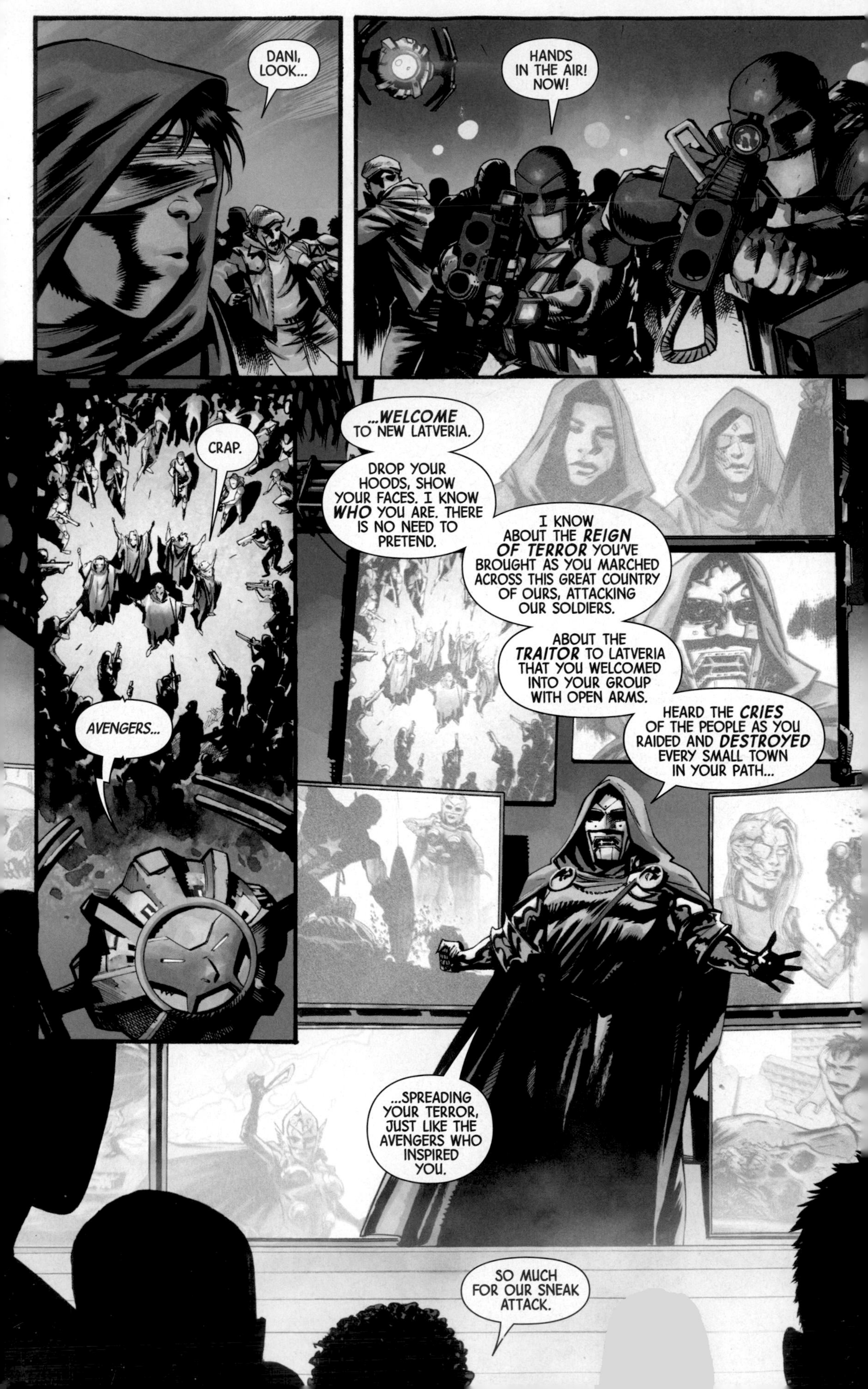
DANI, LOOK...
HANDS IN THE AIR! NOW!
CRAP.
AVENGERS...
...WELCOME TO NEW LATVERIA.
DROP YOUR HOODS, SHOW YOUR FACES. I KNOW WHO YOU ARE. THERE IS NO NEED TO PRETEND.
I KNOW ABOUT THE REIGN OF TERROR YOU'VE BROUGHT AS YOU MARCHED ACROSS THIS GREAT COUNTRY OF OURS, ATTACKING OUR SOLDIERS.
ABOUT THE TRAITOR TO LATVERIA THAT YOU WELCOMED INTO YOUR GROUP WITH OPEN ARMS.
HEARD THE CRIES OF THE PEOPLE AS YOU RAIDED AND DESTROYED EVERY SMALL TOWN IN YOUR PATH...
...SPREADING YOUR TERROR, JUST LIKE THE AVENGERS WHO INSPIRED YOU.
SO MUCH FOR OUR SNEAK ATTACK.

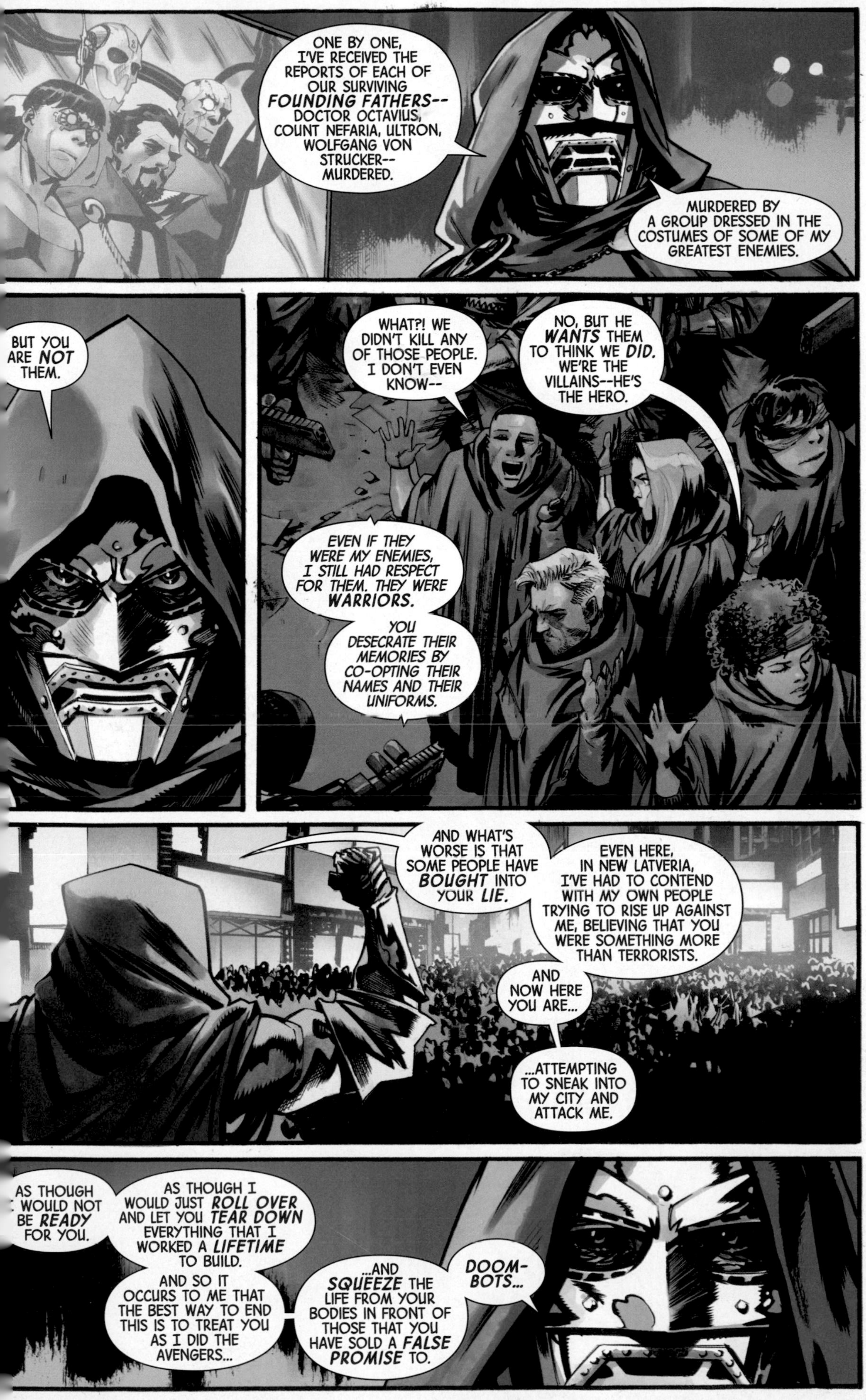
ONE BY ONE, I'VE RECEIVED THE REPORTS OF EACH OF OUR SURVIVING FOUNDING FATHERS-- DOCTOR OCTAVIUS, COUNT NEFARIA, ULTRON, WOLFGANG VON STRUCKER-- MURDERED.
MURDERED BY A GROUP DRESSED IN THE COSTUMES OF SOME OF MY GREATEST ENEMIES.
BUT YOU ARE NOT THEM.
WHAT?! WE DIDN'T KILL ANY OF THOSE PEOPLE. I DON'T EVEN KNOW--
NO, BUT HE WANTS THEM TO THINK WE DID. WE'RE THE VILLAINS--HE'S THE HERO.
EVEN IF THEY WERE MY ENEMIES, I STILL HAD RESPECT FOR THEM. THEY WERE WARRIORS.
YOU DESECRATE THEIR MEMORIES BY CO-OPTING THEIR NAMES AND THEIR UNIFORMS.
AND WHAT'S WORSE IS THAT SOME PEOPLE HAVE BOUGHT INTO YOUR LIE.
EVEN HERE, IN NEW LATVERIA, I'VE HAD TO CONTEND WITH MY OWN PEOPLE TRYING TO RISE UP AGAINST ME, BELIEVING THAT YOU WERE SOMETHING MORE THAN TERRORISTS.
AND NOW HERE YOU ARE...
...ATTEMPTING TO SNEAK INTO MY CITY AND ATTACK ME.
AS THOUGH I WOULD NOT BE READY FOR YOU.
AS THOUGH I WOULD JUST ROLL OVER AND LET YOU TEAR DOWN EVERYTHING THAT I WORKED A LIFETIME TO BUILD.
AND SO IT OCCURS TO ME THAT THE BEST WAY TO END THIS IS TO TREAT YOU AS I DID THE AVENGERS...
...AND SQUEEZE THE LIFE FROM YOUR BODIES IN FRONT OF THOSE THAT YOU HAVE SOLD A FALSE PROMISE TO.
DOOM-BOTS...

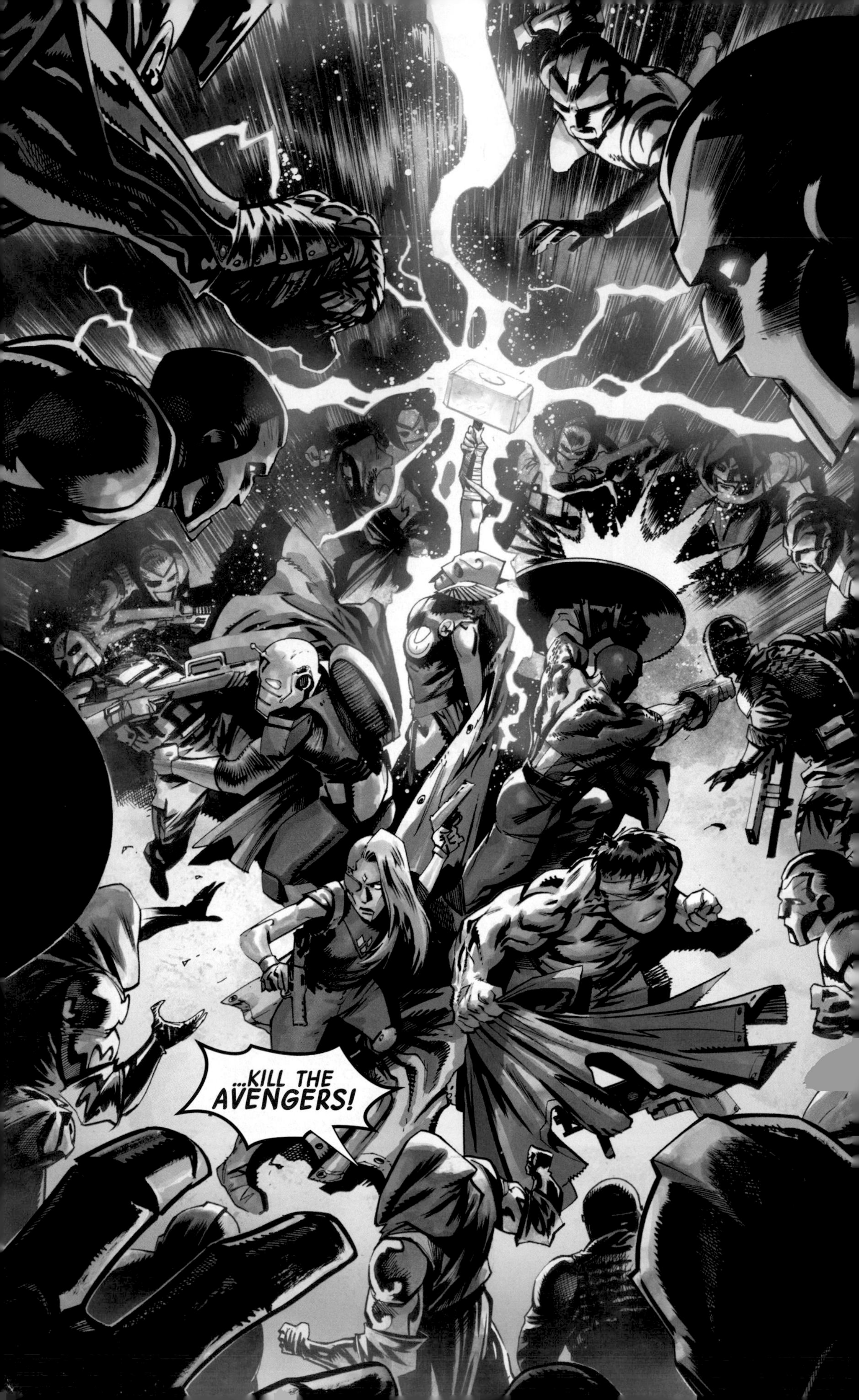
...KILL THE AVENGERS!

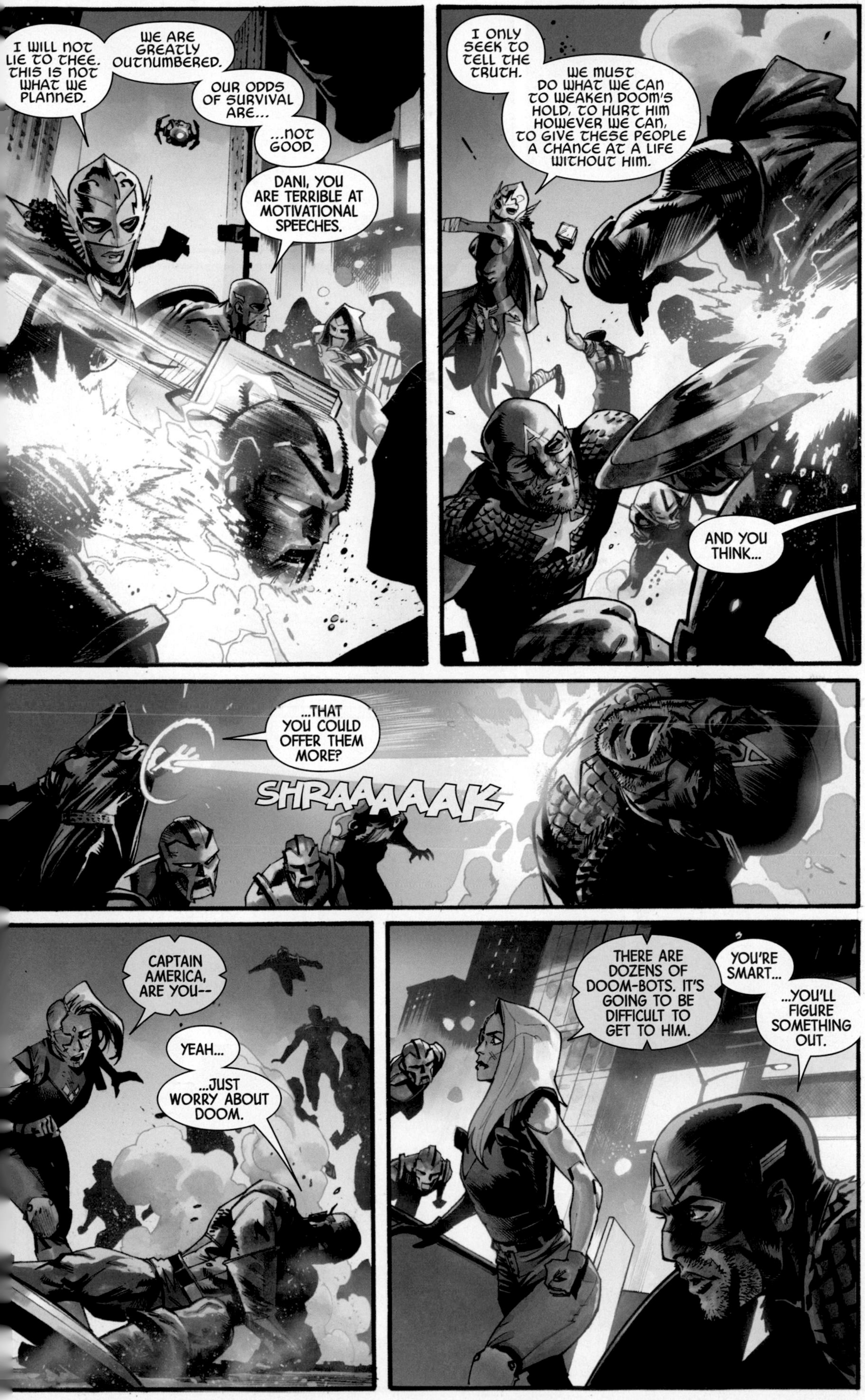
I WILL NOT LIE TO THEE. THIS IS NOT WHAT WE PLANNED.
WE ARE GREATLY OUTNUMBERED.
OUR ODDS OF SURVIVAL ARE...
...NOT GOOD.
DANI, YOU ARE TERRIBLE AT MOTIVATIONAL SPEECHES.
I ONLY SEEK TO TELL THE TRUTH.
WE MUST DO WHAT WE CAN TO WEAKEN DOOM'S HOLD, TO HURT HIM HOWEVER WE CAN, TO GIVE THESE PEOPLE A CHANCE AT A LIFE WITHOUT HIM.
AND YOU THINK...
...THAT YOU COULD OFFER THEM MORE?
SHRAAAAAK
CAPTAIN AMERICA, ARE YOU--
YEAH...
...JUST WORRY ABOUT DOOM.
THERE ARE DOZENS OF DOOM-BOTS. IT'S GOING TO BE DIFFICULT TO GET TO HIM.
YOU'RE SMART...
...YOU'LL FIGURE SOMETHING OUT.

STOP HIDING BEHIND YOUR ROBOTS, DOOM. FACE ME DIRECTLY!

VERY WELL.

SHRRRAAAK

I... OVERESTIMATED YOU.

AFTER ALL THAT YOU...HAVE DONE TO REACH THIS...MOMENT.

TO FALL SO EASILY.

I AM DISAPPOINTED. I'D HOPED FOR MORE.

WHERE...

...ARE THE PRISONERS YOU TOOK FROM MY VILLAGE?!

SLAM

AH...

→COUGH←
→COUGH←

...FINALLY... A SPARK... PERHAPS THERE IS SOME FIGHT LEFT.

I BROUGHT THE AVENGERS HER LIKE YOU ASKED. YO SAID THAT IF I DID T YOU'D LET THEM G

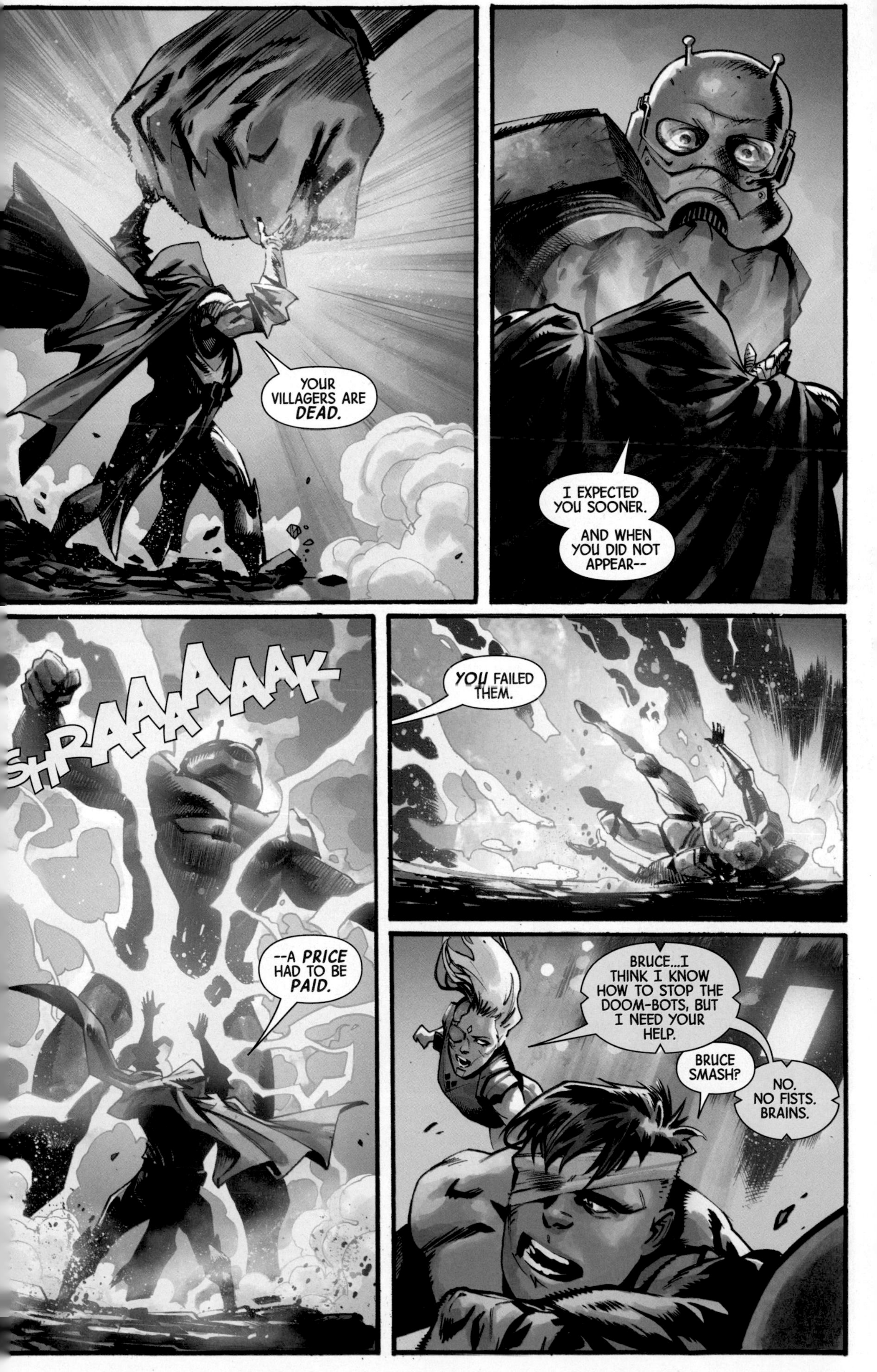
YOUR VILLAGERS ARE DEAD.
I EXPECTED YOU SOONER.
AND WHEN YOU DID NOT APPEAR--
SHRAAAAAAK
--A PRICE HAD TO BE PAID.
YOU FAILED THEM.
BRUCE...I THINK I KNOW HOW TO STOP THE DOOM-BOTS, BUT I NEED YOUR HELP.
BRUCE SMASH?
NO. NO FISTS. BRAINS.

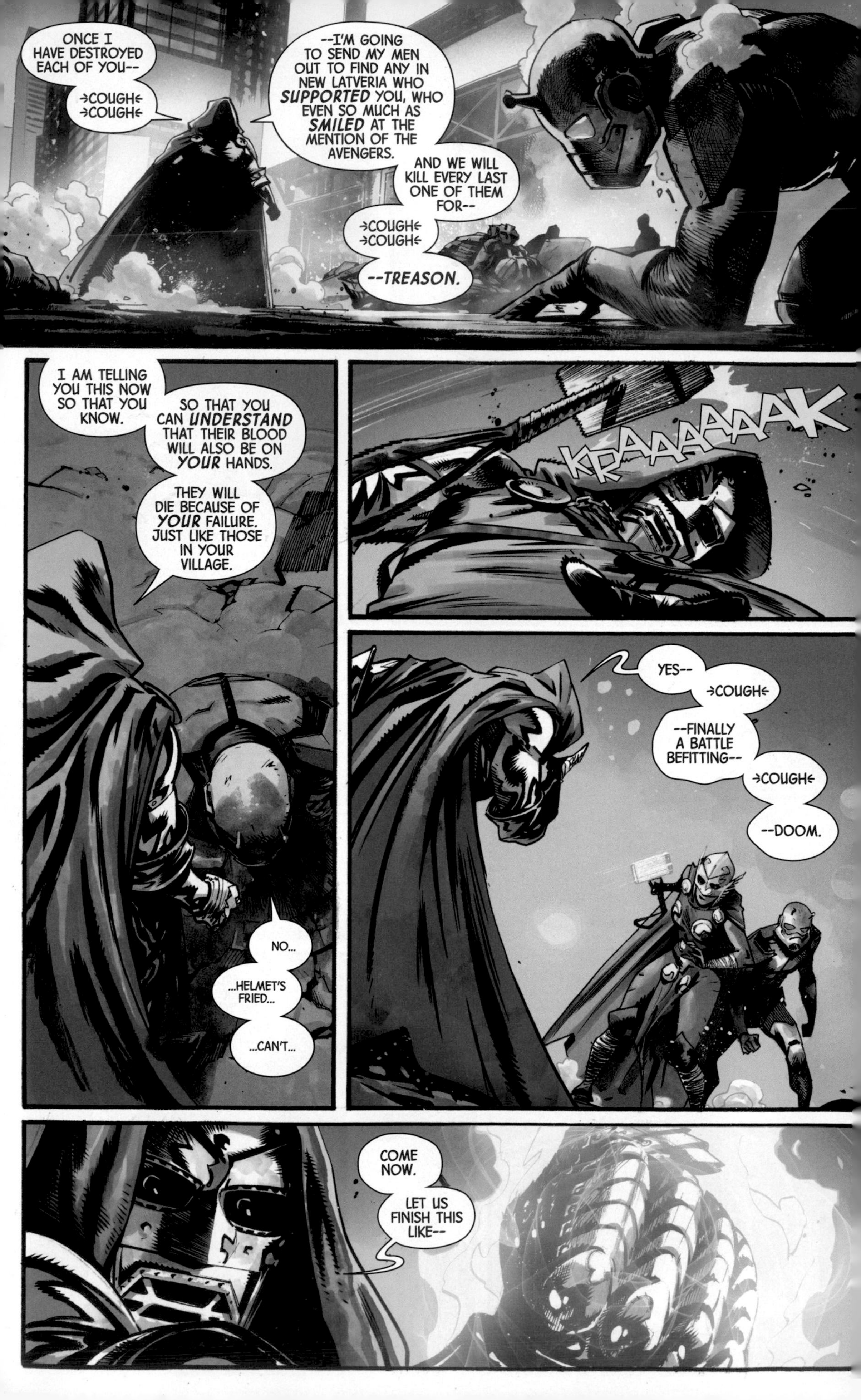
ONCE I HAVE DESTROYED EACH OF YOU--
→COUGH← →COUGH←
--I'M GOING TO SEND MY MEN OUT TO FIND ANY IN NEW LATVERIA WHO SUPPORTED YOU, WHO EVEN SO MUCH AS SMILED AT THE MENTION OF THE AVENGERS.
AND WE WILL KILL EVERY LAST ONE OF THEM FOR--
→COUGH← →COUGH←
--TREASON.
I AM TELLING YOU THIS NOW SO THAT YOU KNOW.
SO THAT YOU CAN UNDERSTAND THAT THEIR BLOOD WILL ALSO BE ON YOUR HANDS.
THEY WILL DIE BECAUSE OF YOUR FAILURE. JUST LIKE THOSE IN YOUR VILLAGE.
NO...
...HELMET'S FRIED...
...CAN'T...
KRAAAAAAK
YES--
→COUGH←
--FINALLY A BATTLE BEFITTING--
→COUGH←
--DOOM.
COME NOW.
LET US FINISH THIS LIKE--

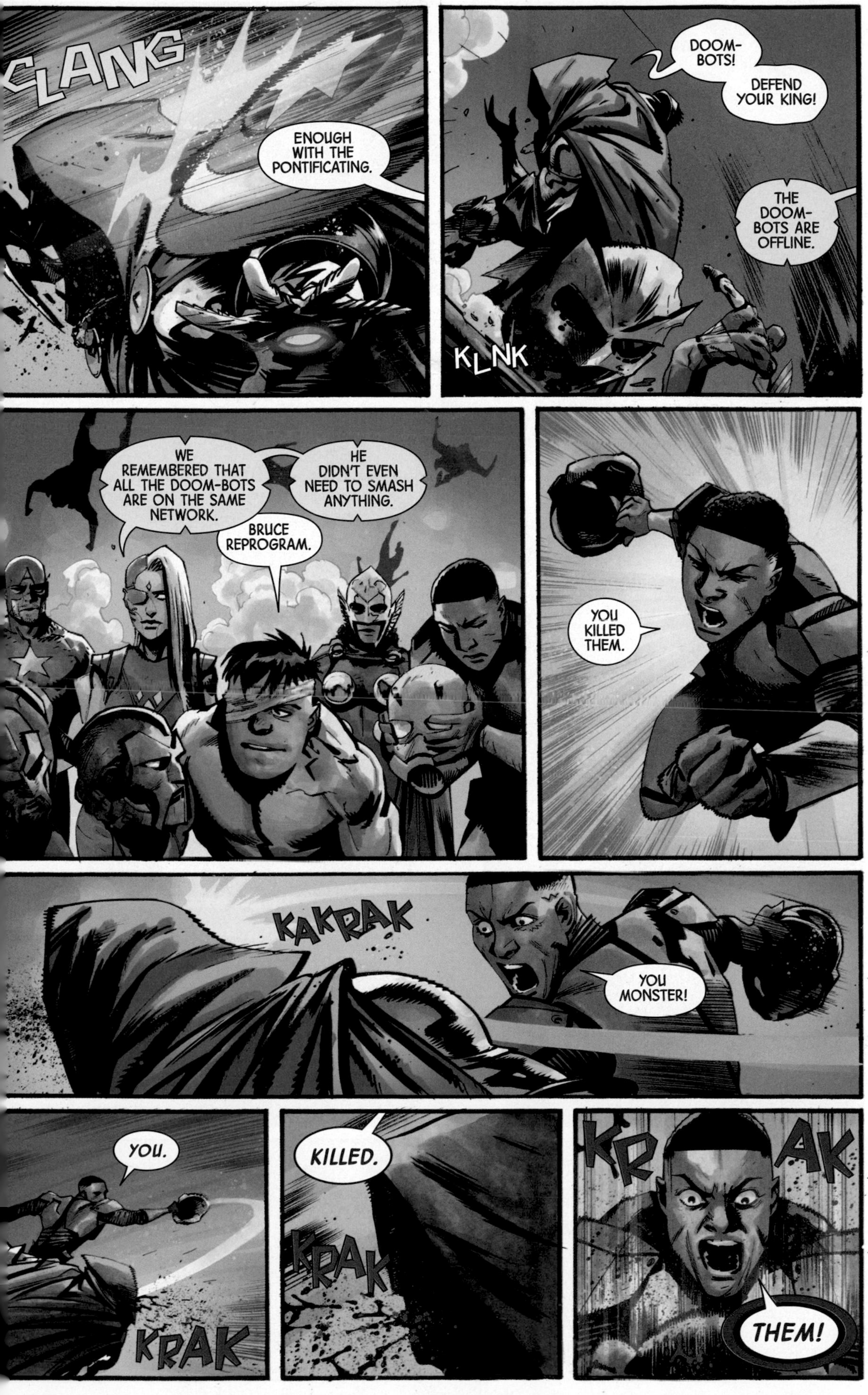
CLANG
ENOUGH WITH THE PONTIFICATING.
DOOM-BOTS!
DEFEND YOUR KING!
THE DOOM-BOTS ARE OFFLINE.
KLNK
WE REMEMBERED THAT ALL THE DOOM-BOTS ARE ON THE SAME NETWORK.
HE DIDN'T EVEN NEED TO SMASH ANYTHING.
BRUCE REPROGRAM.
YOU KILLED THEM.
KAKRAK
YOU MONSTER!
YOU.
KRAK
KILLED.
KRAK
KR AK
THEM!

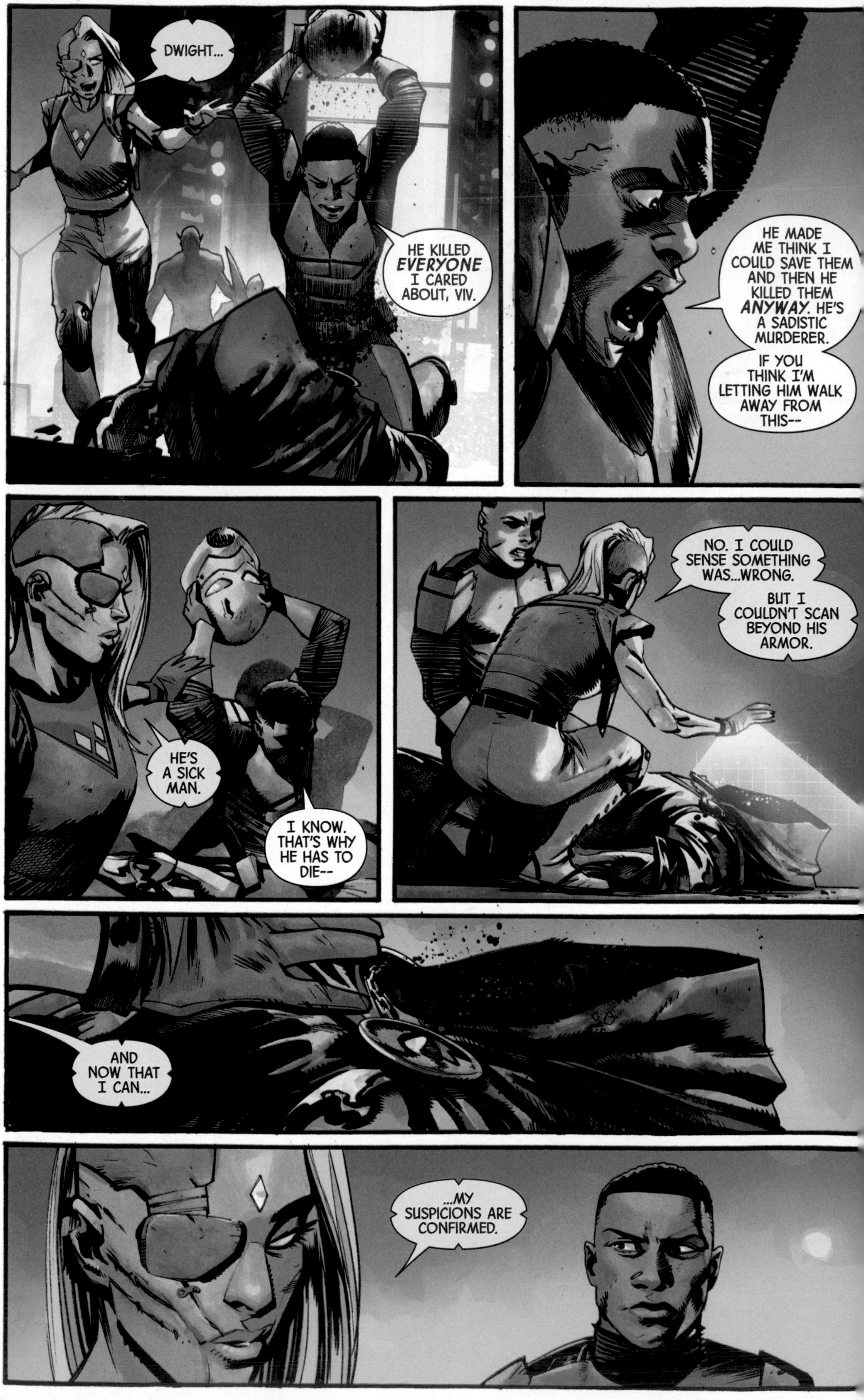
DWIGHT...
HE KILLED EVERYONE I CARED ABOUT, VIV.
HE MADE ME THINK I COULD SAVE THEM AND THEN HE KILLED THEM ANYWAY. HE'S A SADISTIC MURDERER.
IF YOU THINK I'M LETTING HIM WALK AWAY FROM THIS--
HE'S A SICK MAN.
I KNOW. THAT'S WHY HE HAS TO DIE--
NO. I COULD SENSE SOMETHING WAS...WRONG.
BUT I COULDN'T SCAN BEYOND HIS ARMOR.
AND NOW THAT I CAN...
...MY SUSPICIONS ARE CONFIRMED.

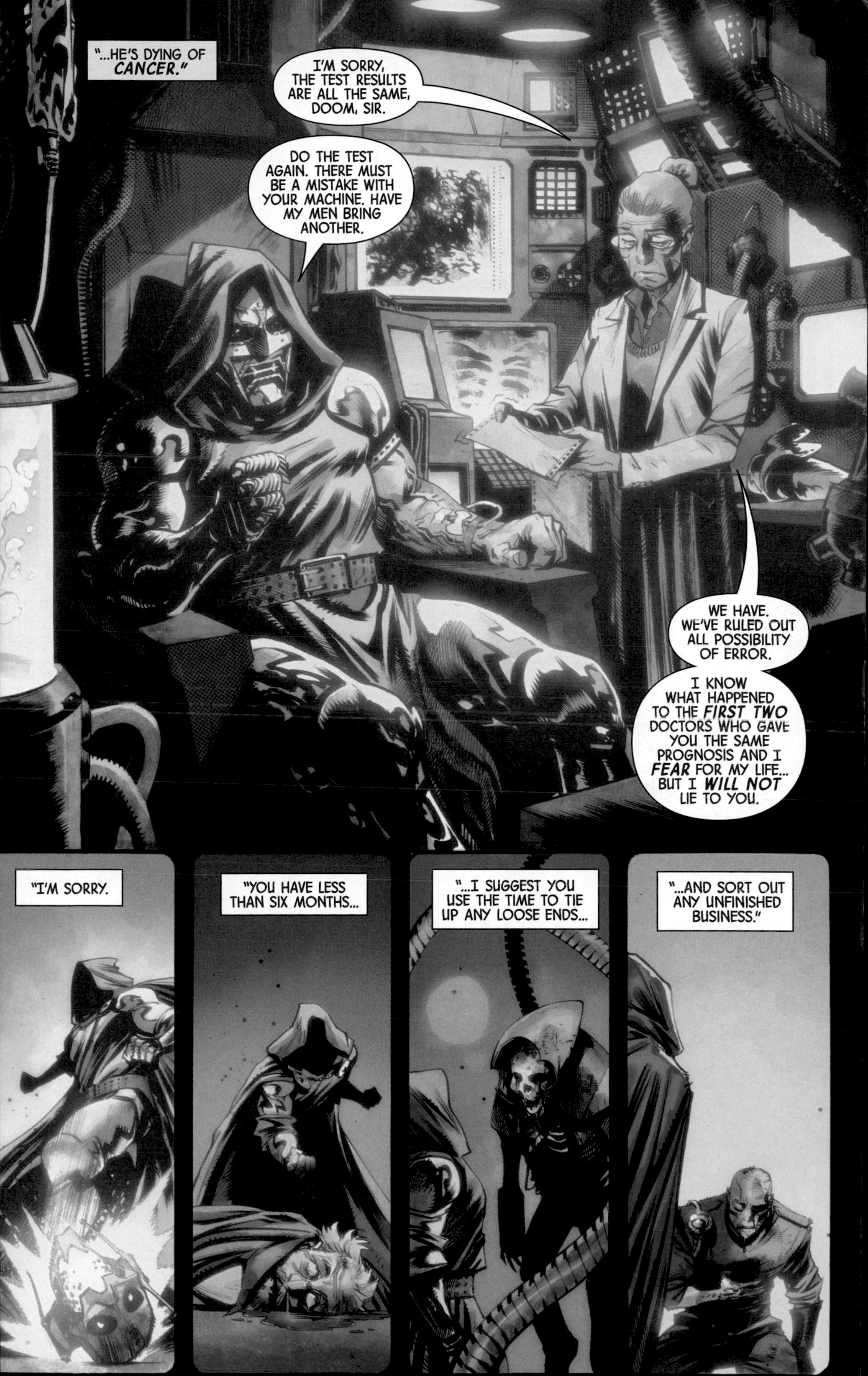
"...HE'S DYING OF CANCER."
I'M SORRY, THE TEST RESULTS ARE ALL THE SAME, DOOM, SIR.
DO THE TEST AGAIN. THERE MUST BE A MISTAKE WITH YOUR MACHINE. HAVE MY MEN BRING ANOTHER.
WE HAVE. WE'VE RULED OUT ALL POSSIBILITY OF ERROR.
I KNOW WHAT HAPPENED TO THE FIRST TWO DOCTORS WHO GAVE YOU THE SAME PROGNOSIS AND I FEAR FOR MY LIFE... BUT I WILL NOT LIE TO YOU.
"I'M SORRY.
"YOU HAVE LESS THAN SIX MONTHS...
"...I SUGGEST YOU USE THE TIME TO TIE UP ANY LOOSE ENDS...
"...AND SORT OUT ANY UNFINISHED BUSINESS."

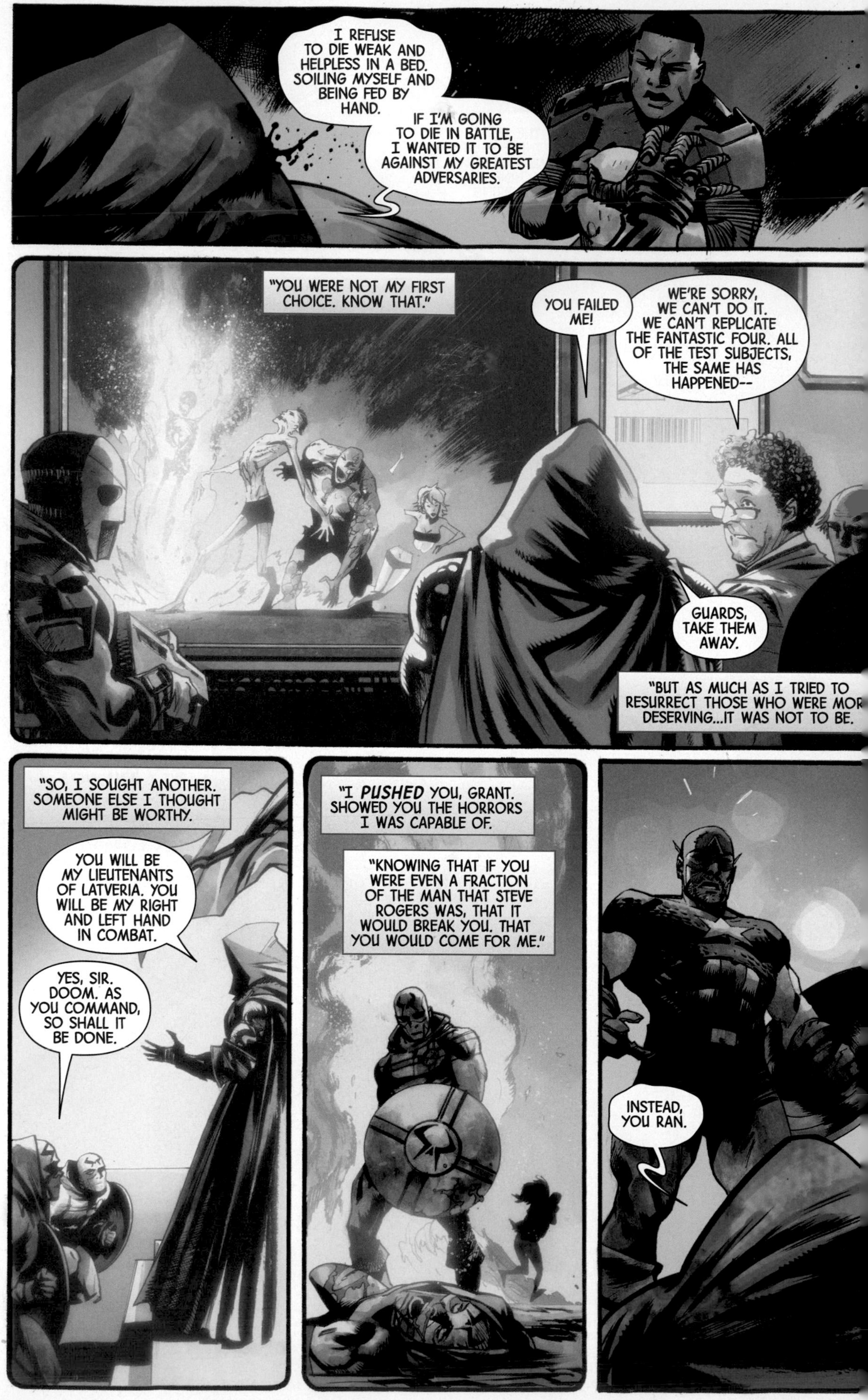
I REFUSE TO DIE WEAK AND HELPLESS IN A BED. SOILING MYSELF AND BEING FED BY HAND.
IF I'M GOING TO DIE IN BATTLE, I WANTED IT TO BE AGAINST MY GREATEST ADVERSARIES.
"YOU WERE NOT MY FIRST CHOICE. KNOW THAT."
YOU FAILED ME!
WE'RE SORRY, WE CAN'T DO IT. WE CAN'T REPLICATE THE FANTASTIC FOUR. ALL OF THE TEST SUBJECTS, THE SAME HAS HAPPENED--
GUARDS, TAKE THEM AWAY.
"BUT AS MUCH AS I TRIED TO RESURRECT THOSE WHO WERE MOR DESERVING...IT WAS NOT TO BE.
"SO, I SOUGHT ANOTHER. SOMEONE ELSE I THOUGHT MIGHT BE WORTHY.
YOU WILL BE MY LIEUTENANTS OF LATVERIA. YOU WILL BE MY RIGHT AND LEFT HAND IN COMBAT.
YES, SIR. DOOM. AS YOU COMMAND, SO SHALL IT BE DONE.
"I *PUSHED* YOU, GRANT. SHOWED YOU THE HORRORS I WAS CAPABLE OF.
"KNOWING THAT IF YOU WERE EVEN A FRACTION OF THE MAN THAT STEVE ROGERS WAS, THAT IT WOULD BREAK YOU. THAT YOU WOULD COME FOR ME."
INSTEAD, YOU RAN.

"JUST WHEN I THOUGHT THERE WERE NONE LEFT WORTHY OF ENTERING INTO BATTLE WITH DOOM...

"YOU APPEARED."

A THOR. A HULK. AN ANT-MAN. A VISION.

AVENGERS, THOUGH NOT YET *WORTHY* OF THE NAME.

"IF MY DEATH WERE TO HAVE ANY MEANING..."

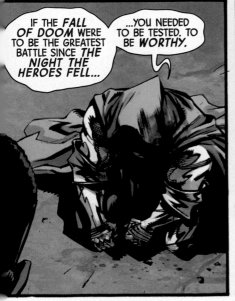

IF THE *FALL OF DOOM* WERE TO BE THE GREATEST BATTLE SINCE *THE NIGHT THE HEROES FELL*...

...YOU NEEDED TO BE TESTED. TO BE *WORTHY.*

I'M THE LAST ONE LEFT. THE LAST SOUL WHO WIPED OUT YOUR KIND. I OUTLIVED THEM ALL!

THAT SHOULD BE MY LEGACY...NOT SUCCUMBING TO THE DEATH OF AN AVERAGE MAN.

MY DEATH SHOULD BE *GLORIOUS.* IN BATTLE.

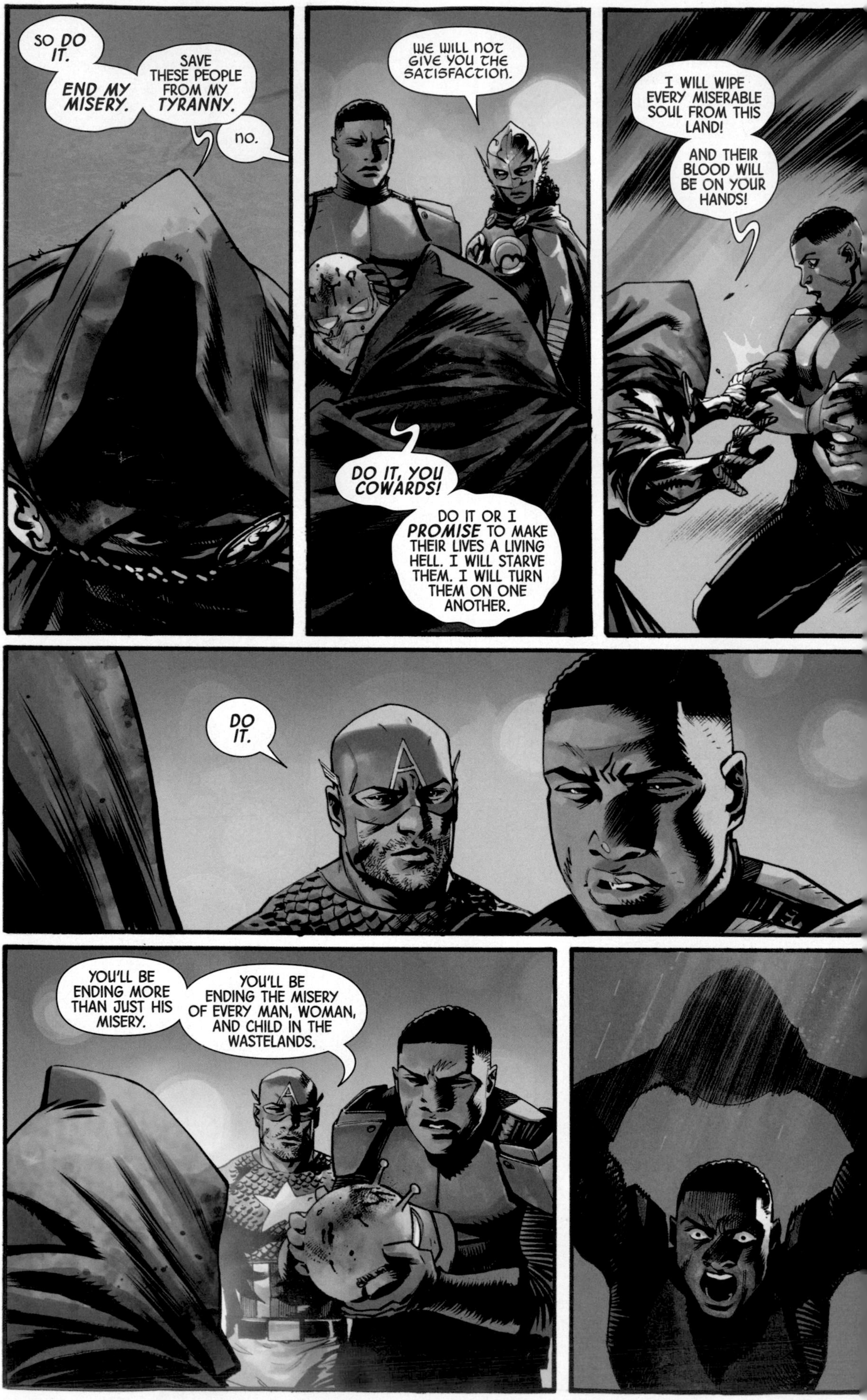
SO DO IT.
END MY MISERY.
SAVE THESE PEOPLE FROM MY TYRANNY.
no.
WE WILL NOT GIVE YOU THE SATISFACTION.
DO IT, YOU COWARDS!
DO IT OR I PROMISE TO MAKE THEIR LIVES A LIVING HELL. I WILL STARVE THEM. I WILL TURN THEM ON ONE ANOTHER.
I WILL WIPE EVERY MISERABLE SOUL FROM THIS LAND!
AND THEIR BLOOD WILL BE ON YOUR HANDS!
DO IT.
YOU'LL BE ENDING MORE THAN JUST HIS MISERY.
YOU'LL BE ENDING THE MISERY OF EVERY MAN, WOMAN, AND CHILD IN THE WASTELANDS.

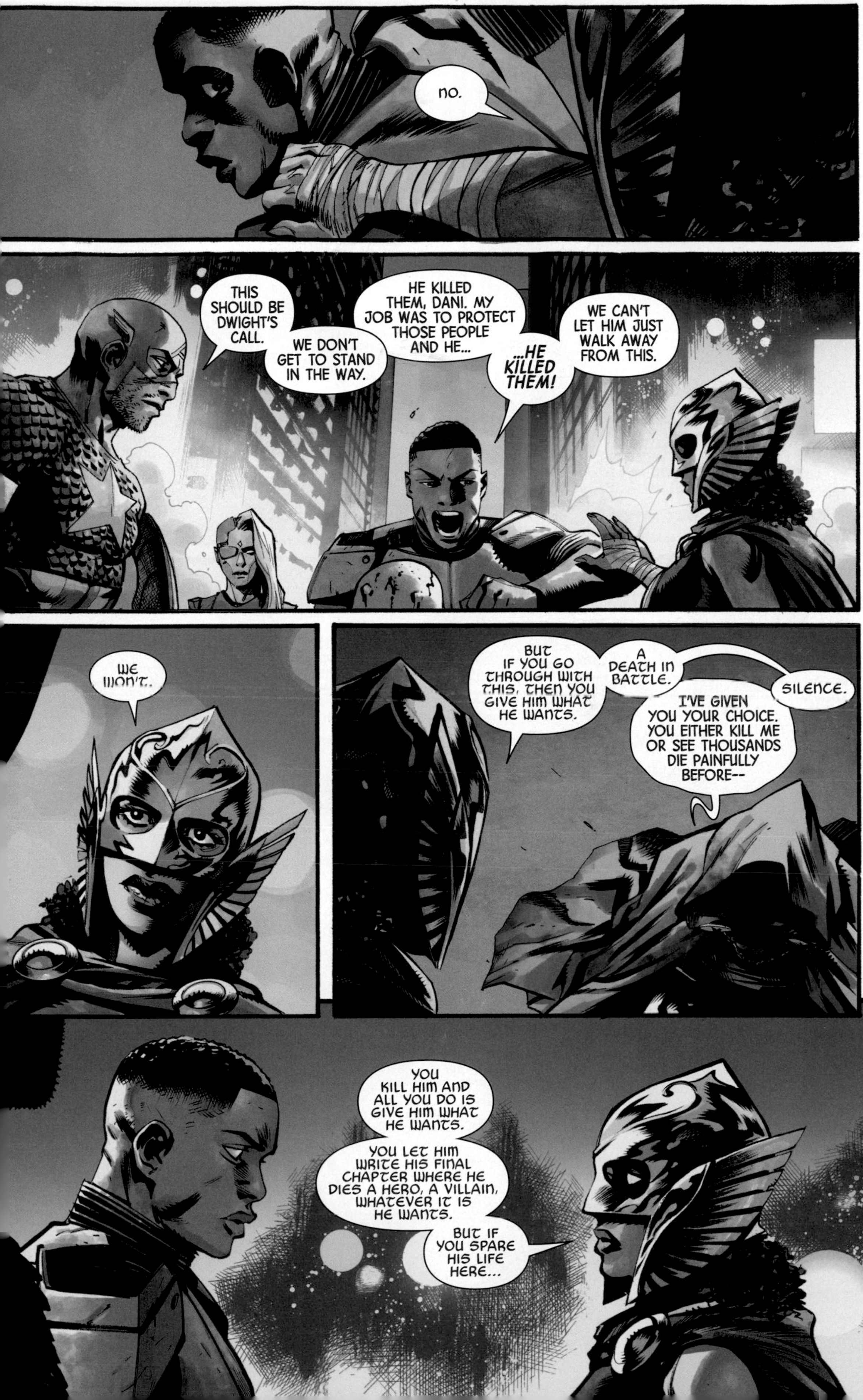
no.
THIS SHOULD BE DWIGHT'S CALL.
WE DON'T GET TO STAND IN THE WAY.
HE KILLED THEM, DANI. MY JOB WAS TO PROTECT THOSE PEOPLE AND HE...
...HE KILLED THEM!
WE CAN'T LET HIM JUST WALK AWAY FROM THIS.
WE WON'T.
BUT IF YOU GO THROUGH WITH THIS, THEN YOU GIVE HIM WHAT HE WANTS.
A DEATH IN BATTLE.
SILENCE.
I'VE GIVEN YOU YOUR CHOICE. YOU EITHER KILL ME OR SEE THOUSANDS DIE PAINFULLY BEFORE--
YOU KILL HIM AND ALL YOU DO IS GIVE HIM WHAT HE WANTS.
YOU LET HIM WRITE HIS FINAL CHAPTER WHERE HE DIES A HERO, A VILLAIN, WHATEVER IT IS HE WANTS.
BUT IF YOU SPARE HIS LIFE HERE...

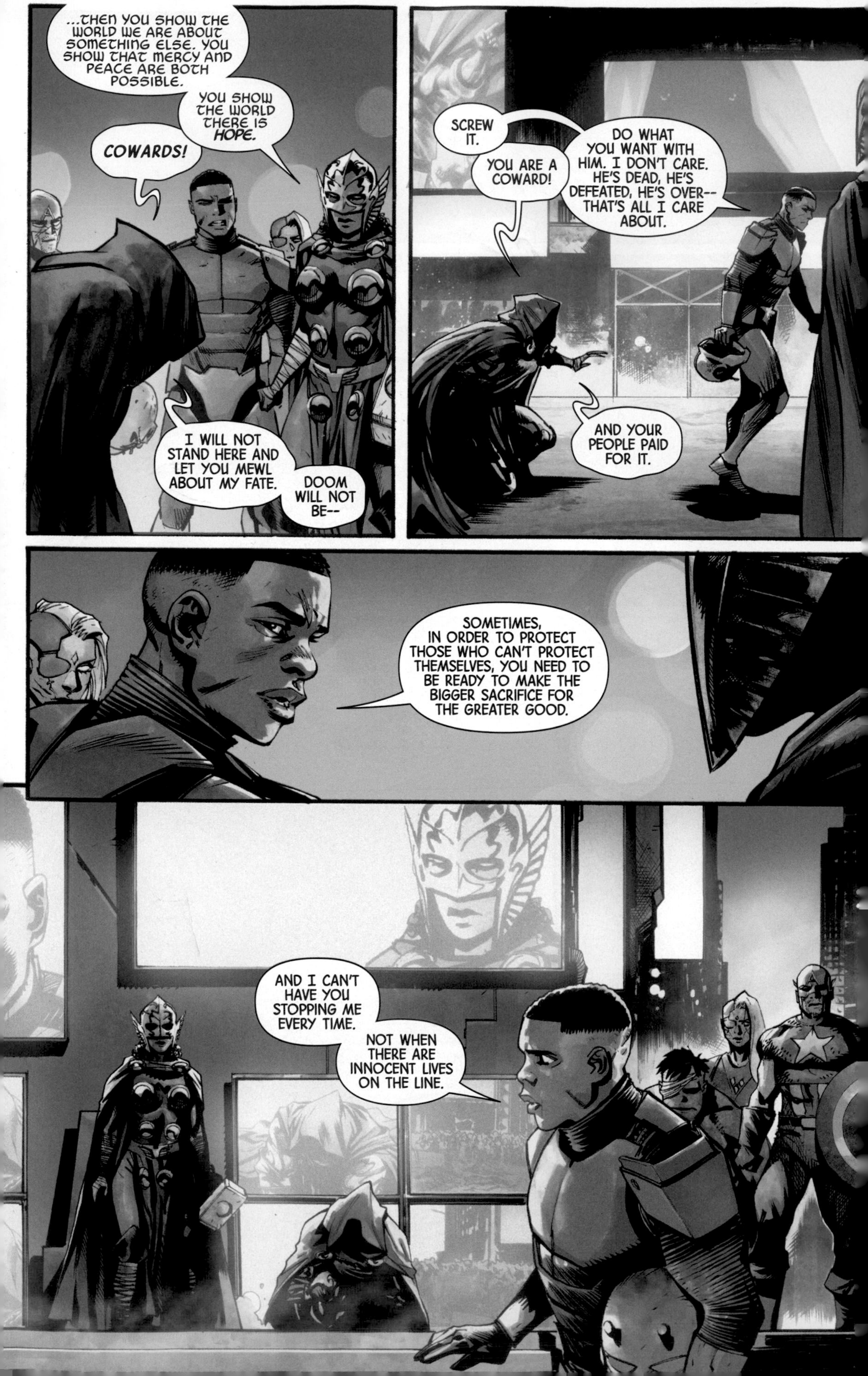
...THEN YOU SHOW THE WORLD WE ARE ABOUT SOMETHING ELSE. YOU SHOW THAT MERCY AND PEACE ARE BOTH POSSIBLE.
YOU SHOW THE WORLD THERE IS HOPE.
COWARDS!
I WILL NOT STAND HERE AND LET YOU MEWL ABOUT MY FATE.
DOOM WILL NOT BE--
SCREW IT.
YOU ARE A COWARD!
DO WHAT YOU WANT WITH HIM. I DON'T CARE. HE'S DEAD, HE'S DEFEATED, HE'S OVER-- THAT'S ALL I CARE ABOUT.
AND YOUR PEOPLE PAID FOR IT.
SOMETIMES, IN ORDER TO PROTECT THOSE WHO CAN'T PROTECT THEMSELVES, YOU NEED TO BE READY TO MAKE THE BIGGER SACRIFICE FOR THE GREATER GOOD.
AND I CAN'T HAVE YOU STOPPING ME EVERY TIME.
NOT WHEN THERE ARE INNOCENT LIVES ON THE LINE.

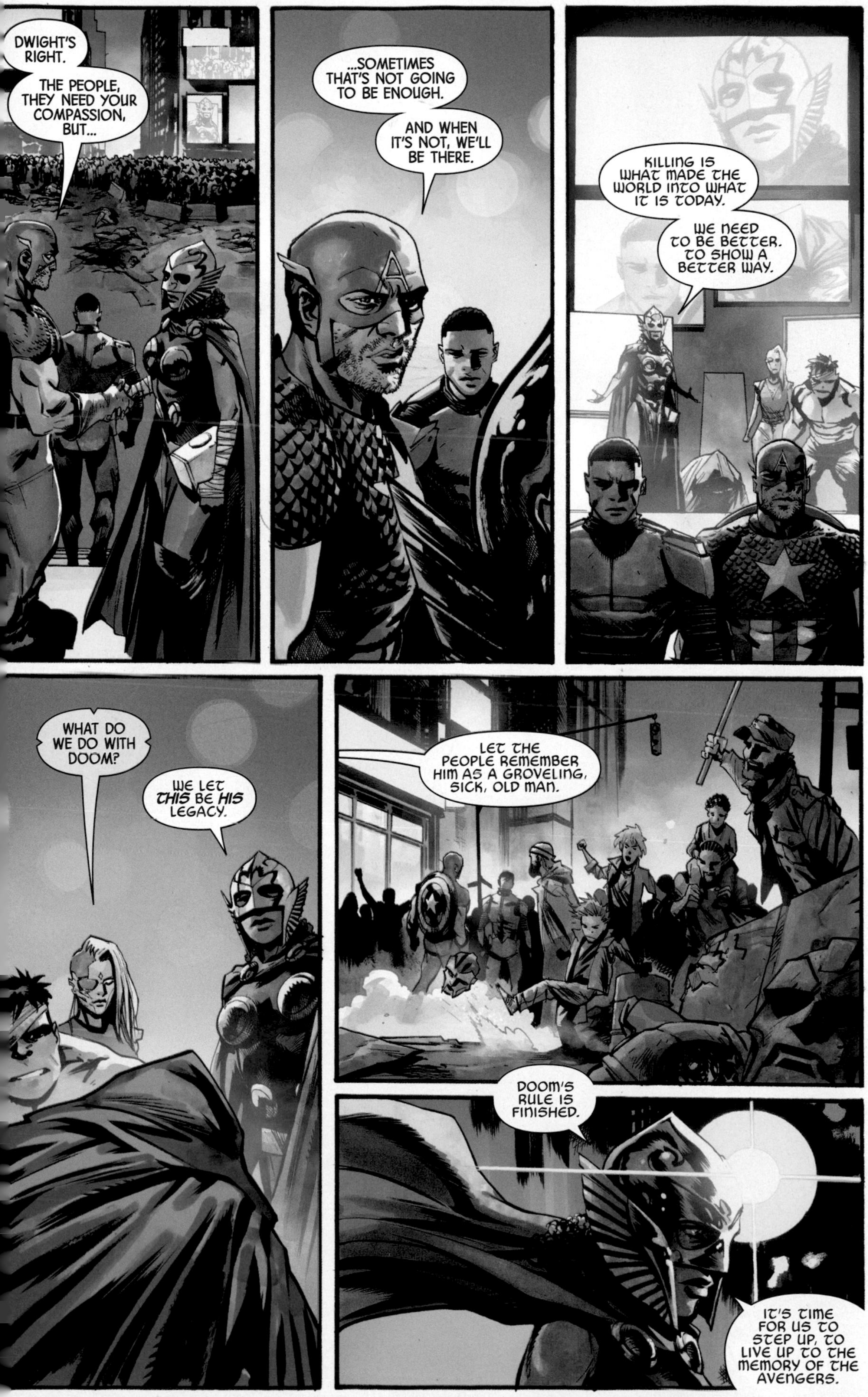
DWIGHT'S RIGHT.
THE PEOPLE, THEY NEED YOUR COMPASSION, BUT...
...SOMETIMES THAT'S NOT GOING TO BE ENOUGH.
AND WHEN IT'S NOT, WE'LL BE THERE.
KILLING IS WHAT MADE THE WORLD INTO WHAT IT IS TODAY.
WE NEED TO BE BETTER. TO SHOW A BETTER WAY.
WHAT DO WE DO WITH DOOM?
WE LET THIS BE HIS LEGACY.
LET THE PEOPLE REMEMBER HIM AS A GROVELING, SICK, OLD MAN.
DOOM'S RULE IS FINISHED.
IT'S TIME FOR US TO STEP UP, TO LIVE UP TO THE MEMORY OF THE AVENGERS.

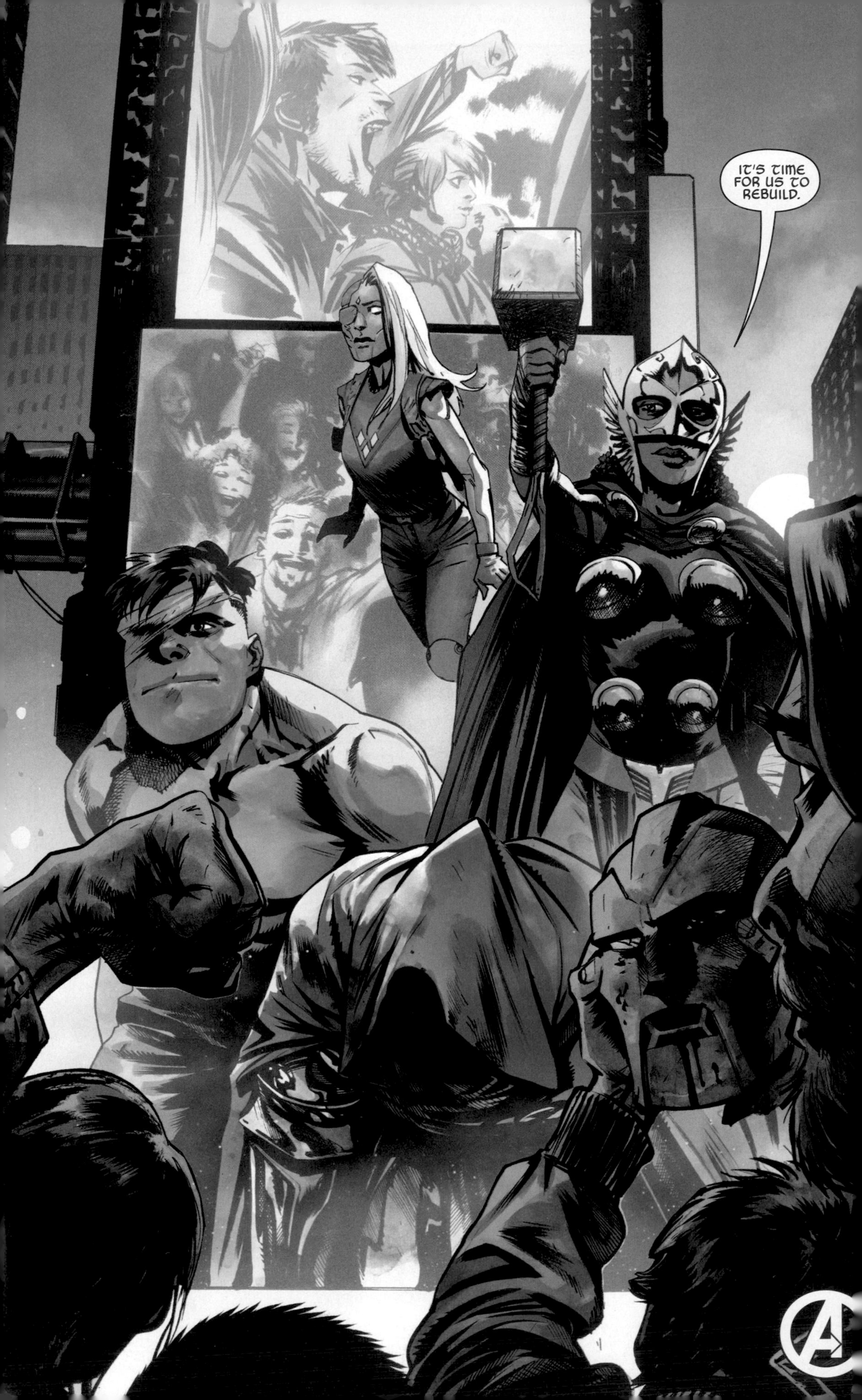
IT'S TIME FOR US TO REBUILD.

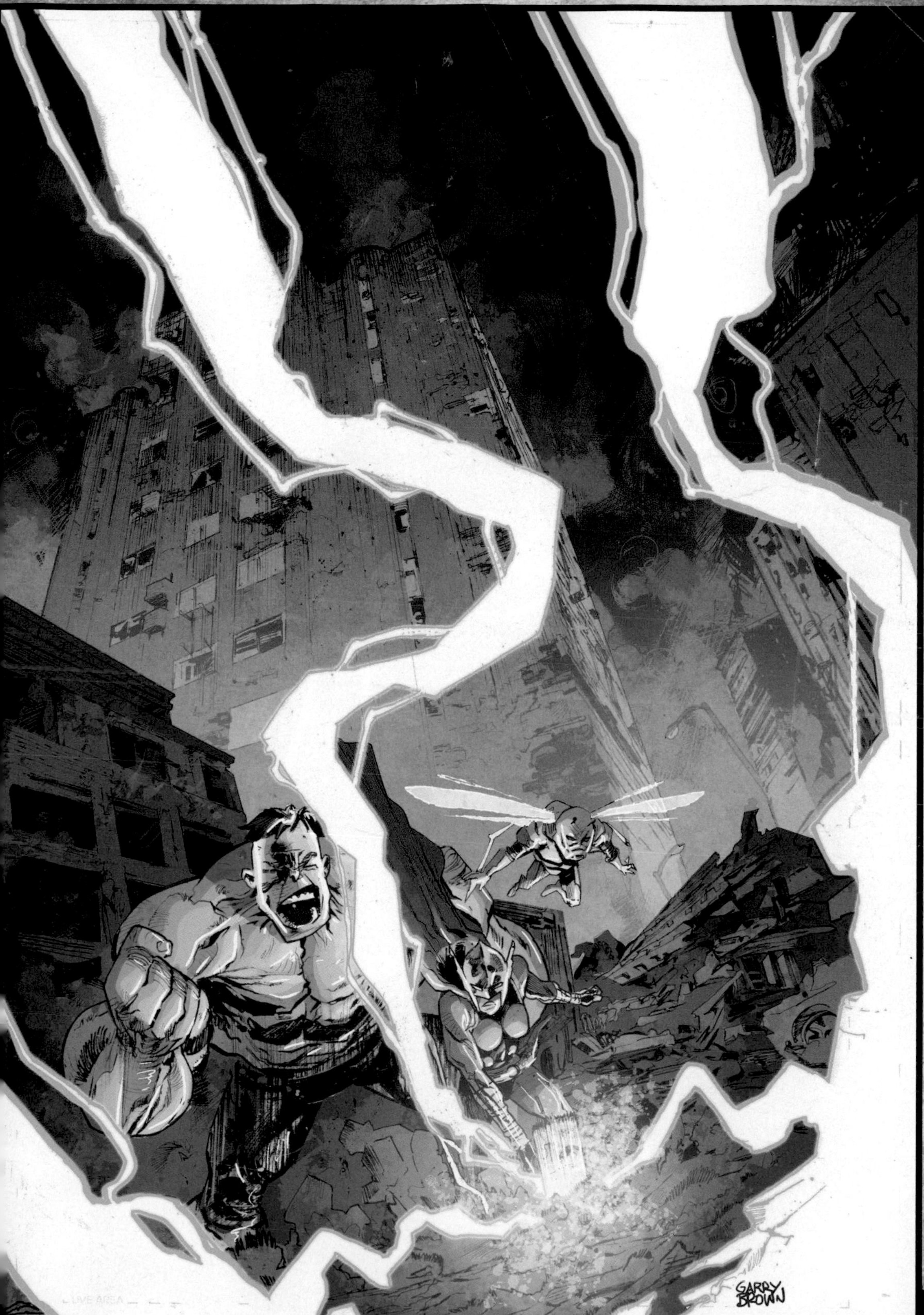
GARRY
BROWN

#1 variant .... **WILL SLINEY** & **DAVID CURIEL**

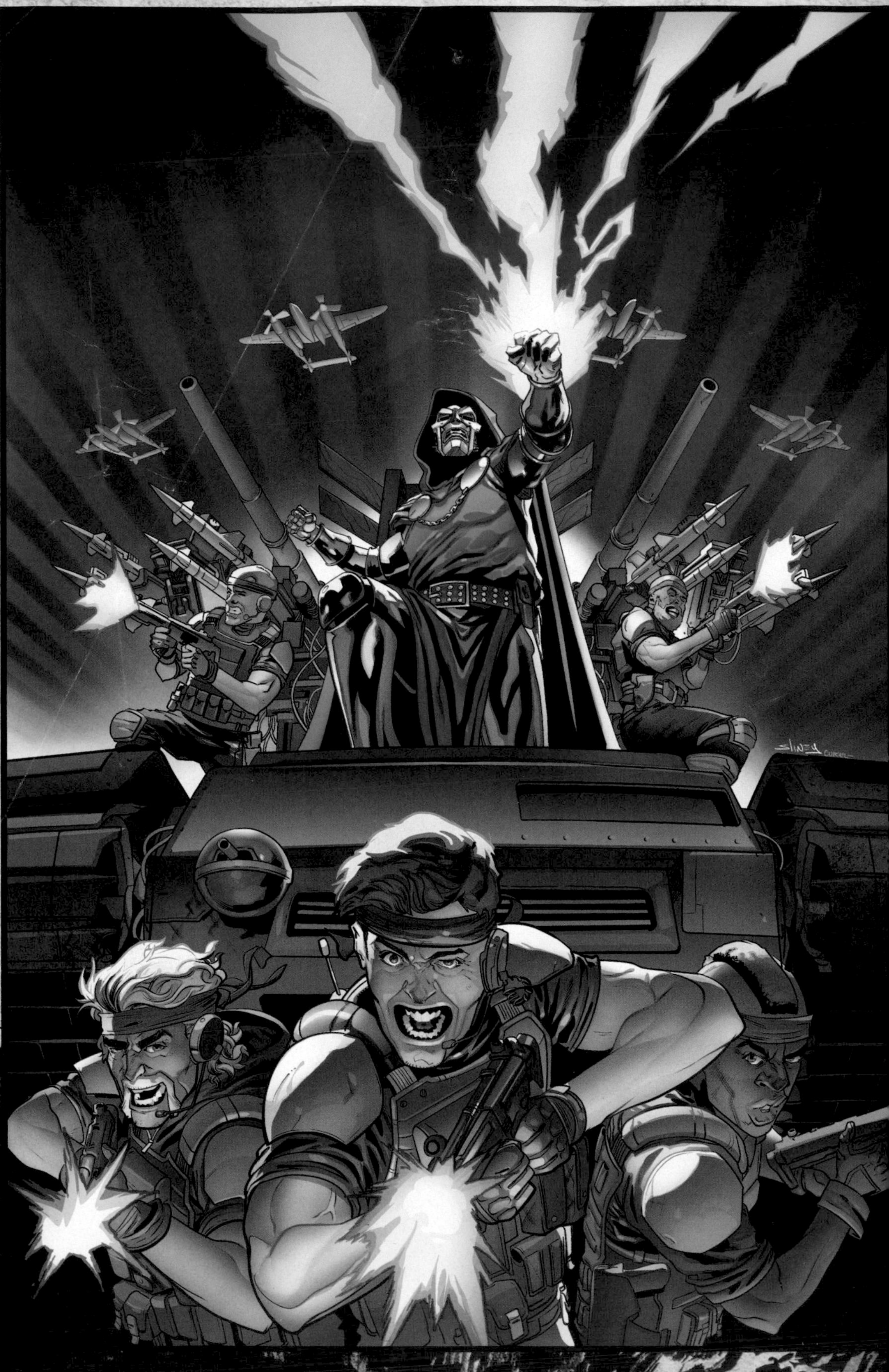

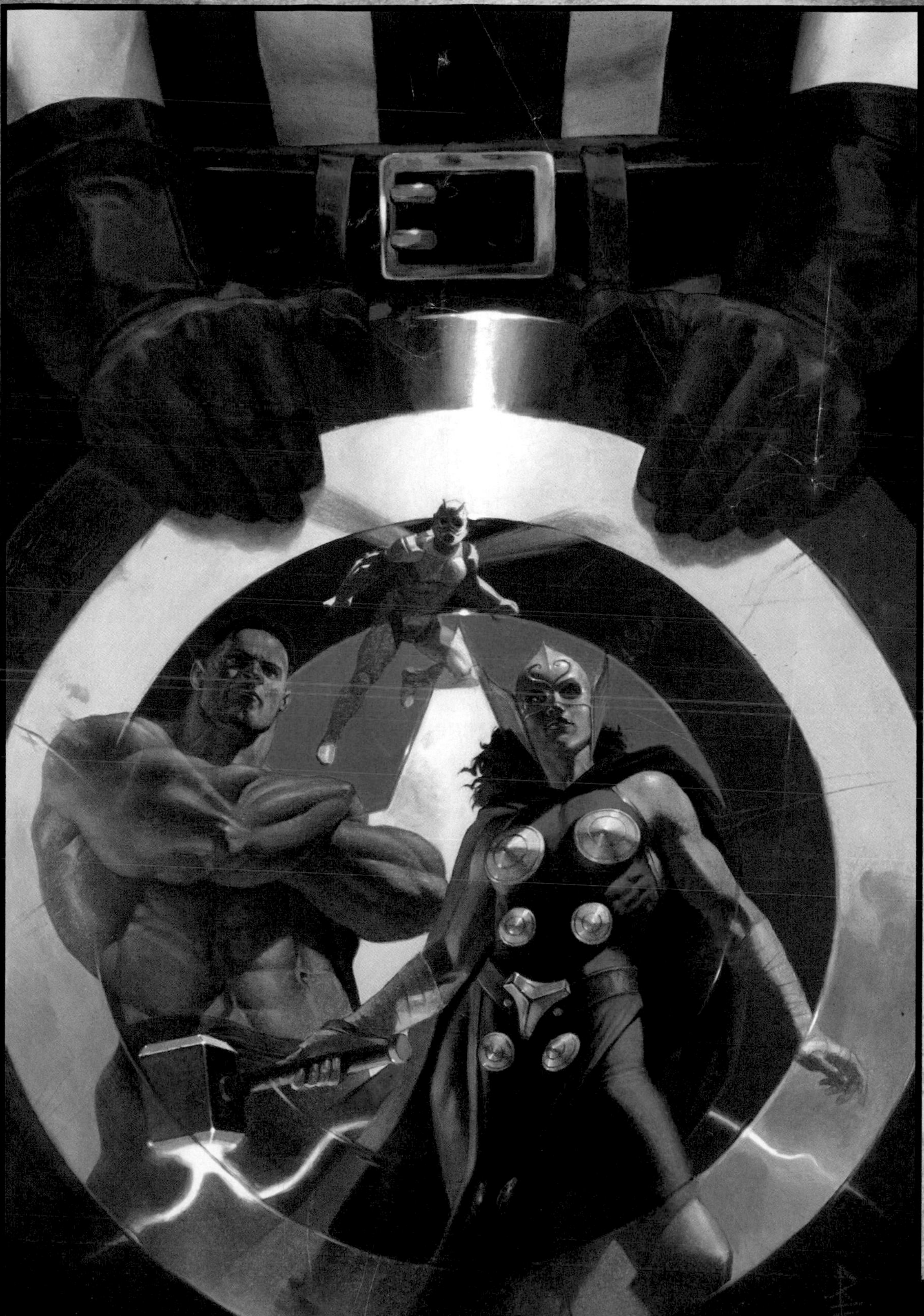

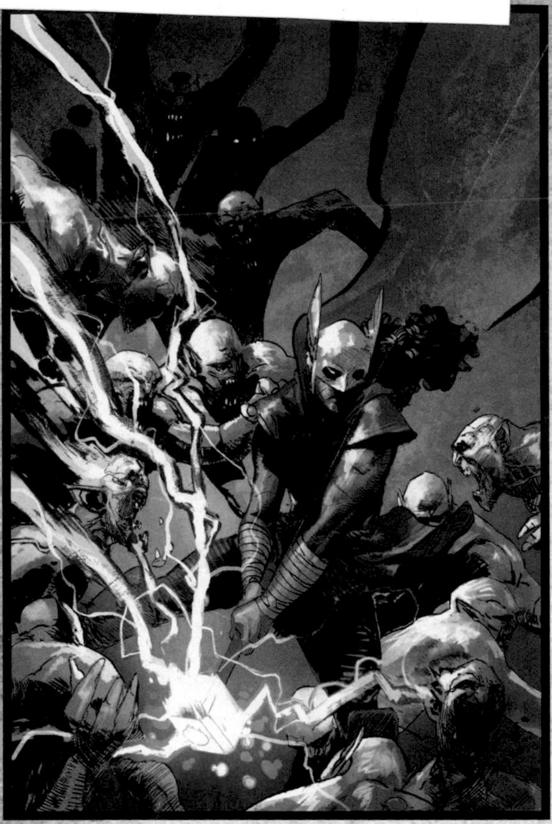

#4 variant by
IVAN SHAVRIN

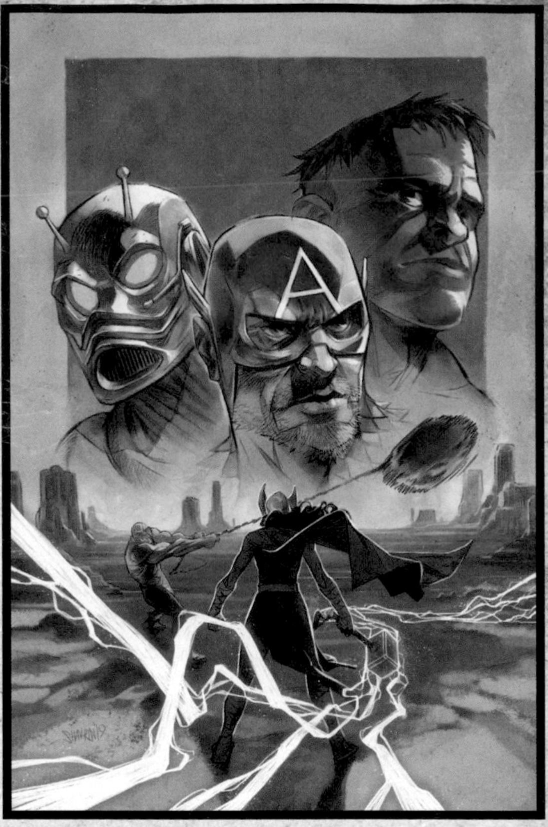

#3 variant by
TODD NAUCK & RACHELLE ROSENBERG

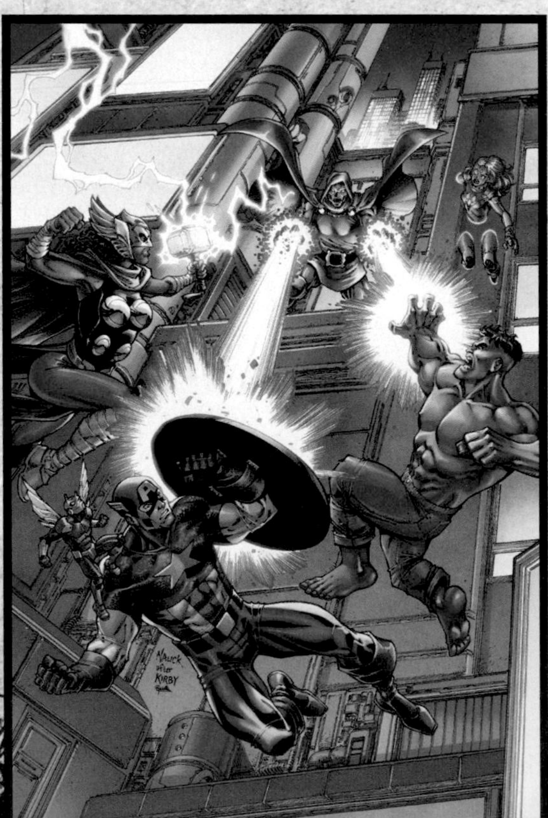